WOMEN ON SEX

Other books by Susan Quilliam

*The Eternal Triangle*
*Sexual Body Talk*
*Supervirility*

# Women on SEX

Susan Quilliam

SMITH GRYPHON
PUBLISHERS

First published in Great Britain in 1994 by
SMITH GRYPHON LIMITED
Swallow House, 11-21 Northdown Street
London N1 9BN

Concept for the work devised by David Sloane and Lorna Hastings

A CIP catalogue record for this book is available from the British Library

ISBN 1 85685 066 8 (Paper)
ISBN 1 85685 070 6 (Cased)

Designed by Hammond Hammond
Typeset by BMD Graphics, Hemel Hempstead
Printed in Great Britain by Hartnolls Ltd, Bodmin

To all women, in the
hope that their thoughts, dreams and
feelings on sex are given voice
in this book

# Contents

# Acknowledgements

This book has been so much of a cooperative venture that it seems odd to 'acknowledge' many of the people involved – as if they merely assisted me in writing the book, when the truth is that without them I would never even have had the chance to write it. However, I would like to thank, in roughly chronological order: David Sloane and Lorna Hastings for having the idea and designing the original questionnaire; Robert Smith for providing the superb publishing machine to produce and market the book; my agent Barbara Levy for putting us all in contact with each other and skilfully negotiating the ways we have worked together; Trevor Day for validating the questionnaire; Ros Maher for typing in all the questionnaires at a pace that sounded like a machine gun firing; Ian Grove-Stephensen for designing and maintaining the computer data base; Sue Linge and Alf Egan for analysing and coding all the responses; June Bulley, my assistant, for her tireless organization.

I would also like to acknowledge, more than anything, the contribution of the 200 women who generously gave of their time and energy to complete the questionnaire, often over several months, and later to talk to me about their answers. Because most of them have chosen to remain anonymous and the rest gave their names to me in confidence, I cannot thank anyone specifically. But I know how much honesty, joy and pain went into their task – and, for that, I thank you.

Finally, I should like to thank my mother who first showed me how to be a sexual woman, and my husband Ian who helps me continue to be one.

All figures given that relate to the survey refer to the number of women who have answered each individual question. On occasion this is less than the total sample.

# Introduction
# First Words

In 1960, the first contraceptive pill for women went on the market. As a result, the sex life of every woman who came of age at that time and thereafter would never be the same again. Because of the pill, women would no longer have to fear pregnancy. Because they didn't have to fear pregnancy, they could claim a sexual freedom that, throughout history, only men had previously enjoyed. And because of that sexual freedom, women's experience of and attitudes to sex changed irrevocably.

Over thirty years into that revolution, it's a good time to take stock. Hence this book, not a philosophy treatise or a sociological thesis, but a direct statement of the way women see sex today. It's based on a qualitative survey that asked women about their sex lives, using questions that demanded they be courageously honest: How would you describe your love-making? What do you do? How do you feel? Do you enjoy sex? What are you frightened of? What do you enjoy, and what do you hate? How many partners have you had? Have you always been faithful? What are your sexual rules?

In response to these questions 200 women spent hours, days, often months, writing in detail what they really felt and thought about their sex lives. They found the experience scary, challenging, exciting, worrying and very arousing. More than one woman, on returning her questionnaire – often running to ten of thousands of words – reported needing to stop halfway through writing, *'because I felt horny, and went away and did something about it'.*

## THEIR MOTIVATION

Women chose to take the risk of being part of this book for a number of reasons. First, in today's world, they wanted to communicate about sex. Even now, in the emancipated nineties, there is still some sense of taboo left about posing the questions that we all want to ask. We actually want *'to know honestly how other women feel . . . to give and receive advice and comfort . . . to stop feeling like isolated freaks . . . to know whether everyone else out there is really bonking their head off except me'!* We want to speak to other women and to hear what they have to say. We want to communicate with men, to tell them what we think and feel, to tell them what we really need and desire.

For many women the experience of filling in the questionnaire has also been a journey of self-communication and, so, of self-discovery. The sexual revolution may be over thirty years old, but society has several thousand years of catching up to do. And therefore many women are confused, hurt and distressed. They responded to the questionnaire to *'see what my views on sex actually were ... to put my relationships into perspective ... to gain healing'.* And many say that they achieved just these things, that writing their own account of their own sex life was helpful to them: *'I remembered some nice experiences and some deep shit ... been forced to think about ways I am unhappy ... finally told my partner that ... understood how things have shaped my sexuality ... dramatically changed my attitudes to men, sex and myself.'*

## WHAT IS NEW?

What does this book reveal about women and sex today? Above all it gives us a celebration of women's sexuality. Whatever else the current shift in attitudes has brought women, it's given us the freedom to enjoy ourselves in bed and to discover the potential we have for love-making. Along with new attitudes to sex, we've developed – and are still developing – a whole new set of skills in communication, in sensuality, in sexuality. We've gained a new range of definitions concerning love and sex; and a new list of sexual rules to govern our behaviour. We now take many lovers, do exciting things in bed, have orgasms – or realize we have a right to them. We are starting to find out what we really want from sex, ask for it, get it and revel in it.

We still, however, feel bad about sexuality. We feel guilty about a whole range of things; wary and angry about others. For the sexual revolution has brought its backlash. We are now free to enjoy sex, but we are also free to feel inferior if we don't have a sexually attractive body, to be pressured to make love whether we want to or not, to be increasingly loved and left. And we are still learning to adapt to what is happening – so we may find it difficult to reconcile our views with our actions, may alternate between love and hate for our new found liberation, may alternately cling to and run from our partners, may run double standards that are just as illogical as those that men have practised over the centuries. And, in this sense, though it may be hard to hear, women may have some sexual development still to do.

Despite all these problems, however, the overall picture is incredibly positive. We are coming to terms with the changes. We are beginning to adapt and grow. We are overcoming the difficulties. And this book, hopefully will help the process – for, in the end, only by total honesty and direct communication can women get the sex lives that they deserve.

VITAL STATISTICS

21 per cent of women are sexually aware before the age of 9

51.8 per cent have masturbated by the age of 14

64.6 per cent orgasm the first time they masturbate

13.7 per cent have felt sexual about a member of their own family

31.2 per cent have orgasmed before the age of 14

# 1. First Knowledge

*I think subconsciously I have always been sexually aware. I felt sexual sensations from quite an early age, probably around the age of 5. I can remember as a child putting blankets between my legs and rubbing myself against them.*

WOMEN ACTUALLY KNOW about sexuality right from the start. They've always known. The sexual revolution has made a difference to our knowledge; we are now far more aware of our sexuality. Had we been born half a century earlier, we would probably have been strongly discouraged from exploring sexual pleasure until we lost our virginity to our husband. So we would have ignored any sexual thoughts and blocked out any sexual feelings. But, in fact, we do know what feels good, and what we can do to make it feel even better, right from childhood.

The women who answered the questionnaire remember having sexual knowlege from an early age. They describe getting aroused in infancy, lying on their stomachs in bed and moving slowly against the mattress or rubbing up against soft toys (bears seem to be a favourite). They remember how, in childhood, they lulled themselves to sleep at night by putting their hand between their legs. They recall strange, pleasurable feelings that they didn't understand. We may be under the impression that sexuality begins in adolescence, but in fact 3.6 per cent of women believe that they had felt sexual before they were 5 and 21 per cent before they were 9. By the age of 14, when many of us are only just reaching puberty, 76.1 per cent reckon they have felt sexually aroused. The memories are clear and undeniable.

*I remember at about 5, I used to like lying on my front in bed and squirming about. I wanted to have my bottom stroked.*

*When I was 11 or 12, riding my pony bareback I felt a strange feeling which made me want to relax and just flop, made my head feel heavy and swim in a terribly nice way. My pony was galloping up a hill, and I was leaning into the movement. He was very tired when I'd done it four or five times.*

## PLEASURING OURSELVES

The sensations are irresistible. And it takes very little indeed for them to turn into self-pleasuring, building on the sensation all the way through to orgasm. Again, we start early. By the time they were 14, over half of the women in the survey say they'd already masturbated – usually working purely from instinct. Occasionally, but rarely, they find out how by talking it through with a girlfriend, perhaps showing each other what to do during a 'sleepover' party. Or, they may read about it in books: *'I worked it out from a vague description in a teenage novel . . . I read somewhere in a magazine that women like to put things in their vagina.'*

Most of us, though, find out about masturbation instinctively: *'I learnt by accident . . . it just seemed to happen . . . it was natural . . . it seemed like fun.'* We slip our hand down our pyjamas while going to sleep, touch our clitoris, and the movements just naturally develop. We use the soap in the bath or accidentally arouse ourselves with the jet from the shower-head. Several women talk about sliding up and down the ropes in the gym.

We're not often tempted to penetrate ourselves; that doesn't feel nearly as nice as touching our clitoris, though one woman does say that: *'[I] had sex with a hairbrush when I was about 8 and was terrified afterwards that I might be pregnant!'* But we don't simply copy adults making love. In fact hardly any of us have any opportunity to learn about sex directly. We find out all by ourselves that masturbation feels good. Then we carry on putting our knowledge into practice.

*I was probably 5 when I masturbated by stimulating my clitoris with my finger over my knickers. I remember thinking it was a nice sensation, like wanting to go to the toilet.*

*I must have been about 7 when I had my first experience of sexual sensations. I remember pulling back the hood of my clitoris and touching it; it was almost painful, but I had to do it again. So I suppose I became increasingly sexually aware from that point.*

*I remember masturbating at the age of about 8, though it took a couple of years before I connected it to sex. I am not aware of having any sudden discoveries of feelings connected to my genitals, therefore I believe that I must have been masturbating in some form from a very young age.*

One proof that we instinctively know how to arouse ourselves is that we usually end up orgasming when we masturbate. As many as 64.6 per cent of women report that they climaxed on their first attempt, and almost all of them learnt within the first few times they pleasured themselves. If we simply relax and allow the sensations to take over, at an age when we are unworried by what we should do or what our partner will think, we come easily and without effort: *'I think I just concentrated very hard and pulled my knickers up tight.'* Our climax may be weak, or undeveloped – most women say that adult orgasms are stronger and somehow different – but it is so spontaneous and overpowering that it often takes us aback: *'I freaked out when on the brink because I thought I was going to have a heart attack!'*

## EARLY EXPERIMENTS

Our next step may well be practical experimentation with other people. At first, this has little to do with sexual pleasure; we usually just want to confirm our suspicions about the mechanics of sex. We've learnt about these basics from books, parents or teachers, and usually we've been shocked by them – more than one woman uses the word *'horrified'* when she writes about discovering what intercourse really was.

Who do we do this experimenting with? Most of us will at a very early age have looked at a boy and seen how different he is from us – either because we have brothers or because we mix with boys: *'I was about 7 when a boy in my class decided to pull down his trousers and show me what he had! . . . I often found my knickers down and the boys having a good look and vice versa, but it was all very naïve and innocent.'*

But because we mix more with girls and because girls seem that much safer, it's more likely that we'll do our hands-on experimentation with them. We look, we touch; we are looked at and touched in turn. Many women report examining breasts, or putting things into their vagina to see what that looked and felt like.

*At about the same age, I used to play games with three or four girlfriends. We'd look at each other's genitals and insert pencils and things like that. We were caught in my bedroom one day by my mum who sent the other girls home. The incident was never discussed, but it was obvious to me I shouldn't have been doing it.*

We're also sometimes on the receiving end of sex play. This is commonly with slightly older female relatives, sisters and cousins who use us for experimentation, to 'practise on' or play with. This doesn't seem to feel abusive, only confusing; we usually aren't aroused by it, and we don't link it with sexual feeling.

*My elder cousin sometimes played doctors and nurses with my brother and myself. While my brother would wait in the bedroom, my cousin would tell me to lie down on the landing floor and then pull down my knickers. She would then open my legs and insert one of those round plastic counters from a board game against my clitoris. She would then close my legs and spent ages in the bedroom with my brother.*

Some of us take things further. We kiss and hug closely when playing with our girlfriends. We sleep over in the same bed and end up stroking each other's breasts, lying on top of one another, rubbing each other between the legs. We get pleasure from this, though it's more sensuous than sexual. The majority of us, in fact, realize quickly that we prefer men, and when we look back and remember these early adventures, we say that what we did with girls was not passionate but only exploration and practice: *'I do not count this a true lesbian experience because we were young and experimenting on each other.'*

But through these experiences we do learn about our own female sexuality, usually in a relaxed and unthreatening situation. Experimenting with girls is cooperative; it's learning about our own bodies by exploring someone who is just like us. It repeats the lesson we learnt when self-pleasuring that, actually, sex is instinctive, fun and easy.

## FINDING OUR SEXUAL FOCUS

At this point, early in our adolescence, just before or just after puberty, there's a sexual turning point. We finally start to identify the focus of our attraction. Some of us, having pleasured ourselves and maybe experimented with friends, look around and spontaneously feel aroused by someone 'other', someone very different to us. Many women say they remembered a specific moment in their childhood when they became aware of boys (or girls) as different and exciting.

Often the feeling comes first in dreams. For some of us it's stimulated by night arousal. We dream of watching or being watched, of being touched or kissed. We feel a rush of desire – even if we don't realize what that is and don't connect it with sex until later.

*I dreamed, from about the age of 9, of boys older than I was just being there, watching me and being powerful. They never touched me sexually, but they looked and watched and waited for me. I was scared and felt wonderfully trembly at the same time.*

Then, we feel the same thing in real life. We look at our brothers' friends and *'get butterflies'*. We watch love scenes on the television and feel aroused ourselves by the actor (or actress).

*I felt excited when I was hidden behind a curtain in my friend's older brother's bedroom while he weight lifted nude. I found it a big turn-on although I didn't realize this until later.*

*I remember being 7 and fancying a boy at school and wanting to kiss him – properly – lying in bed at night passionately kissing the pillow wishing it was him.*

This arousal is often a frightening feeling. For the first time we realize that other people can create sensations in us that we can't stop, can make us feel pleasure that we can't control. They have sexual power over us. We begin to be a little wary, to fight shy of potential partners while at the same time desperately wanting them to pay us attention.

## MAKING CONTACT

Slowly, what has been sensuality becomes sexuality. What was experimentation and exploration begins to have a bite to it. We begin to feel sexual when we fight friends in the playground. We begin to think of what would happen if we didn't just look at our brothers' friends but also touched them. We watch television and breathe heavily at the love scenes, *'read naughty paperbacks and feel hot under the collar, imagining myself as the heroine'*. We look through books and get *'a strong sexual thrill through my fanny'*.

It will be a while yet before we are ready to pair off sexually, to take a 'real partner' even in the short term. But we do manage to make contact. We may take our female explorations a stage further: *'I was about 12, and we had oral sex with each other. I enjoyed it thoroughly and experienced my first orgasm.'* Or we play kissing contests with the lads in the class above us: *'A lot of the boys used to want to touch me. So if I let them get a bit closer it was a real nice sensation.'* These are no longer games, even though they are nowhere near adult passion. We know very well that they are something different, but we are not quite sure where they are supposed to lead.

And so we find ourselves, perhaps at puberty, perhaps a little earlier or a little later, on the brink of a wonderful discovery – partnership sex.

*When I was about 10 there was a little boy who used to play Black Magic, White Magic with me. In this game, which was surprisingly complex, we had to rub against each other, fusing the power of black and white magic. I noticed I got very, very aroused when we did it, but I was amazed rather than frightened and wanted more and more.*

From them on we begin the move from childhood sexuality, where our main focus is ourselves and our own capacity for pleasure, to sex with a partner, where we begin to learn about mutual sexual fulfilment. Over the following years we will probably expand our potential through taking many partners, beginning with the ultimate aim of every adolescent girl – the boyfriend (see chapter 3).

When we look back on our early childhood experiences, most of us feel good about them. Though, as we shall see in the next chapter, external influences may tarnish and spoil things, when women experience physical pleasure under their direct control, it rarely feels anything but normal and wonderful.

This surely is nothing new; for centuries before the sexual revolution, children played with themselves quite happily until they were punished. What is different is that now, with our adult lives full of rich and varied sexual experience, we are more and more able to give ourselves permission to be aware of the good sensations we felt as children and to celebrate those sensations in adult life. We look back delightedly to our early masturbation experiences. We smile at the memory of childhood kisses. We are able to retell happily, in surveys like this one, the story of the first time we felt sexual. We are, slowly, beginning to be proud of our childhood sexuality – and to recognize that it is a vital part of what makes us a sexual woman.

*I definitely had sexual sensations from about the age of 9. It is hard to explain; sometimes when I thought about a boy and tried to imagine kissing them, I would feel involuntary rhythmic contractions in my vagina, a little milder than an orgasm. I was aware of the pleasurable sensation even then.*

VITAL STATISTICS

63 per cent of women feel their sexual attitudes were mainly influenced by their family

48.2 per cent feel their sexual attitudes were mainly influenced by their friends

66 per cent influenced by their family feel bad about what they learnt

13 per cent said their main models of sexual behaviour were books, magazines and films

# 2. Sexual Messages

*My family have shaped my outlook, not by enforcing morals on me but by letting me make my own decisions about relationships and by being there for me if I have something I want to discuss. My friends influence the way I think about sex; through talking and expressing our opinions we can learn about ourselves as well as as about sex.*

THE INSTINCTIVE SEXUAL knowledge we have as children never develops entirely freely. We constantly take in messages about sex from the world around us, messages about sensuousness, about sexuality, about relationships, about what is good and bad. Very often, these messages totally contradict what our bodies are telling us. The result, particularly in a society that's in the middle of changing from sexual restriction to sexual freedom, is often confusing and distressing.

Women participating in the survey are remarkably clear about where their sexual messages come from. And feelings about those messages are equally unambiguous. Just a few women say that they've been influenced by school lessons or teachers, though they report that they really only learnt the facts of life rather than any moral judgements about sex or love. Some 13 per cent feel they got their attitudes mainly from

the media, particularly teenage photolove comics and romantic novels.
They say that as teenagers, these media sources really affected their
attitudes to men and to sex; but that now, as adults, they've revised
those views, and now think they were over romantic and completely
unrealistic. At the other extreme, just a few learnt from pornographic
material:

> *My father was a book salesman and used to deliver all kinds of books,
> including pornographic magazines, to newsagents all over the country.
> He would come home with the van still loaded, and my sister and I used
> to sneak in and look at the magazines; we were about 8 and very curious.*

The majority of our messages, however, came from family and
friends. Our family gave us our basic beliefs about sex: what to think, what
to feel, how to judge. And even those of us who say that we haven't taken
on our family's messages seem to have been influenced by them, if only
because we have dissented so consistently and so strongly. We say that our
peer group, by contrast, taught us the nuts and bolts of sex: how to behave,
what to do, how to look as if we know what we are doing: *'I was taught
the basic facts of life from my mother, but my friends gave me far more
detailed and lurid accounts.'*

## FAMILY NEGATIVES

But the sad fact is this. Out of all these influences, we look back and think
of only a few as positive. While our accounts of early sexual pleasure feel
good, right and fun, our accounts of what other people have taught us
about this pleasure are full of confusion, unhappiness and blame. It is as
if, looking back now at the negative messages we were given about sex
and realizing that they are wrong, we also realize how destructive their
effect was. We know not only that we were lied to but that those lies have
also affected our ability to enjoy sex to its full potential. And, in many
ways, we can never forgive that.

Some 66 per cent of women who think they've been influenced by their
families feel bad about what they have been taught. They blame parents,
particularly mothers, for not having given them the information they
needed about sex. They blame their families because, in the end, they
were left wanting to know and needing to know.

Women answering the questions about childhood experiences write
so consistently about lack of information that their accounts could have
been written in the Victorian age: *'Sex did not exist for my parents ...
I was given no information ... I was simply handed a book, which I threw
in the bin.'* These accounts come not only from older women, whose

mothers grew up before the sexual revolution and so who may be expected to have a traditional viewpoint, but also from women who are still in their teens and whose parents, therefore, are post-pill. The past thirty years, it seems, has not achieved much in terms of positive early experiences. For both sets of respondents, total lack of information about all aspects of being female has led to real fear, embarrassment and lack of confidence, first about having to cope with sexual feelings at all, then about the transition from girl to woman, lastly about the prospect of having intercourse.

*I was not given any information about menstruation. So when I was 14 and began having menstrual cramps, I believed that I had contracted venereal disease – which I read about in the problem pages of a magazine. I believed that I must have contracted the disease through being kissed by a boy at a Christmas party. I wrote to the problem page and was advised to visit my doctor, but I could not consult an elderly gentleman, who knew my family, about something I was so ashamed of. Later, when I had monthly bleeding, I resigned myself to the belief that the disease had reached an incurable stage.*

Where we were given information about sex as children, we say that it was almost always negative. Whether it came to us directly through words or indirectly through the way our families behaved, the underlying messages were overwhelmingly pessimistic – about us as women, about our relationship to boys and to men, about the moral correctness of heterosexual love alone, about what love is and about how it relates to sex: *'My family instilled shame in me at being a woman ... Men were portrayed as the master while I was worthless ... My mother taught me that all men are bastards ... My father was unfaithful, so I knew what men were like ... My father was absent, and the only time I saw my mother was in bed with a man.'* Now, as adults, we are fully aware of how these childhood messages have affected us, and how negative that effect was.

*I was brought up to believe sex was a chore, men were bad, and women had to fight all the time. Consequently I made bad choices in men; my husband was violent and verbally abusive, resulting in my losing all self-confidence. I can only sleep with a man who wants sex not involvement. I feel unworthy of love.*

## SEX AND SIN

Many of us complain that we were told that sex is morally wrong; some of us even say that we were given the impression that it is wrong whether or not we are in a long-term committed relationship. When we played childhood sex games, we were told we were wicked: *'Playing Mummies and Daddies was severely punished ... I first remember examining my genitals at a very young age, when my mother was washing my hair in the bath. She told me it was very naughty and slapped my hand.'* When we were older, we learnt that sex has much longer term punishments attached to it than simply a slap: *'Sex was never mentioned at home, except when my cousins had to get married. Then it was scorned upon. I got the impression that sex was dirty, and that only wicked people had sex and paid the price by having babies.'*

Sadder than all this, when we got to the age where sex was a possibility, we may also have been constantly told that it wasn't going to be fun: *'I learnt that sex was a duty that a wife has to suffer ... Sex is for men to enjoy and women to endure.'*

The truly tragic thing, of course, is that such teaching sometimes ruins sex for us. If, when we get this kind of message, we haven't already felt sexual pleasure, then our minds are an open book. We believe what we are told, and when we have the chance to experience sex, we are wary of it. If we have already felt aroused, then we probably believe sex is a good thing. But faced with negative messages from adults whom we respect, we start to think that maybe sex is bad after all. At this point many of us mix the two beliefs and become convinced that to feel good is something to feel bad about. Our instinctive knowledge of sexual pleasure begins to be undermined.

## FAMILY POSITIVES

Not all women receive negative messages from their family. Some 24 per cent of respondents feel positive about what their families taught them. They feel good largely because their mothers were open and honest. She *'talked to me naturally ... was there for me when I wanted to talk through problems ... gave me information freely'.*

If we are in this group, most of our mothers are post-pill. But this isn't always true: the oldest, 69-year-old survey respondent says that, by the standards of the 1930s, her widowed mother was practical and able to communicate well. And another woman writes:

*I was a teenager in the fifties/early sixties when sex as a subject of conversation was still taboo. I was lucky. Mothers of girls about to enter the local grammar school were advised to tell their daughters the facts of life. I cannot remember being told these facts, probably because my mother had answered my questions openly and honestly from an early age. When I menstruated shortly after my eleventh birthday, I knew what was happening and was prepared. When I was 15 and in a book-*

*shop with my parents. I found a Teach Yourself book on sex, which my father bought and paid for. I was encouraged to borrow library books on sex and ask both my parents questions. So while I never witnessed any intimacy between my parents I was brought up to have a healthy attitude to sex – though not before marriage.*

Such positive mothers informed us early on about the facts of life, usually in a way that was not only factually correct but also emotionally positive. When it comes to puberty, they gave us both information and the idea that menstruating is a good thing. In contrast with the terrified girl described on page 11, we feel *'happy ... excited ... proud ... keen to start'.*

*I returned home from school to find blood on my pants. I felt a little bemused, but my mother seemed very happy – and it was a close time for us as she showed me how, what and when to do things.*

When it came to the how, what and when of making love, these positive mothers typically liked sex themselves. They not only told us what we need to know but also gave us the impression that love-making is pleasurable: *'My mother taught us that sex was a wonderful thing ... My parents have always had an excellent, loving relationship; my mother always told me that sex was a good thing and that I would enjoy it.'* This either fitted in with what we had already experienced for ourselves when masturbating or laid the foundations for what we were going to experience when we actually started feeling sexual. Whichever way round things happen, the result was a self-fulfilling prophecy: sex was said to be wonderful, and so it usually proved.

## ENCOURAGING PROMISCUITY?

There's a current belief that talking to young people about sex just encourages them to do it sooner, more often and more irresponsibly. But that's certainly not what this survey shows. Those women who received detailed information and encouraging messages about sex from their mothers seem less likely to have had casual boyfriends and are less likely to have lost their virginity hurriedly – even if they are more likely to have lost it willingly and enjoyably. If our parents confirmed our experiences of sex as pleasurable, then we believed them when they told us that we should wait to experience it – simply because what they were saying about sex fitted in with what we had experienced for ourselves. So the mother who said sex was *'a wonderful thing'* also told her daughter that it was therefore *'not to be taken lightly'*; her daughter took these comments

seriously and followed the advice. The mothers who kept information
back through fear, on the other hand, seem to have laid the foundations
for their daughters to experiment with sex as soon as possible, in order
to find out for themselves.

*I practised sex later than most, but that was because I understood sex
more than my friends and didn't have to rush into it. They, on the other
hand, hardly knew anything, practised sex early and didn't know what
they were doing. That is why most of them fell pregnant at an early age,
and I didn't.*

*My family, to a significant extent I believe, shaped my sexual outlook.
I was never told sex was dirty or bad, it was never rude to speak about,
and therefore I never felt odd thinking about it and eventually doing it.
I was never taught marriage was a prerequisite to sex – except at school
– so I never thought pre-marital sex wrong. I was taught it was something to be enjoyed, enjoyed with the right person, someone chosen. And
I believe this.*

A large majority of women in the survey who receive positive
messages from their mothers seem to have made up their own minds about
sexuality, to become what one might call 'sexual decision-makers'. They
were supported to work out what they wanted from sex, to make their
own choices and not to give in to pressure from peers or from boyfriends.
Not surprisingly, women who report this are likely to be younger than the
average survey respondent and have parents who grew up in the post-pill
age. And because they were in control, doing what they wanted when they
wanted, they typically not only waited until they were really ready before
having intercourse but also enjoyed what they were doing far more than
their peers did. They seem to get the best of both worlds.

## THE INFLUENCE OF FRIENDS

We often feel that we were less influenced by our peer group than we
were by our family. Some 51.8 per cent of women say they weren't
influenced at all by friends in their beliefs. This is often because they felt
they didn't have many friends as children, and often because they had
already formed their own opinions about sex by the time they discussed
it with their peer group.

We often feel wary about the way our peers thought about sex. They
seemed to know only as much as we did or less. Their views and their
opinions were sometimes inconsistent, often wrong, often ill-advised:
*'You're supposed to groan to pretend you're enjoying it.'* Many women,

when talking about the influence of their peers, end by saying, 'but I tended to do what I wanted, regardless of other people's opinions'. And quite a few hold up their family's beliefs as being much more valuable than those of their friends: 'My mother taught me that I should value my body; all my friends were sleeping with their boyfriends long before I was.'

If we do feel that we were influenced by our peers, we may feel unhappy about that. First of all, we may have felt pressured by friends. They seemed to be much more advanced than we were sexually: they had boyfriends long before we did; they told us in gory detail about last night's wrestling match; they bragged a lot. There was a great deal of emotional blackmail, not only to be sexually active but also to be completely 'het', as one lesbian respondent pointed out. There was also a lot of competition.

*At school I was always going to parties. It was the in-thing to drink and see who could score with the best-looking guy. We'd have a system to see who would go the furthest with a guy but without actually having intercourse with him. It put a lot of pressure on everybody.*

We were aware at the time that there were double standards, and this put us in a double bind. On the one hand, we had to keep up with the crowd or be damned as boring. On the other hand, we couldn't be seen to have too many boyfriends, to go too far. There was a 'contradictory contempt for promiscuity', as one woman put it. The safest thing all round was usually to be seen to do exactly what everyone else did at precisely the same time. The fact that we may not have been ready to go that far, that fast, with that particular boy was irrelevant. The main thing was to be seen to be normal.

*My friends at school influenced me to a certain degree. If a girl had too many boyfriends, she was called names, and if she had none, she was unpopular, so I guess that maybe pushed me towards trying to be in the middle.*

Many of us have a final criticism. Our friends' kind of sexuality often sounded either awful or just too good to be true. Constant boasting about passion made sex seem either so disgusting that we were frightened, or so totally wonderful that we felt we could never match that. And indeed (see chapter 4), when our turn came to have sex, this could well be true: fear and disillusionment were some of the most common emotions reported when a girl loses her virginity.

## HELPFUL FRIENDS

The quarter of women who feel that their peers did influence them positively feel that's largely because they were able to discuss sex with them. If we fall into this category, we're likely not to have been able to get information about puberty and sex at home; friends were our only source of knowledge. The words *'insight ... education ... sharing ... discussion'* occur time and again in women's accounts. With friends, they were able to gain information openly and to swap experiences.

Also, if we talked to other girls who went through what we were going through, we could feel we were normal. We were not the only ones to feel wary, not the only ones to worry about what to do, not the only ones to want sex and to be aroused by boys. Friends gave us reassurance at a time when we were feeling particularly insecure. Often, they were also the ones who gave us 'permission' to feel passion. If our families forbade it, friends told us that *'it was OK to have sex ... it was not wrong.'*

Finally, peers made us curious about what sex is like. They encouraged us to start, *'they said it was good so I wanted to try it out for myself.'* And while friends could, wrongly, pressure us into trying before we were ready, they could also help us gain the confidence to follow our instincts. We swapped notes with them about what happens, what to do, how to handle the practicalities of kissing and petting. And, if things went wrong, good friends reassured us, helped us, told us that we were not stupid or unattractive. If we were able to steer clear of the double standards, friends could be an endless fund of knowledge and support. As one woman said, *'My friends taught me everything.'*

## BAD INFLUENCES

There's a third category of people who may have influenced our childhood sexuality and given us messages that we remember even today. It was unsurprising, though saddening, to discover that 9 per cent of respondents were abused as children. Their abusers were almost all members of their own family or known to them: neighbours, parents' friends, brothers, uncles, stepfathers, fathers, grandfathers. The abuse involved kissing, masturbation, oral sex, anal sex and actual intercourse. These women's accounts are detailed and often particularly horrifying because many of them say that they have never dared to tell anyone up to now – or, even worse, that they tried to tell someone and that *'didn't help at all'*.

It's obvious, surely, how much abuse can ruin sexuality for life. The messages of forced sex, particularly at such an early age, undermines a child's instinctive knowledge that sex is good even more than verbal negatives from those around her. She is not only being forced to feel sexual sensations unwillingly. She is not only being forced to do sexual acts to other people against her will. But she may also be pressured to keep the whole thing a secret — often by the worst sort of emotional blackmail. The result is often a loss of all confidence in sex as a pleasurable activity.

> *I was abused by my stepfather for a couple of years. He performed anal sex on me. He tried to get me to give him oral sex and when I could not he ejaculated all over my face. This occurred most days when my mum was at work. I did not tell anyone. My mum would not have believed it, and, apart from that, my stepfather said that if I told, I and my half brother and sisters, who were babies, would be taken away.*

Many, though happily not all the women who have been abused, say that their sex lives still suffer: *'I try to remember, but the memory ends ... I feel dirty and wrong about touching myself ... I have difficulty trusting people, and sometimes I can't make love to my fiancé because of the memories. Luckily he understands and helps me through the difficult times.'*

## FOR THE NEXT GENERATION

Whether our upbringing was destructive or supportive, one thing is clear: we take our thoughts, feelings, attitudes and beliefs about sexuality to a large extent from our past. We leave childhood with a particular attitude to sexuality, and this influences us as we move on to adolescence and begin to take sexual partners. There is an interesting postscript to women's accounts of their childhood influences. One of the survey questions asks what respondents want to say to children, what messages they want to pass on to the next generation about sex and its place in life.

In many ways, respondents' comments do attempt to improve on experience. We are desperate to avoid giving children the same negative messages we had. Where we were blocked from information, we want children to have it: *'It's important that they can talk to me about everything.'* Where we were told by our families to follow the rules, or urged by our friends to rebel, we are keen that children make their own unbiased decisions: *'Don't do anything you don't want to ... your body is your own ... don't feel pressured into doing anything you feel uncomfortable with.'* And where we got confused about love and sex, we want to tell children not only to distinguish between the two but also to hold out for both: *'Only get involved with someone you care deeply for ... don't just have sex for affection ... don't use sex as a weapon.'*

## FEAR AND OPTIMISM

Underneath all this good advice, however, there is an undercurrent of fear. The sexual revolution has meant that many of us have got hurt, and so we preface our comments with a warning: *'Make sure you use contraception . . . practise safe sex . . . be wary of AIDS . . . if you can't be good, be careful . . . don't sleep around . . . never trust a man.'* We have learnt the hard way that sex can mean trouble. We are desperately concerned that our children learn from our mistakes.

This is understandable but sad. So many of these warnings seem to parallel the negative messages that our parents originally gave us and that we now resent so much. Is there a danger that our children in turn will hear only the negatives in our advice, not realize the concern that lies behind them and end up rebelling as we did? Could it be even that what we think of as negative messages from our parents were in fact just the product of fear — from their own sexual problems, 'before the revolution'?

Happily, though, things have changed somewhat. Respondents' advice to girls growing up includes many statements of encouragement and positivity. We do want to pass on to them a sense of the sheer pleasure of sex, the complete delight in it that we've had throughout our lives: *'Sex is to be enjoyed . . . it's totally natural . . . it's good for you . . . it's great . . . loving . . . brilliant.'*

So perhaps the next generation will receive a different set of messages. Maybe our daughters will look back happily on the ways we influenced them and be able to begin their sexual lives with a positive and optimistic outlook. We can only hope so.

*I find it quite difficult to deal with my children's sexuality. For example my 6-year-old daughter masturbates by crossing her legs very hard and moving up and down. I don't want her to masturbate in public — but neither do I want to make her ashamed of masturbation. Yet I want to be as open as I can with her. I want to explain that her body is her own, and that she shouldn't be pressured into doing anything that she feels uncomfortable with. I want to answer her questions honestly and not leave her ignorant.*

VITAL STATISTICS

15.4 per cent of women had more than 11 partners before they lost their virginity

21.8 per cent received oral sex before they first had intercourse

20.8 per cent had given oral sex before they first had intercourse

30.5 per cent had pre-intercourse sex in front of other people

When heavy petting, 63.2 per cent did things they actively didn't like

# 3. Boyfriends

*I had about eight boyfriends before sexual intercourse occurred. I suppose when I was very young things did progress with each partner, though when you reach a certain stage you've done all there is apart from IT.*

SEX BEFORE INTERCOURSE is all about boyfriends. We may have experimented with girls up to now because they feel safe and are available. (Later, when we have more self-confidence and real self-knowledge, of course, we might turn to women again, if that's what we really want.) But in early adolescence what is normal nowadays is to get pre-sexual experience with boys, and 93.8 per cent of the women took that option.

For some of us simple hormones focus attention. We look across at the boy in the next desk, and, without knowing why, we feel weak. We *'get dizzy'* when we hear boys' voices or see them moving. We start finding excuses to talk, to tease, to fight – anything to get to touch them or to get them to touch us. We want contact with boys because some part of us knows that it will feel good.

*I remember going swimming on holiday with my parents and meeting a boy of about 14. I was 12. I really liked him and, without knowing*

*why, felt strange inside when he came near me. I was very embarrassed.*

And, whether or not we are excited by boys, in this day and age we also need them in order to be seen as successful and to be accepted by our friends. Sex is now a status symbol, in the way it wasn't for our grandmothers. So women often write of the confusion and unhappiness of suffering peer pressure about sex at this time in their lives. Going out with boys is what everyone does, and so we want to do it too. Being sexual with boys is what everyone claims they have done, and so we aim for that as well.

## IS IT LOVE?

There is a myth that says that all teenagers are in love all the time. Teenage girls only go out with boys they are in love with and they only have sex with boys they are passionate about.

*I fell in love for the first time at 15 years old. There was no sexual relationship except kissing. I felt dizzy about him, high from the ground all the time. Our relationship lasted three months, but I still loved him from afar for three years.*

*I looked on him as a big brother at first. Then I fell in love with him, but it was never a sexual relationship. I can't really answer that many questions on him as he died in a motorbike accident. Now my relationships with men are not really important to me anymore, as really I only tell them now that I love them to keep them happy. He took my love with him when he went.*

In fact it isn't like this at all – if indeed it ever were. These women are two of only a very few who mention being in love when asked about adolescent relationships. Quite simply, when we are very young, only a few of us are lucky enough to fall in love at first sight. We are far more likely to choose a partner through opportunity rather than true compatibility or sexual attraction because we are still learning what those things are. And even if we do feel attraction, and even if it is reciprocated, often we are just not socially skilled enough to get together and form a partnership. Many of us settle, at least at first, for going out with with any boy we meet who wants to go out with us and with whom we feel comfortable. We go out with classmates, boys at the youth club, our older brother's friends, or someone else who works at the same Saturday job.

Most of us are between 11 and 17 when we have our first boyfriend. In most accounts of early boyfriends, women speak of going out with boys older than them. Where we are in one class at school, he is in the class higher. If we are at school, he is at college. And, very occasionally, the age gap is wide. He is not our friend, but our parents' friend, someone who has drawn us to one side after a family party or a wedding and suggested that we meet later, in secret. This is deliciously dangerous and also feels especially good. For we're not just going out with a boy – we're going out with a man. He will know what to do, particularly when it comes to sex.

Even when our partner is no older than we are, he is undoubtedly more experienced – undoubtedly because 63.9 per cent of women say that they don't doubt it. Certainly it is what our partners want us to believe. They never seem to be ignorant, confused or uncertain. They enjoy everything we do. They push us on to go further and to do more. They try to persuade us to go through sexual barriers. Only a few women remember that *'I initiated my pre-sexual experiences, mainly with partners who were as green as I was,'* or *'They were all a lot younger than I was . . . we used to fumble.'*

In fact the truth is that, at the time, probably many of our partners know as little as we do. They are probably just as uncertain as we are and twice as scared of being rejected. But they put on a good show: *'The man always initiated things. I don't know if they were more sexually experienced than I, although certainly that was the impression they liked to give.'*

## THE NUMBERS GAME

When it comes to how many boyfriends we have before we finally lose our virginity, they are some very distinct patterns. Some 11 per cent of respondents have just one boyfriend before intercourse. He is *'the one'* who we feel is the right person to take our virginity, and he does. This partner is probably someone we've known for a while, a friend from school or the boy next door. We've got similar interests and are great friends; so we probably talk through sex with each other and discover it together. Then we wait until we're both old enough to feel like intercourse, which is probably a few months or a year after we've started going out.

*I had no boyfriends before sex, just casual childish dates. The one I lost my virginity to was the first one. I loved him for a year before doing it, so I wasn't really interested in anyone else.*

Most women, about 68.7 per cent, have up to half a dozen boyfriends. We possibly begin with playground contact, where 'going out with' means talking, walking home, meeting at the school disco or going, chaperoned, to the cinema. We may have contact, and it may feel exciting, but we often don't take it seriously.

*I think my first experience of sexual sensations was when, at the age of 12-ish I had my first 'proper' kiss, and the fella pushed himself right up close to me and felt my breasts.*

We usually go out with each boy for quite a short time, one or two months. We may keep sexual contact at a very low level – holding hands or kissing. We don't feel particularly aroused by our partner, and we wait to progress to real sex until we are old enough to meet a boy we feel truly passionate about.

If we do sexually advance with each partner, this progression follows a different pattern from that with a single boyfriend. Then, we discovered together how to please each other, and there was a great sense of cooperation. With several boyfriends we spend a lot of our time holding back and holding out. For boys nowadays know that they can expect to have sex with a girl – and they don't want to wait. They suggest, persuade, protest. We turn away, move wandering hands and resist – until eventually the boyfriend realizes that he isn't going to get any further.

*When I was 15, a 16-year-old boy, with whom I'd formed a relationship through letters, fingered me in a secluded alleyway at a train station. He got his willy out and wanted me to play with him, but I was too scared. It was the first time I'd seen an erect penis, and it was enormous! I went home incredibly sore and bruised. I can't remember enjoying it much, but he was a wonderful kisser! He never wrote to me again.*

## LOSING INTEREST

The bottom line may well be this: if we don't go at the pace our boyfriend wants, he's simply not interested in us. The first time this happens is shocking; we can't believe that anyone would leave us simply because we said no. But when it happens two or three times, we know what to expect. Then we either start saying yes or accept that boys will leave in the end: *'Those who were obviously after one thing then gave me the elbow when I refused to be touched on the breasts.'*

At this point many of us do start saying yes. Sometimes that's because we are being pressured, but often it's because partnership sex is actually starting to feel good. When we get to the point of mutual masturbation, all of a sudden there doesn't seem to be any point in holding out. In any case, most of our friends are already saying that they have gone 'the whole way', so we know that it must be time for us to do the same. With the next boyfriend that we feel we can trust – or the first boyfriend to dare to ask for everything – we say yes.

Or we may be part of that group of girls who, however many partners they go out with, seem to take control of what is happening. The number of partners we have varies – from just a couple to 'lots and lots'. We may progress steadily with each partner, or we may have a 'hand-holding' relationship with the first few and then suddenly leap forward, as we start to get more aroused, to masturbation, oral sex and then on to intercourse.

These are the 'sexual decision-makers', we spoke of in chapter 2, often part of a younger age group of respondents, the daughters of informed, sexually aware mothers, and almost a new breed, a new generation. They may still gain more sexual experience earlier than, for example, their grandmothers did, but they go at their own pace, take control of their relationships, keep saying no until they are ready to say yes. They leave partners who pressure them and accept being left by partners who want more. They find that they get more pleasure with every new relationship, and they want to keep finding out what really works in sex: *'With each boyfriend I experimented more ... I got more adventurous with age and with experience ... Braver, more experienced, more conscious of what I wanted.'*

## WHERE DO WE GO?

The questionnaire asks whether any pre-sexual experiences took place in public, and 63.2 per cent of women answer a horrified, no, of course they didn't. The other 36.8 per cent, however, explain that they had nowhere private to be with their partners, so the only option was to do their love-making *'at parties ... on school trips ... in the car ... on the field ... behind the bike shed ... in the bus shelter ... at the back row in the cinema'*. And when they do have to go to these places, there's a sort of ostrich effect of doing these wonderful, passionate things for the first time; they don't feel that they are in public, or that they are being watched. They imagine that they are in their own private place, doing their own private things. And, because of this, they can be wonderfully outrageous.

*My second partner and I used to be as daring as we could, without anyone else noticing. I remember at school, when we used to be in class together, we would flirt with each other, and I would let him see parts of my body from across the room, without others noticing. I would usually pull my skirt a little higher or unbutton my blouse so that he could see my underwear.*

*For several years we used to gather at a friend's house on a Monday evening, about eight or ten young people. I was always with one particular guy. We would kiss in the room and then go over on to the landing to indulge in full petting. At any time people could and would walk past us.*

## WHAT DO WE DO?

Before we lose our virginity, one step after another, we do everything. Everything, that is, except oral sex. We begin with cuddling and kissing: kissing is most girls' *'favourite thing'* at this age. It's something we know about and have seen other people do, at least on television. It feels nice, makes us feel loved and wanted but also safe. We press lips softly or very hard. (French kissing, with the tongue, if often felt to be *'common'* or going a little too far.) Along with kissing, we are happy to hug and cuddle, although we may prefer gentle, almost non-sexual touches, while the boy will prefer to *'push up close to me ... thrust ... hug urgently'*.

We're not really aware at this stage of how our partner is trying to recreate his own masturbation experiences, the forcefulness in kissing and holding that he may need in order to turn him on. We're only conscious of his strength and force, and it may worry or even frighten us a bit. It doesn't seem to us much like loving. The women who speak most happily of their pre-intercourse experiences consistently used words like *'gentle ... slow ... sensitive ... affectionate'* about their partners, boys who were probably either naturally gentle or had learnt how to reassure a beginner.

The next step is fondling breasts. Perhaps at the cinema, with arm round shoulders, his hand moves down to cup a breast. Even though with a first or second boyfriend some of us may say no, this step quickly becomes acceptable, though for a boy to nuzzle at rather than touch breasts is seen as rather *'experienced'*. What is not quite so acceptable, a real watershed in a relationship, is the removal of clothes above the waist. This step is, for many of us, the point at which sexual feeling starts to replace sensual feeling: *'I first felt sexual when I was 16, and my boyfriend lifted up my top slightly and touched my stomach.'* Removing clothes gives a sense of real intimacy and is certainly a bargaining counter to offer in order to please a boy, persuade him to stay even though we are not prepared to go the whole way. At the same time it still feels safe and under control.

*My partner at the time initiated everything and was generally more experienced than myself. I would allow petting and kissing and was happy to do whatever he wanted. I remember enjoying having my nipples sucked, as this couldn't get you pregnant!*

## GENITAL TOUCHING

The next stage is touching each others' 'parts'. And, at this point, accounts of what happen start to sound just a little more wary and unwilling. Many women use words like, *'I allowed ... I was on the receiving end of ...'*, phrases that sound as if they are simply keeping still and letting things happen rather than participating and enjoying. What is happening is somewhat scary. Perhaps they're reaching the limit of what they are happy doing. It feels like a watershed. If we are going to stop, we probably stop now.

> *I was on the receiving end of upper and lower body petting. I was aware of what we were doing, and it was always in the back of cars, cinema or doorways. I would not allow French kissing. I was happy to be touched and kissed but was not happy to touch a boy's genitals. I think I enjoyed kissing most.*

Also, up to now, what has been done has been mutual. Our partner has kissed; we have kissed back. And while his touching our breasts has seemed a bit naughty, our touching his chest is simply affectionate and definitely acceptable. But when we move to genital contact, things start to get challenging. For while having your vagina and clitoris stroked feels nice, having to touch his penis feels strange and frightening: *'Genitals felt revolting, and I didn't know what to do with them ... I wasn't too impressed with male secretions ... I was always comfortable with the exploration of my body but hesitant to discover my boyfriends ... I remember being very uncomfortable when I saw my first erect penis. The idea of masturbating a man was disturbing.'*

## STOP POINT

At this point, the majority of us have gone as far as we are happy to go before intercourse. 'Below the waist petting', usually with clothes on, sometimes without, is the last common stage before going the whole way; all but 20 per cent of respondents drew the line here. It takes a great deal more experience and a great deal more self-confidence before most of us are happy with oral sex. The questionnaire answers aren't really clear why this should be. Many women who said no to oral sex before intercourse are later in life happy to do it and are aroused by it. But, at this age, at this stage, somehow receiving oral sex seems too intrusive and giving it seems very offputting.

Who goes further? It's a minority of us who do everything, up to and including oral sex, before losing our virginity. But this minority seems to feel subtly differently from other girls. We take to sex like ducks to water, know what we like and want, seem enthusiastic to 'do everything' and indeed want to do so before we actually go on to have intercourse: *'He did the whole works, oral, everything. I was aware of what he was doing, and what it was doing to me, and I loved it all ... Before I lost my virginity, I went as far as I possibly could – mutual masturbation, mutual oral sex, massage etc.'*

These women are often those 'sexual decision-makers' who took their time and didn't rush into full sex. But that doesn't mean to say that they don't take full advantage of what happens before intercourse. It is as if they want to spin out the pleasure, to learn how to make love fully before actually doing so. In many cases they have actually discussed the issue with their partner and have decided to wait a while before going on to penetration – not because they aren't enjoying themselves, but because it doesn't feel right yet: *'Yes, I definitely progressed with each partner and had very exciting and satisfying sex without intercourse.'*

## ENJOYABLE OR NOT?

It all sounds wonderful. And, in many cases, it is. At this stage in the sex game, before going the whole way, many of us have night after night of passionate, mutual, orgasmic sex with our partner. Many of us enjoy ourselves a great deal. We do get sexual pleasure. Nearly a third have orgasms.

Emotionally, too, it is often great fun. We love feeling close to our partners and wanted by them. Or we like being approved of and feeling emotionally powerful. Quite apart from, and often more than, the physical pleasure, we like the attention and the affection: *'I enjoyed the contact and affection more than the sex ... I enjoyed the comfort ... the sex was less exciting than the tension, flirtation and closeness ... I enjoyed seeing them excited, and I enjoyed them being pleased with me.'*

But one fact that emerges very clearly from the questionnaire responses is that not every girl revels in what she's doing as much as this. For perhaps one of the most worrying set of statistics in the whole survey is that at some time before they have intercourse 63.2 per cent of women do something that they don't like and don't want to do.

In terms of sexual sensation we often don't enjoy ourselves all that much. Some of us actually dislike everything we do with our partners apart from kissing. Particular hates were *'having men slobbering over me ... being undressed ... having my lower body touched ... I didn't like him touching my breasts because I didn't have any ... I was happy to talk but unhappy about touching.'* This woman's account is very typical.

*We lived in the country, and we used to go into the fields. He expected me to give him blow jobs, which I did, but didn't enjoy it. He would touch me between the legs but never licked me, would finger me as well, which I didn't enjoy. I never had an orgasm, and I didn't really enjoy any of this, which looking back was probably due to his inexperience. I wasn't really aware of what I was doing, but he seemed to enjoy it.*

## WHY NO PLEASURE?

What is the problem? Most of us have already felt good sexually when we are masturbating. Many of us are having regular orgasm by ourselves. The unhappiness of our partnership experiences seems to be caused far more by what is happening with our emotions than in our sensations, far more to do with learning to have sex with a partner than with simply being able to have pleasure.

A key element is fear of failure: *'I was so scared of doing something wrong . . . I felt awkward . . . I didn't know how, and I didn't want to look silly . . . I felt totally helpless and useless.'* We know what to do with our own genitals, but have no idea what to do with a penis. In these early experiences success is all important. No one has shown us, and we are terrified of getting it wrong. Of course, a boy who seems very experienced, or one who pressures rather than encourages us, just makes things worse.

Secondly, lack of experience on both sides means that very often, there isn't actually much sexual pleasure for us in what's happening. Our partners may claim to be experienced, but *'fumbled . . . had no expertise'.* For our part we may feel unable to introduce into the proceedings our own sexual knowledge, our awareness of what works for us.

*No, I never had an orgasm on these occasions, although I had already discovered masturbation and have always been able to have orgasms very easily that way.*

*I didn't orgasm with male partners, though I did with female ones.*

Also, many of us at this point feel guilty about what we're doing. Surprisingly there was no clear association between how guilty women feel and how strict or inhibited their parents have been – though, certainly, for some women there is a link. What seems to be very clear, though, is the connection between girls being pressured to do something sexually and their feeling guilty about it. And this is true whether that sexual pressure is happening here and now or has happened in the past. So girls who are pushed by their boyfriends to go further than they want feel more guilty than those who are allowed to make their own decisions freely. And those who have been abused as children feel more guilty about sex than those who have not.

Of course it doesn't seem fair that it is the person on the receiving end of the pressure who feels bad, but there it is. It is as if in these situations guilt is our body's way of saying that something unpleasant has happened, but not being precise about who has committed the crime. Instead of feeling critical of the person who is pressuring us, we feel critical of ourselves for giving in. Instead of feeling angry at our abuser, we guilt-trip ourselves out of sexual pleasure as a form of punishment.

*I was almost raped at the age of 13 by an older boy who made me masturbate him first. From the age of 13 to 18 I never indulged in any form of petting. I went out with lots of boys but only kissed. Occasionally they would try and feel my breasts, and I would be very angry and never allow it. From the age of 14 to 18 I would have different boyfriends ranging from weeks to a few months relationships. I enjoyed kissing but never felt any further sexual urges. In fact I was rather repelled by the thought of sex and intercourse. At 16 other friends would tease me about it. I thought I was frigid, because I could not think of doing any form of petting or intercourse with anyone.*

## THE SECRET OF ENJOYMENT

It's very clear from every respondent's account of these pre-intercourse experiences that to enjoy them, we have to feel in control of the process. For it isn't a case of instant sexual awakening – only half a dozen women in the whole 200 kiss and are then immediately ready to take the step to intercourse. We need to progress step by step, taking our time until things feel right.

It usually does feel right in the end (unless, of course, we are experimenting with a sex to whom we are not really attracted). Respondent after respondent describes how, having at first been wary of some sexual act, with some particular partner – or with one particular sexual move – it suddenly begins to feel good: *'I first felt sexual when I was 17, and this boy kissed me – and it was actually nice. Up until then men kissing had actually repulsed me ... I had kissed a few boys before him but kissing him was different, and he was the first one I would let touch my body ... I would allow a little more each time, and I wanted a little more each time.'*

But this natural process of adjustment has to happen freely. If we are pushed to override our natural fear – and, of course, being pushed to do so is much more typical nowadays, when sex is seen to be the expectable norm – then we feel threatened. Passion becomes blocked. Sex can become permanently disagreeable rather than increasingly enjoyable.

On the other hand, where we are in control of the process, then passion develops easily and steadily. Where we can do what we want, and only what we find pleasurable, where we can take the initiative and are able to introduce our own sexual knowledge, then we get aroused. And many women – the sexual decision-makers described earlier – do just this. They decide how fast and how far they go: *'I said no to ... I wouldn't let anything be done to me until ... No taking clothes off below the waist, until I felt ready ... I wouldn't go to full intercourse yet.'* It sounds as if they are inhibited – but, in fact, they are staying in control. And, in the end, because of this, they often become the most uninhibited lovers.

## THE SUPPORTIVE SEDUCER

If boyfriends support us to stay in control, then we often develop sexually even more quickly and easily. Where a partner is happy to take his time and go at a pace that is right for us, we can relax and begin to enjoy ourselves. Perhaps all the adolescent boys who want so desperately to get their girlfriends' knickers off should remember this.

*My boyfriend was not more experienced than I was, but he knew a lot more. He understood more about the emotions and feelings of sex. Before we had sex we masturbated together, gave each other oral sex and petted each other. It took me a while to be comfortable, but I was not pressured. My boyfriend was patient and suggested things and was happy to wait until I was comfortable.*

The result of such support is an equality in sexual development. We gain in confidence and are increasingly able to use our sexual knowledge to show our partners what we need and what pleases us. He, in turn, relieved of the burden of having to take the lead all the time, becomes more relaxed, more sensual and more expert. Both of us respond to our mutual pleasure. And where both we and our partners go at a pace that is right, where we build up trust and experience without pressure, then quite simply, everything is possible.

*After I had known him for two or three months, things really got moving. He showed me how to give him pleasure by masturbation and then gradually oral sex. I was happy to do all that was asked of me, this was mostly oral sex. I liked to be touched and masturbated by my partner but could only reach orgasm if I masturbated myself. I wasn't sure if I'd had an orgasm the first time, but I soon realized afterwards that it must have been the real thing because it made me feel so excited and breathless.*

VITAL STATISTICS

40 per cent of women lose their virginity below the legal age of consent

38.9 per cent don't use contraception when they lose their virginity

Only 22 per cent physically enjoy the experience of losing their virginity

Only 5.7 per cent orgasmed when they lost their virginity

26.1 per cent of women never have sex again with the person to whom they lose their virginity

80.9 per cent of women are glad they have lost their virginity

# 4. The first time

*The family were away, and he came over specifically to take my virginity – we arranged it. I bought beautiful white-lace flowing lingerie, and he brought a condom or two. I was so nervous and excited. He was telling me not to be afraid and being so nice. Then it was going in, and it was so painful. I was lying there thinking: I am never doing this again if this is what it's like. Physically it was excruciating, though I didn't want him to stop or withdraw. Emotionally it was one of the most amazing experiences ever.*

LOSING OUR VIRGINITY is still important to us as women. Things may have changed from when the 'first time' was a once-and-for-all step only to be taken after marriage. But for the vast majority of the women who answered the questionnaire, first intercourse is still a change point, a step to be taken carefully. We believe it will be wonderful, and we want it to be special.

The main reason we lose our virginity is because we feel the time has come for us to do so. We may be in our mid-teens – 68.8 per cent of respondents were between the ages of 14 and 17 when they first had sex – and want to grow up. We have been told that intercourse is the way to make 'the transition from girl to woman'. We sense that now is the right time to do that.

Or we may feel panicked because all our friends tell us about sleeping with their boyfriends, and we don't want to be left behind. Although many say, '*I would have preferred to wait,*' a lot of women comment that '*I lost my virginity because everyone else had . . . I felt left out . . . If you were a virgin, you were considered strange.*' When we feel like this, we sleep with '*the first one I was happy to sleep with*'. This decision often has no relation to any social guidelines or even any law: 37.5 per cent of women who answered the questionnaire lost their virginity before they were 16, the age of legal sexual consent. And the decision also has little link to where our true passions lie: even the committed lesbians in the survey lost their virginity when the time came.

## PARTNER PRESSURE

We also have intercourse with a partner because he wants it. In this case we are usually in our late teens. We've done most things we're happy to do before full sex. We are in a relationship that we like and that involves our emotions. We love our partner and want to give him what he wants. And, often, we agree not only because '*I thought the world of him*' but also because '*I felt sure that this would cement the relationship.*' As we'll see later, our certainty may or may not be well judged.

Sometimes we give in to pressure. Our partner is desperate for the experience, for the pleasure, for the chance to lose his own virginity. And there seems no reason not to agree to penetration when in fact we're doing everything else. Pre-intercourse boyfriends may have left if we said no, but the partner to whom we decide to lose our virginity is often sufficiently emotionally involved to stay with us regardless. By now, though, he is really distressed if we keep refusing; many women report that their partners pleaded or were angry if they wouldn't give in: '*He wanted it . . . he begged me to let him do it . . . he pestered and at last I gave in . . . he had spent many hours weekly trying to persuade me.*' Finally, we add up the pros and cons; we reckon that keeping our virginity may not be worth it after all.

> *We'd spent the evening in front of the TV, and finally we were alone. I started to feel annoyed and tried to get him to go, but he made excuse after excuse and kept on and on at me to have intercourse with him. I think that in the end I gave in because I knew the atmosphere would become intolerable.*

Some of us quite simply want to lose our virginity because we feel that we never will. Once past the age of 20 the reasons that we give for first intercourse suddenly shift. We stop talking about how much our friends or partners are pressurizing us and start talking about how bad we ourselves feel because we are virgins. We become frightened that we aren't attractive, that we're lacking sexually, that we're different from other women. We're frightened that we will never have sex, and we make up our minds to have it as soon as possible – often with the first man with whom we have the opportunity, whether we like him or not, whether we fancy him or not, whether we know him or not.

The interesting thing about all these reasons for having first sex is that none of them is linked to pure pleasure. Only a handful of women out of the whole 200 say that they were overcome with passion and so longed for penetration. For a large number of us, having intercourse is the result of a mental decision, not of physical passion.

## CHOOSING NOT TO LOSE

Technically speaking, just two respondents say that they never had a virginity to lose. One *'took my own virginity with a recorder though I was never aware of this as being sexual'*, and another *'had my hymen removed by a gynaecologist (thanks to a liberal mother and that being a bit of a fashion at the time in Germany)'*.

Just a few of us wait until we meet a man we are certain we'll remain with for life, and only sleep with that man after we are engaged or married. For us, penetration is the outward sign of a lifelong commitment and has to be delayed until that commitment is made. Most of us, however, go *'almost the whole way'* with that same partner before we are married, and many 'jump the gun' by having intercourse in the week preceding the formal ceremony. Only three women from the whole survey waited until after they were married to have sex – one older, pre-pill and two younger, post-pill respondents.

Many of us, usually younger women, discuss having sex with our boyfriends and decide to wait until it feels completely right. We want to be sure that we will enjoy intercourse, and as described in Chapter 3 we often want to do a wide variety of sexual things before penetration. In some ways then, even though we have no expectation that the partner to whom we lose our virginity will be our partner for life, we follow the same road as the women who 'save themselves' – though we do it because of an inner sense of what feels right rather than because of social or religious pressures.

## STAYING A VIRGIN

Just two respondents were virgins at the time they filled in the questionnaire. Both, contrary to common myth, say that they are fully sexually aware, masturbate regularly and are far from frigid. They want other women to realize that their view of sexuality is just as valid as the majority view, and that their decision to remain virgins is just as much of a conscious choice as that of women who opt to have sex. One, aged 25, challenges the view of first sex as a transition point from girl to woman.

*It's something I feel strongly about, this question of virginity. I don't want to be ignored or dismissed just because I've never met a man with whom I want to have sex . . . . Womanhood does not come from sex, or blood, hormones or age but from maturity and mental outlook.*

The other woman, aged 40, writes that she tends to get involved with unsuitable men. So although she has enjoyed a full range of non-penetrative options – this is a woman who loves to come anything up to ten times in each masturbation session – she has so far not found someone with whom she wants to have intercourse.

These respondents' choice is deliberate and voluntary. And, however much we may feel that they are missing out, their decision is an interesting lesson for all those of us who feel we have spent our sexual lives having our decisions made for us.

## WHO TAKES OUR VIRGINITY?

The man we choose to have first-time sex with is usually one who we know and trust. Over 80 per cent of women choose men whom they have known for months or years rather than for weeks or hours. Over half of them will choose a regular boyfriend, though only 14 per cent will choose a man who will later become their husband.

*I was just 18, and my partner was 19. I had known him for about 18 months. He had been out with my older sister for a short time, and about four months later, we started going out together. When he took my virginity, we had been together for nine months.*

*I was 14, and he was 18. I had known him for two years, been dating him for six months, and he was my future husband.*

Of course some women don't follow this pattern – usually for one of three reasons. They may suddenly and for the first time with a brand new partner realize what sex is all about and after that simply see no need to wait. Or they may sleep with a man who isn't a boyfriend but who has status: *'I had known him a few weeks, but he wasn't a proper boyfriend, just the local lad all the girls fancied.'* And just a few women, whose main aim is simply to lose their virginity, will choose a casual partner because they don't want to wait for a long-term relationship – three respondents said that it happened on a one-night stand: *'I was 17, and he was 23. He was a casual acquaintance, I had known him about an hour, and we were very drunk.'*

Just as we choose pre-intercourse partners slightly older than we are, we also usually lose our virginity to someone older. If it happens when we are below the age of 14, he is likely to be more than just a few years our senior because boys of our own age are not usually ready for full sex. (Though one woman says she lost her virginity at age 10 to a boy aged 11: *'I don't know that he was a virgin, but I presume so.'*) If our first time happens in our mid-teens, it's usually with someone a few months or years older, a member of our own peer group, from our circle.

And there is a curious age watershed when we are about 17. Once we are older than this, the age gap between us and our partner widens again. Some of us, wary of losing our virginity, find that only an older, more experienced partner can give us the pleasure and encouragement we need to go the whole way. Others, desperate to get rid of 'it', choose the first man we meet, without really worrying about how old he is.

## PARTNER EXPERIENCE

It is no surprise that 70 per cent of women lose their virginity to a man who isn't a virgin. Either his prior experience leads him to expect that we will 'go the whole way' – and, often with very little thought for our feelings, he pushes on regardless, and the deed is done. Or his prior experience allows him to hold back, to teach, to lead, to guide us into full sex. If he isn't experienced, it's much more likely that we are long-term partners, who after going out for a while have now finally decided that this is the right step for both of us to take together.

Contrary to the myth that a woman likes to lose her virginity to an experienced man, we don't seem to feel strongly about whether our partner is a virgin or not. We feel best about a man who takes the initiative without pressure and makes us feel safe – but this man can be a virgin of

16 or a highly experienced 30 year old. Respondents don't comment on a man's having an advanced technique, either for or against. They do feel bad about men who lie about their past experience: *'He said he was a virgin ... but now I don't think he was.'* And just one woman wryly says:

> *We'd known each other for four and a half months. We were both virgins. I had been pestering him to have sex, but he was the one who was saving himself for Mrs Right.*

We will probably lose our virginity on our partner's territory – his bedsit, flat or his parent's house. Sometimes this is because there he feels sufficiently in control to make a move, and sometimes it is simply that he has more freedom to have sex on his home ground than we do on ours. Far fewer do it in 'her bedroom' and just a few in 'her parents' house' – often when a boyfriend has been allowed to stay over and has crept into 'her bedroom' in the early hours of the morning. Cars, once the traditional place to have sex, only account for 5.2 per cent of first experiences – almost always in 'his car' rather than 'hers'. And most of the other locations were on 'neutral ground', well away from both sets of eagle-eyed parents: hotel bedrooms, friends' spare bedrooms, parties, a swimming pool, an orchard, the grounds of a stately home, behind a bus shelter, against a wall, behind a shed in the school grounds during the disco, and under the snooker table.

## WHO INITIATES IT?

It is very often the boy who starts things off, or at any rate that's our experience at the time. Some 56.4 per cent of women say that the boy suggested intercourse, and a remarkable number of partners do check out verbally before the act.

> *He asked if I wanted to go all the way, and I agreed. It was dark in the room, and I think we both had all our clothes off. He turned away to face a lamp while putting on a condom. I felt anxious but expectant. I don't think it occurred to me I could have said no.*

In some ways, simply asking just a few minutes ahead of time isn't the best option. Discussions in advance and preparation for the event usually works: both partners have time to be sure that this is really what they want. But a simple question and answer a few minutes beforehand leaves room for mistakes. For most of us make the decision with our minds and not our bodies; then, having actually said the word yes, we feel unable to change our minds if, during love-making, full sex suddenly doesn't feel

right. What might be better for women, even if frustrating for men, would
be to check out at the moment just before penetration or the few seconds
just afterwards whether this is really what we want, whether full intercourse is what feels right physically to us now.

Just a few women, usually the younger ones, say that it was they
who initiated first intercourse rather than their partner. They're usually
already sexually intimate with him, and intercourse is just the next step,
which they confidently suggest just when they're ready. Their partner
happily agrees.

*We got a bit drunk at his room in a squat nearby. I asked him to*
*accompany me to my own room. I initiated it because I didn't want to*
*be a virgin any longer.*

In longer-term relationships the majority of women say that the
decision is fully mutual. They have often discussed it with their partner
months in advance, decided to wait until the time was right, arranged the
contraception – in many cases waiting several weeks until the birth-
control pill took effect – and planned the occasion. They feel totally in
control, enjoy the actual event a good deal and are able to ride out any
possible disappointments.

## THE RITUAL

Once we've decided that we're going to have full sex, we move into the
ritual that we have already established with our partner or have experienced with other boys. Kissing first, getting more and more passionate,
then some fondling of breasts.

We may undress at this point – 51.4 per cent of respondents do,
while the rest take off enough clothing to allow the boy to enter them:
'*I still had my dress on, but it was pulled up.*' Just exactly how much we
take off is linked mainly with whether we have sex in less-than-private
places: far more couples took their clothes off when the sexual act
happened indoors and in private. But it's also linked to whether, before
losing our virginity, we have ever stripped off completely in front of
anyone. Those of us who do remove everything have often done so before
as part of a developing relationship; we revel in being naked and feel it
to be only natural.

Having taken our clothes off, we continue to kiss and to fondle for
a minute or two. We are aware, perhaps, that our partner is getting
aroused. If we are used to masturbating him, we may hold his penis,
though most of us don't need to help our partner get an erection: the
thought of intercourse is enough. We ourselves start to get aroused, and

we feel the excitement building at the thought of what will happen. We wonder how it will be.

But, then, a totally unexpected thing happens. Instead of the touching and fondling that felt so safe; instead of the delicious feeling and licking that we have learnt to enjoy; instead of the rising passion that many of us have experienced over time, we have penetration: *'He got on top of me, penetrated me, jumped up and down.'* As many as 96.7 per cent of women report that when they made love for the first time, foreplay was almost non-existent. Once penetration was possible, everything else was forgotten. Just a few say that their first time included mutual masturbation and oral sex, while only a handful more make it clear that there was enough kissing and fondling for them to be really aroused. For the rest, suddenly all the exciting kissing, touching and fondling disappears, and what is left is simple penetration.

> *His parents had gone to bed, and we were kissing and petting on the sofa. We both got very excited and rolled off on to the floor. He got his penis out and put it between my legs; it was wet. He said 'It's going to happen', and he pulled my pants down, though we were both still dressed. He was pushing hard to enter me, but it was very difficult. I said, 'I don't think it will go in.' He said, 'It's got to happen sometime, so it might as well be now,' and gave another push.*

## WHEN IT FEELS GOOD

For some of us being penetrated feels wonderful. We move with our partner, we enjoy the novelty of the sensations. We like the closeness and warmth. We welcome the meaning it gives to our relationship, or the fact that it is finally happening, and that we are finally a woman. We love the fact that it is 'real sex'.

> *My mother was out at work, and we were petting naked in the bedroom. He was very gentle and very encouraging, trying hard not to hurt me although he was very turned on. He made sure I was aroused and inserted two fingers inside my vagina; normally in petting I think he only used one. Then he penetrated me. I remember enjoying making love immensely, although it was quite quick. I remember thinking how much more beautiful and natural it was than the furtive masturbating we had enjoyed up till then.*

For 22 per cent of women, there is sexual pleasure. Some have been with a partner for a while and got to know each other's bodies and the specific techniques they need. Others are able to get that knowledge during first-time penetration simply because there is real trust and care between them. If our partner is encouraging, gentle and able to take his time, then we may get increasingly aroused. Penetration may hurt, and we may bleed – but if we feel good about the decision and are enjoying the event, the pain and the blood are largely something to be proud of.

*It was a week after my sixteenth birthday As it was outside we only removed the clothes we had to, and as we forgot the foreplay I was far too dry, and he couldn't really enter. So we gave up. Later that night we were in my grandmother's kitchen saying goodnight and had one last try. Thinking nothing had happened, we turned on the light to find the wall and floor covered in blood. After frantically tidying it up, I spent the rest of the night giggling to myself.*

There is even a tiny chance we may orgasm – though only 5.7 per cent of women do. We are more likely to climax if we are one of those women who has been in control of her sexual development and has planned to lose her virginity in advance. We are more likely to if we have developed our sexual knowledge already through mutual masturbation and oral sex. We are more likely to if we are one of the very few women who included a lot of genital touching in the moments before penetration. We are more likely to if we have orgasmed before, often, with our partner. When all these things happen, then losing our virginity can be a good experience.

*We had planned to have full sex at some point but didn't know when or where. My parents owned a shop and downstairs was a long hallway; he always used to see me home, and we'd kiss and touch in the hall for hours.*
*We came home after a party one night, and I remember that we were laughing. This time, I was against the wall and he asked if it was time to try. I said, yes – the curiosity was killing me. He gently entered me and we were both still standing; I remember looking at the moon through the skylight above the front door. Eventually, we lay down and carried on. I remember really into getting into it and loving it. It was very delicate and beautiful, as we were both discovering each other's bodies. He came very quickly, but we stayed in that position for ages and just held on to each other; I was very wet and had an orgasm. I enjoyed it immensely, felt as if I was really a woman and remember thinking, Wow! This is what everyone goes on about. It's great!*

## WHEN IT FEELS BAD

Unfortunately that woman's experience isn't typical. The myth – believed by adults as well as teenagers, perpetuated by traditional literature as much as by the popular media – is that losing your virginity is always a wonderful event, and that through it you discover what passion is. That certainly isn't what the women in this survey say. For while certainly many women are glad they had had intercourse, in fact 56.7 per cent didn't physically enjoy it, and another 20.5 per cent found it a very mixed experience. Only 22 per cent of women rated it positively. (Six women, in fact, said that they lost their virginity as a result of being raped; these women's experience will be dealt with more completely in chapter 20, on Saying No.)

Emotionally the experience may be very disappointing. We expected 'real sex' to be very loving. But many of us, particularly those who know our partners for only a short while, find that it isn't. Intercourse can be affectionate, but it can also be thrusting and violent – and a man in the middle of a long-awaited penetrative orgasm may not be the gentle and sensitive partner of whom we dreamt. So woman after woman comments that *'there was no emotion, or caring or kissing.'*

Physically our disappointment can be even greater. We've probably known since we first touched ourselves or started petting with a partner that we were capable of pleasure. Many of us even know that we can come. We've heard how good 'real sex' can be, not only from the media but also from our partners, as they try to persuade us, and from our friends, as they boast of what they have done. We know that sex should feel amazing – and often it's not: *'I thought that it would feel much nicer, an earth-shattering experience, but it was not . . . I felt very sore and and uncomfortable and totally disillusioned . . . I experienced no sensation whatever except boredom . . . I can remember lying there and thinking, God, is this what all the fuss is about? I am not doing this again . . . I used to read a lot of Mills and Boon books and thought the first time was going to be wonderful. It was crap!'*

In hindsight it's obvious why. Penetration just by itself is likely to pleasure a woman physically only with the right positions, movements and clitoral contact. The first time we have sex we and our partners may not know this, and, even if we do, we may not have the time to find out what they are for us. Also, moving from minimal foreplay direct to intercourse, as most women say they did when they lost their virginity, is rarely the way to guarantee enjoyment, let alone climax. It's no coincidence that those women who do report pleasure and orgasm are those who say that first sex was an event that lasted a while, took place in relaxed circumstances and included a range of sexual options such as mutual masturbation and oral sex.

There's a final reason why losing our virginity may be unpleasant. If we aren't aroused, then the actual physical trauma of breaking the hymen is worse. More women who don't enjoy the experience comment on the discomfort involved and remember it as *'violent . . . I screamed with the pain . . . I hated it.'* More surprisingly they also remember the bleeding as more upsetting, while women who enjoy the experience often see the bleeding as something to giggle about proudly.

## LATER THE SAME DAY...

It should be clear by now that the accounts of women's first experience of penetration are often quite mixed. Many of them would be forgiven for never bothering again. But women are very resilient, and time changes minds. So while well over three-quarters of respondents feel bad or mixed during the actual event, when asked about their emotions later the same day, only half still feel negative.

Those women who feel bad after losing their virginity report feeling *'stupid . . . embarrassed . . . scared'*. Some, even those who used contraception (see chapter 17), are worried about possible pregnancy. Many feel guilty and angry – and often turn this feeling against their partner.

*Later that night I felt a bit guilty and ashamed, as if I had done something wrong. I blamed my boyfriend. The next night he stayed over. I would not let him touch me at all. I felt actually repulsed by him.*

These negative feelings may be why many of us who before first intercourse felt that we had a stable relationship often suddenly find ourselves splitting up with our boyfriends very soon afterwards. As many as 26.1 per cent of women never have sex again with the partner to whom they lost their virginity. So while many of us expect that having full intercourse with a partner is going to be the way to cement the relationship, 25 per cent of us will be proved completely wrong.

Some of these relationship endings do seem to be down to 'screw and run' partners.

*I came down to earth when I realized he didn't really want a serious girlfriend. I had been naïve; he never lied. I was just stupid, but went on loving him and dreaming of when we'd be together again.*

But more than a few women describe how first sex with a partner was last sex because of negative emotions that spring to the surface.

*I had been with him for seven months. He was my steady boyfriend, and we had discussed intercourse beforehand. But we never had sex again. After the experience, there began to be problems in the relationship, and two or three months later we split up.*

These events, along with the physical and emotional disappointment, can affect us long-term: *'I actually went backwards sexually ... I took a large step backwards.'* After the extremely pleasant times we've spent masturbating ourselves or orgasming through foreplay with our partners, the experience of unpleasurable intercourse may start us doubting whether we like 'real sex' or not. We may blame ourselves for not climaxing – after all our partner seems to have no problem, so it must be our fault.

And we may start to doubt our own sexual knowledge, may abandon our own self-touching techniques in favour of our partner's thrusting – which at first, in fact, may not give us as much pleasure. It may take us years to reclaim our own ways of gaining pleasure and to incorporate them in partnership love-making. Only one woman says that *'I enjoyed the heavy petting sessions better, so went back to them for a while'*, a brave move, and one that probably allowed her to enjoy intercourse more fully when she eventually felt ready to try again.

## A WELCOME LOSS?

Women who feel good in the long term about losing their virginity usually do so largely because they feel good about their partner: *'I really loved my boyfriend and felt it had been right.'* They probably stay together for a while and build on their relationship.

Other reasons why we feel good about it are to do with our original reasons for having first intercourse: we want to grow up and be like other people. So many of us talk about the feeling of transition: *'like a woman at last ... initiated into the adult world ... I remember standing at the cooker next to my mum later that evening and wondering if she could tell. I suppose I felt grown up.'* Others write about wanting to gain status by spreading the news: *'The next day I wanted to tell everyone ... As teenagers do I rushed to tell my best friend.'*

Long term we are usually glad to have had intercourse. Only a handful of women when asked if they wished they'd remained a virgin say yes. For losing our virginity does open the door to a new form of sex – and, for most of us, the one that feels closest and most intimate, the one that most reflects our love for our partner.

Many of us take a while to contact the actual pleasure of intercourse, but most of us do so in the end. We speak of beginning to blend our previous sexual knowledge and masturbation techniques with the act of penetration. We move on further with our partner to mutual masturbation and oral sex. We learn to combine what we know about our own sexual needs, our own techniques for gaining pleasure, with those of intercourse. Over time we become able to enjoy intercourse and regard it as the peak of sexual fulfilment.

And what of our partner? Only a handful of women are still with their first sexual partner, most of these being older women who married him, or very young women who have not yet moved on. But, as a generation, we have adapted very quickly to the new expectation that the man who takes our virginity won't stay with us for life − or for even a few weeks. We rarely regret having had the experience of full sex or of having lost the partner with whom we shared the experience. We accept that losing our virginity is no longer the seal on a life-long relationship, but the start of a long and varied sex life with more than one partner. We not only accept that − we also welcome it. And so, in the end, though our virginity is important, we are glad we've lost it.

*Why should women hang on to their virginity? It's important to experiment to see what you like sexually in a partner. And we want sex too. So, wish I'd remained a virgin? No, definitely not.*

VITAL STATISTICS

13.1 per cent of women don't think sex is important, 81.7 per cent think it is

95.1 per cent have been in love at some time during their lives

37.3 per cent do not need love and affection in order to get sexually aroused

86.5 per cent of women find touching other people very important

33 per cent of women have, at some time in their lives, had sex just for a cuddle

90.5 per cent of women would choose cuddles rather than orgasms for the rest of their lives

# 5. Sex and love

*I think that there is a difference between making love and just having sexual intercourse. Caring, attentive, more pleasurable sex is part of a special relationship. Quick, basic, sexual intercourse also has a place in a special relationship, but I see it more as part of a casual relationship. As I don't particularly place any emphasis on a relationship before making love or having sexual intercourse, I do what I feel right with at the time.*

NOW THAT WE are free to have it, sex is essential to us as women. Some 81.7 per cent of respondents say that sex is important or very important to them. They see it as *'vital as eating and sleeping'*. They say that they *'couldn't possibly live without it'*. Particularly at the start of a relationship, they want it all the time. Particularly when they're not in a relationship, or their partner is away, they *'think about it fifty times a day'*. Particularly when they're young, they seek it out constantly. When they're old, they value it increasingly.

But very few of these feelings centre around the sheer physical pleasure of sex. Hardly anyone, when asked about the importance of sex in their lives, actually talks about the sensations, the passion, the orgasms. Of course these things are important, but it is the relationship that surrounds them that really matters to women, which makes the pleasure mean something.

The sexual revolution may have made us more free and easy about sex, but it has, if anything, made us more intense about relationships. If sex is important to us, it's because it is *an extension of my affection and emotions ... a chance to show my love ... an opportunity to feel completely close together*. If it's not important to us, we explain that in terms of relationships, too, saying that sex *isn't as central as friendship ... companionship ... making one another happy*. When sex changes in importance to us over the course of our lives, we say that this is because our relationships have changed, or because one particular relationship has influenced us. We don't separate sex from the people with whom we have it – and we don't want to. This means that in order to understand women's sexuality, we have to understand the way they love.

## WHAT'S LOVE?

So, first, what do we mean by love? All the women in the survey talk about it differently. Many of them question whether they know what it is. Despite this, 95.1 per cent reckon they've felt it – significantly, many considering that they are only just now feeling it for the first time, with their current partner.

> *The relationship I'm in now is the first time I've really been in love. I feel an ache inside when I'm not with him, sort of soft. I don't care how he looks, he whips me up to the most wonderful peaks of excitement. I want to hold him all the time. Does that describe love? It's very difficult to write it down.*

Whether or not we know what love is, we certainly do know when we experience it: *'I felt really good in myself ... really solid grounded feeling, warm, secure, brill! ... I feel special and wanted ... want to be with him 24 hours a day ... butterflies ... nothing can upset me ... totally secure ... heightened perceptions and a sense of unreality'*. Many speak of phases in love, with an eventual feeling of settling down, thinking particularly about the future, and a *'comfortable togetherness. I feel he is a part of me and I of him.'* And others express the darker side of love, when it's not returned, or it goes wrong, and we feel *'confused, disturbed, depressed'*.

*Yes, I have been in love with someone I went out with and eventually lived with for three years. I felt happy and miserable at the same time and at different times. It was a very explosive and passionate relationship, making me feel the extremes of love and lust, to nearly dislike.*

Whatever our definition of love, we universally see it as involving sex. And if we are heterosexual, 'love' particularly means having intercourse with our partner, because we see that as the closest we ever come to being at one with him. Mutual masturbation and oral sex are pleasurable and loving, but when we write about 'making love', we almost always mean the act of penetration. And, because we link sex and love so closely, it follows that when we feel love for a partner, we want to have sex with them. When we don't feel love, we often don't want to have sex.

## SEX WITHOUT LOVE

Or do we? In fact, within the responses, there were definite indications that while these attitudes form the baseline of women's belief about sexuality, our views are changing. We are post-pill women, and even the older respondents make distinctions between love and sex that weren't being made thirty years ago, distinctions that maybe no generation of women has ever before made. Up to 37.3 per cent of women say that they can have sex with their partner without feeling loving and affectionate, especially at the very start of a relationship, and particularly when their sex drive is high. Many say that within a love relationship, the *'zipless, affectionless fuck'* is nice in its own way. Instant sex, when we bump into each other coming out of the shower or wake up feeling horny, is a valuable part of the wide range of things we can do with our partner: *'We have a loving relationship but like a quickie now and again.'*

Just a very few of us opt for long-term sexual relationships without love. Our reason is almost always that we are recovering from some trauma, emotional or sexual, and simply do not feel able to be intimate: *'I find it difficult to mix emotional affection with sex – maybe due to rejection or the fear of it.'* We want sex and see no reason why we should not have it even if we don't want love. Or we want companionship and are happy to include sex in the bargain. We are able to separate our passion from our love – and often report finding this a more satisfying option than linking the two.

Many of us in the nineties also feel that we have a right to sex outside the context of a relationship – 'casual sex'. Some 22.9 per cent of women feel good about it, with another 27.9 per cent feeling mixed but generally positive. We reconcile our belief in love's involving sex but sex's not necessarily involving love in an interesting way. Woman after woman uses the phrase that *'having sex and making love are two different things'*. We seem to be separating the two functions in a way that we weren't able to even a single generation ago.

Now it's acceptable for women to have sex without a loving relationship, and we may well want that. We want it because we want straightforward sex; because we can't find a permanent partner; because it's a way of gaining wider sexual experience. In fact, some women who haven't had 'casual sex' feel positively envious of those who have: *'Lucky . . . she should enjoy herself . . . knows what she wants and goes for it.'* And even women who say they wouldn't have sex casually themselves said that it was up to each individual woman to make her own decisions, to *'draw the line when you are not happy with yourself and be honest about that'*. We are unwilling to criticize others, even if their behaviour differs from ours.

> *Is a woman cheap if she has sex outside a relationship? There is no such thing as 'cheap' in my dictionary: women are women are women. If they enjoy sex, then what's the problem?*

## THE UNWRITTEN GUIDELINES

But while attitudes to casual sex may have changed over the past years, there are still firm guidelines attached to the way that we think that sex and love should be balanced. For, along with new sexual attitudes, new guidelines have come into force that are just as definite as the old ones, even if they do seem more permissive and even though these rules may be unspoken, are often broken and are different for men and women. For women the rules are these: sleep only with who you really want to, preferably not simply because you're drunk. Practise safe sex. Don't do it with someone else's partner. And don't do it if you're in a long-term relationship yourself, unless you're about to finish that relationship.

If you break these rules, you are in deep trouble: other women will unanimously condemn you. The words leapt off the page with these women's comments: *'Slag is the word, I guess . . . gives other women a bad name . . . slut . . . tramp . . . whore . . . prostitute . . . a tart '*. We resent other women having casual sex and not using protection: *'They put everyone in danger.'* We're equally angry when women sleep around while in a committed relationship or with partners who are committed elsewhere. Some respondents try to understand, but even their most compassionate explanations of rule-breaking behaviour show that they feel critical: *'A woman like that must be insecure . . . immature . . . sad . . . looking for attention . . . can't be feeling good about herself'*. The majority of us don't even want to understand; we close ranks against irresponsible casual sex and completely condemn it.

*Women are by nature more fussy about whom they sleep with. A woman has more dignity in doing this; she proves her femininity. A woman who sleeps around is one who often sleeps with men she feels absolutely nothing for; I feel she has no self-respect or dignity. Women should take pride in their sexuality and only sleep with those good enough for them.*

## LOVE WITHOUT SEX

While love and passion are almost always linked, just a few women report that they have loved without sex. Some say that they were very young – sex wasn't really in their minds, they weren't ready for it or the sexual part of the relationship never fully developed.

*I fell in love with him when I was 16 and got over him when I was about 19. Yes, I felt confused, disturbed, sometimes very happy and sometimes depressed. He did not reciprocate, but he was only 14. He was never cruel or nasty about it but very honest. There was no sex, not even a kiss; he did try to kiss me, but I didn't like it. I still think of him, but I'm not in love with him any more.*

Other women were already committed to a sexual relationship when they fell in love with someone else; they desperately wanted to be with the person they loved but felt they had to stay with husband or family. They could have had an affair or even a one-night stand, but they decided not to; instead their choice is to stick with their previous commitment, remain sexually faithful and simply love without consummation: *'No, I nearly was unfaithful but couldn't do it. I felt too guilty and knew it would be stupid and solve nothing, only create more problems.'*

Another, this time larger, group of women are currently experiencing a life with no sex at all. Up to 24.2 per cent of respondents are celibate. Celibacy is not a popular option; usually it isn't an option at all but a state forced upon them by circumstances. They are without a sex life because we have no partner, have simply not met one who appeals to us. And they aren't prepared to go to bed with someone just for the sake of it. Respondents are always unhappy with this and say both clearly and forcefully that they *'would do anything to get out of the situation'.*

Nine women, however, were deliberately celibate at the time they answered the questionnaire, and several others had chosen celibacy at some point in the past. They haven't chosen celibacy within a relationship; that is, no one has a good partnership yet has opted not to have sex. What these women have chosen is to be without a partner entirely and also to avoid casual sexual encounters.

There are a number of reasons for this choice, mostly hinging around the fact that a sexual relationship takes time and energy at the deepest level. These women, at this time in their lives, don't want that. Some want to prioritize other things for a while: moving house, taking exams, developing a career. Some simply want time on their own, to find out what they really need without having to consider a partner's desires. Many have chosen celibacy in order to recover from the ending of a bad relationship. They want to *'sort myself out ... find out about myself ... be more in charge'*. The feeling is that sexual commitment distracts us from concentrating on ourselves, from sorting out our thoughts and feelings. It stirs up the emotions and demands reinvolvement – an involvement that simply isn't appropriate sometimes. Just one woman has been celibate for the past 18 years because early experiences have so traumatized her that she cannot now bear to have sex.

## LOVE AND SEX TOGETHER

But while sex without a relationship is now acceptable, and a life without sex is sometimes a good idea, most of us want sex and love together. No woman considers it necessary to be married before having sex, but 48.6 per cent did feel that a commitment was necessary for sex to be really rewarding. And just a few, 15 per cent, think that a loving marriage would survive even if the couple had not slept together before their wedding night – though a vast majority thought that this was probably asking for trouble. Even those who feel fine about casual sex say that it is only an interim measure. And the majority of celibate women who answer the questionnaire say that their goal is to have a sexual relationship again.

The fact is that loving sex still feels somehow more 'right' to us physically, emotionally and intuitively. The actual physical pleasure of loving sex is consistently greater than that of either casual or lone sex: *'I personally don't get any satisfaction out of sex if the relationship isn't good ... I've only ever orgasmed easily with my husband, and I know it's because I trust him implicitly ... I find it impossible to get aroused if there isn't love.'*

And, as love grows, so pleasure grows. Some 59.3 per cent of women find that the longer a relationship lasts, the better the sex gets. They become more affectionate, more caring, more eager and more able to please. They learn their own and their partner's bodies more fully. They become more relaxed and uninhibited; worries and fears disappear. The central phrase crops up again and again: they are 'making love', not 'having sex'.

*There's a pattern that seems to be present. First, feelings of euphoria, exhilaration, excitement. These settle to comfortable levels. As the sexual relationship develops, familiarity deepens, emotional feelings grow, and these feelings are more binding. Sexual satisfaction becomes more fulfilling as love deepens.*

And, because love and sex are so bound up with each other, as sexual pleasure grows, so the love also grows. Many women make the point that sex *'is one of the roots that keeps a relationship together'*. If our sexual relationship is strong, it's easier to be faithful. Sex increases trust and understanding. The pleasure we get from each other gives us a motivation not to stray. And what more proof could we ask than that if we make love less regularly, we find that the relationship seems to die – and vice versa: *'I found our love changed for the worse when we were stuck in a rut sexually.'*

## MEN ON SEX

Do our partners feel the same as we do about all this? The answer is that, where our partners are men, we are sure that they see sex as more important than we do – but only slightly. Many years ago, perhaps, women and men differed a great deal in their views. In the 1990s we reckon that our partners do rate love as important, often as important as we do. What's changed is that we now feel sex is almost as essential as they do. Up to 87.7 per cent of partners are thought to see sex as vital, to women's 81.7 per cent. Sometimes the traditional roles of man's focusing on sex and woman's focusing on love are actually reversed, as in this response.

*I relayed the questions of whether sex and love are important to each of us to my partner in a transatlantic phone call one evening. He said to say that sex is important to me but not to him. It has less importance to him. He likes to be in control of his sexual needs and not have them control him.*

Where there is a partnership difference in viewpoints about love and sex, is it a problem? In general, as long as our partners feel the same way as we do, then the answer is no. Where couples think the same, whatever their attitudes are, then they can feel good about that and justify it. If both of us feel sex is unimportant, for example, then we say we are a couple who values love. If both of us feel sex is very important, then we report that we are a couple whose love is demonstrated by their sex life. Tension seems to arise only where views are different. If our partner views sex as more vital than we do, then we think of him as regarding it only as a physical thing.

*He always tells me how much better sex is with someone you care about,
but he is more preoccupied with the physical side of sex than I am.
Whereas I would rather masturbate than have sex in a loveless way, he
would be quite happy to shag if he couldn't make love.*

And if our partner sees sex as less important than we do, we feel
rejected and frustrated:

*My partner could always take it or leave it, which astounded me
constantly. If he doesn't want it then wild horses couldn't make him
change his mind. I would be on stand-by though, just in case.*

*I desire my boyfriend all the time, but he just hasn't been interested in
the last three months or so. It used to be so nice in the beginning.
Sometimes I feel very hurt and depressed and wonder what's wrong
with me, why he doesn't desire me.*

When it comes to judging our partner's attitudes to sex within or
outside a love relationship, we are less tolerant. How we react to the
thought of men's sleeping around depends very much on how we have
been affected by men who do. If we haven't been directly harmed by that
sort of behaviour then our comments seem fairly relaxed: *'It's his choice.'*
In contrast, those 48.1 per cent of women who judge men harshly for
having casual sex are usually those who have been hurt by that. They
think back to times where they have had sex with a partner who didn't
love them or have been the partner of men who had casual affairs, and
they seethe: *'My first husband was anybody's. He couldn't help it, but it
gradually killed my love for him.'*

In general, too, while more of us think badly of a man than of a
woman who has casual relationships – 48.1 per cent compared to 42.5
per cent – we tend to excuse men more. We are more likely to try to find
reasons for his behaviour. So where most of us judge a woman who
chooses casual sex as being *'a slut . . . a slag'* and only a few try to explain
her behaviour in terms of insecurity, many of us say that a man who
behaves like that obviously *'isn't getting what he needs at home . . . hasn't
found the right woman yet'.* We do recognize this double standard: *'A
woman is a slag, and a man is a hero if he sleeps around, and that's totally
unacceptable.'* But many of us, nevertheless, still subscribe to it.

## THE FINAL CHOICE

So, in the end, which is more important to women, love or sex? To high-
light the issue the survey includes the following question: 'If you had to

choose between being able to have orgasms only for the rest of your life but no cuddles or loving affection; or being able to have the cuddles and loving affection, but no orgasms, which would you choose?' Most women are utterly horrified at having to make a choice, and 5.8 per cent of them refuse to do so: *'I cannot live without both ... I must have both ... I believe you need both to be happy ... I would be devastated to do without either ... If I had to make a choice I'd kill myself.'* It seems as if we need and want both pleasure and affection, and the ideal is always a combination.

When pushed, though, the bottom line is this. Only 3.7 per cent of women say that they would go for the orgasms, a few because they've never had them, a few because they currently feel they don't need affection from other people.

But an overwhelming 90.5 per cent of women say that they would opt for the cuddles: *'I can enjoy sex without orgasms (many women do), but I can't enjoy life without love and affection.'* They say that affection is far more important than sheer pleasure. The loving lasts longer, can last for ever, whereas the orgasms provide just a few moments of passion. The loving involves another person, is dependent on a partner – whereas we know that we ourselves have the power to orgasm alone. And more than one woman hints that her relationship would certainly survive the loss of sex – but the loss of love and affection would end it completely.

The verdict is clear, then. Sex is important. Love is more important than sex. But sexual loving is more important than anything.

*The two work together. I need affection to build the arousal I need in order to come. I can't choose. If you held a knife to my throat then cuddles ... but only if I could masturbate.*

VITAL STATISTICS

5 per cent of women have only had one partner

52.1 per cent are not happy with the number they've had

33.5 per cent want fewer partners

16.2 per cent want more partners

57.4 per cent have been out with a partner more than ten years older than them

65.7 per cent of women have lived with a partner

# 6. Men in our lives

*There have been eight men in my life.*
*Two relationships were long term, four years and*
*two years respectively. One man I had known and*
*wanted for six years, so even though I only had sex*
*with him twice, I wouldn't call our relationship a*
*casual one. One man was my boyfriend when I was*
*14, and he was 18; when he went away to college*
*he said he would come back for me when I was old*
*enough, and he did. So that's not casual. One was*
*a close friend for two years whom I turned to at a*
*bad time and who gave me solace in his bed.*
*One was a friend, someone I'd fancied at school,*
*and we had a brief relationship eight years after we*
*met. Again, both these relationships weren't casual.*
*That makes six. Two of my relationships were*
*casual. I wish I'd had two less. The last two!*

WHEN WE THINK about the men in our past, the first issue that springs to mind is the numbers. How many lovers have we had? The questionnaire answers show a certain amount of defensiveness, 'This sounds very competitive'; guilt, 'I'm a bad girl!'; or regret, 'I wish I'd had more.'

Let's grit our teeth and get straight down to the hard facts. Just 1 per cent of the women who answered the questionnaire have, at the time of writing, never had intercourse, though one of them has had several sexual partners; one has never had any sexual contact at all. Some 5 per cent of respondents have had one male partner only, 6.5 per cent have had two, and 14.4 per cent have had between three and five. Up to 72.4 per cent of respondents have had more than six male partners; some of these say that they've lost count or stopped counting, and 1 per cent of women say that they have had 'hundreds ... about a hundred and thirty'.

The first and most obvious thing to be acknowledged about these figures is that, by definition, they are far higher than they would have been for any generation of women before us. Our grandmothers, and even our mothers, often had one or at the most two partners. The second thing to be said is that these figures are, in fact, above the statistical norm for the present day. Women who answered the questionnaire – along with all respondents of extended sex surveys – tend to be more sexually experienced, in general, than most people in the population. Experience often gives a sense of confidence that enables people to talk about their sex lives; or it makes them want to tell other people their stories and so come to terms with any distress they've suffered.

## THE MAGIC NUMBER

Yet however many partners they've had, respondents are often just as likely to be satisfied as they are to be dissatisfied with their sexual history. Not so long ago there used to be a 'magic number', an ideal total of sexual partners for a woman: one. But this is no longer true; now, there's no consensus and no magic number, so our reactions differ. Just under half of us are happy with our 'score'. But many of us, far above the average in terms of numbers, wish we'd had more partners, and many women far below the average wish they'd had fewer partners. Several of the lesbian respondents comment that in hindsight, they regret not the number of their partners but the fact that such a large proportion of them were male.

*I have had two sexual partners. Both of these were or are serious relationships. No, I am not happy with this number. I wish I had experimented more with different partners when I had the chance to. In fact, I had at least three other partners with whom sex could easily have been on the agenda. I was asked many times to go all the way, but it didn't feel right for me at the time. But now I wonder whether I had old-fashioned values forced on to me by my mother and perhaps believed I had to remain a virgin until I met the man I would marry. Although, thinking about it, I lost my virginity to a man that I had no idea I would marry. There is one man I seriously wish I had made love to, and we had many opportunities to do this – but we didn't.*

How do we explain our dissatisfaction? Some of us begin our sexual career with a committed partner and then, if this relationship breaks down, take another, then another. If we don't find real fulfilment, we begin to tell ourselves that this is because we haven't slept with enough men, and we start seeking more partners with whom to gain experience. Somewhere along the way that attitude shifts. We find the right person and stop looking. Or it gradually dawns on us that we aren't going to get what we want. And then our minds spontaneously change; we look backwards and start regretting that we haven't had fewer partners.

## ONE OR TWO PARTNERS

The raw numbers hide some clear and significant patterns. Those of us who have had one partner only are either older, pre-pill women who lost our virginity to a husband and, happy or not, have remained faithful ever since. Or we are young women in our teens or very early twenties, who are still with our first sexual partner and are content to explore our sexuality with him alone: *'Partners? I've had one at the moment, and I'm happy with that.'* If we are one-partner women, then in general we are content; the fact that we have made a single choice seems to create a natural acceptance and satisfaction. We aren't contemplating any other possibilities, so we settle to being happy with our situation: *'I've had one partner. Sometimes I think I'd like to have had more, but I don't think about it enough to worry, or do anything about it.'*

There is a shift in attitude when we take a second lover after the first, for having two relationships makes us want to compare partners. Some of us have consecutive relationships, first one partner then another. Some have parallel partnerships; we have taken a lover because our original relationship is becoming unsatisfactory. For whichever reason, when we have slept with two people, our minds seem naturally to move to yet other possibilities. Many of us in this group express a desire to have, or to have had, more partners: *'Sometimes I wish I knew what it would be like to make love with lots of boyfriends ... I'd like more lovers for comparison ... I'd like more experience ... maybe that's why I'm having an affair; the sex is so very good that I realise what I've been missing all these years.'* We are searching, or we would like to search, for what one woman calls *'perfection and sexual fulfilment'*. If we haven't really searched far, we wonder just what we're missing. And however faithful we stay, we probably always will wonder.

## MORE PARTNERS

By the time we move into the range of three to five lovers, a slightly different pattern emerges. For while, up to now, most women have had only love partnerships, in this middle range they are more likely to have had a mixture of relationships and casual sex. So as well as being dissatisfied with the number of lovers, this group suffers more regrets about the kinds of relationship they've had. They regret saying yes when they really wanted to say no. They regret their choice of partners. They regret being unfaithful to one partner with another. They regret having had sex without love. We regret not having had more experience.

> *I've had one long-term teenage boyfriend, two broken marriages, one affair, one successful marriage which is still ongoing. I wish I'd had more short–term affairs when I was younger and had learnt more about men and relationships. If I had, I might have avoided the broken marriages.*

If we've had more than six partners, we describe our relationships as being approximately 50 per cent committed and 50 per cent casual. And in this group we also seem to analyse our partnership patterns more deeply. We offer explanations for them, explanations that are often self-critical but are also often self-forgiving. In hindsight we believe that we were *'insecure'*, or *'looking for something'* that we never found. We comment wryly that *'I'm not particularly impressed with myself,'* but we also seem to understand why we did what we did.

> *I stopped counting at 10 partners, but I can think of 20. Nine of these were casual, and the rest were relationships. I am glad I had them all as I believe that every experience I have had makes me the person I am, and I like the person I am. Also I'm glad that I have had the experience with men so I know I am not missing anything. However, 20 partners does sound a hell of a lot!*

Many of us who fall into this high-number category are post-pill but pre-AIDS. We experimented with casual sex decades ago, when there was no panic about disease and when there was positive social approval in our peer group for having uncommitted sex. In hindsight, particularly if we are certain that we haven't contracted disease, we are happy with our sexual history. We feel that such experiences *'can only make you a better lover,'* and we celebrate our *'great and varied sexual lifetime with men'*.

Because significantly, in many ways, the more partners a woman has had, the more self-accepting she seems to be. Like those women with only one partner, women with very many may well feel that they have made a conscious and deliberate choice. It is their decision; they may now think they were unwise, but they are happy to live with it: *'I've had hundreds of partners, all casual. It's pointless regretting anything about the past because the past cannot be altered.'*

## GETTING TOGETHER

How do we meet the men in our lives? In general, the key factor is opportunity. We meet our lovers in the course of our everyday routine; only one or two women mention dating agencies or classified ads. If we are younger, we meet our partner at school or at college. We grow up next door to them, meet them through the family, pair off from within a larger group of friends: a sexual partner may well be a past partner of a girl-friend. If we are older, we socialize with men through house-mates, share a flat with men, meet men on a course. If we are in our thirties or forties, we often meet lovers or future partners when in a foursome with our current partner. Already in one long-term relationship, we pair off with another couple socially, and gradually find that attraction is a great deal more than friendship: an affair develops, or both pairs split and re-form.

Often we meet at work. Just under half the respondents have met a partner through their job, though, significantly, three-quarters of those who have said they wouldn't repeat the experience: *'I keep work and sex separate now.'* Typically, we go out with someone on the same work level as us or someone who is our senior: several women say they went out with their bosses, while only 14 per cent have been out with people junior to them in a firm. We work near to each other, develop common interests, feel close to each other. This day-to-day partnership is so like the feeling we get with a lover that it is only a very small step to making the relation-ship sexual. And this step can be made whether or not either of us is already in a relationship; more women report starting affairs or having relationships with married men in office environments than anywhere else. There seems to be something about working together that encourages us to override our prior emotional commitments, at least in the short term.

*It was at a disco, and we both knew we wanted each other sexually, as through working together we had grown close. So when it was dark we had sex in the car park. Colleagues knew that we were close, but although they guessed, they never truly knew that we were having sex.*

Very rarely we have holiday romances. We feel wary of these, as they tend to have the reputation of being casual flings, with no relationship attached and with the promise of bad sex: *'Man approaches, go for a quick drink, normal boring routine of questions, back to a room, quick bonk, never see him again.'* Where we do have relationships on holiday, we freely admit that we fall for a combination of the man and the scenery, not simply the man: *'The guy was charming and good looking, the atmosphere and setting were irresistible.'* We are relaxed, we feel beautiful, we aren't in our usual environment, and we feel a bit daring. We take a risk – and sometimes we strike lucky.

> *My holiday romance was the most gorgeous affair ever. I had broken my collar bone, but we still managed it, everywhere. It lasted a week, and we were mad about each other.*

## CHOOSING THE MAN

How do we choose a sexual partner? Looks do count; unfair as it may seem, we make our first decisions on a man's physical appearance. We look at his eyes, closely followed by his hair *'dark and well cared for ... not greasy ... blondes are more fun'*. Good skin, nice hands and *'a chocolate brown voice'* were mentioned often as positive attributes. And these smaller details seem much more important than the perfect body shape that most men worry about and work for. For while many men think that they need to look like a body builder or a pop star in order to be attractive, women are in fact wary of the model man. So while one or two women are turned on by a *'tall, fit man with muscles'*, far more want *'someone slim and sensitive ... I can't stand body builders ... I like my men quite squashy so I'm not intimidated by them being too thin. I like the soft, rounded bits ... I like a man with a bit of weight on, one who I feel can look after me.'*

When it comes to more intimate physical details, the idea that 'bigger is better' is only true for a minority of women. Some 21.2 per cent of women do like a big penis – *'size is important ... whoever said it isn't is a man.'* Many, however, make the point that in fact width, as opposed to length, is the vital factor; we want to feel ourselves stretching to accommodate a partner. Some, though, prefer a small penis, because a big one stretches us too much and is painful. And the majority of us say that size doesn't count at all; it's technique that's important: *'It's what they do with it that counts.'* Or, as one delightful sixty-year-old respondent comments, *'Better the Mini that travels regularly than the Jaguar that comes out once a month.'*

Looks are important, but they are not the heart of the matter. While most of us judge a man at the start on whether he looks right, we make our final decision to sleep with him on whether he feels right. And if we have known a man for a while and begun to appreciate his personality, then even if his looks don't turn us on, we can still become sexually attracted to him. One reason, incidentally, why work relationships often turn into sexual ones seems to be that we get the chance to see a potential partner in a number of situations before we become sexual with him. We see him in action − working, playing, laughing, listening. And what gets us into bed with a man is, in the end, what he does rather than how he looks: *'He can be as ugly as sin if he has a good sense of humour.'*

For contrary to the idea many men hold, and despite our increased sexual freedom, we do still choose our bed partner largely on his potential to be a companion rather than a stud. So we fall for mental outlook, intelligence, education, a compatible background: *'I want someone who ticks along in the same way I do.'* We like gentle, loving personality traits: *'Generosity . . . kindness . . . maturity . . . compassion . . . trust . . . a sense of himself'.* And we are realistic about the danger of falling for looks alone.

*More important than anything is the gut feeling that a person is a nice person. This is vital. There was a guy once who I chased after because he was so good looking. When I got a chance to meet him, he turned out to be such a bore. It destroyed all my illusions. Why couldn't I have kept him just as a guy I fancied?*

When choosing a partner 42.3 per cent of women feel that age is irrelevant: *'I like the eagerness of young men and the confidence of older men . . . I socialize with groups varying in age from 25 to 65 years old.'* But while 51.5 per cent say that on balance they prefer their partners slightly older, only 6.2 per cent prefer younger men. Age seems to appeal because of a man's experience.

*Probably because I am young, only 17, I am generally in contact with people older than myself in my daily life, and I find boys of my age and younger, for the most part, to be immature and unable to have a proper relationship.*

Nevertheless, respondents have gone out with men up to 17 years younger than they are, and up to 41 years older. Many of us, for example, go out with much older men until we are into our twenties; we find that up to that age there is still a maturity gap, both emotionally and sexually, which means that we choose older partners to gain equality of outlook.

Others of us like to feel looked after and protected by an older man. By our mid-twenties, however, we seem to change, possibly because subconsciously we want to start a family and need a man of our own age with whom we can consider a long-term future. If, in our thirties, we re-enter the partner market through divorce or widowhood, we sometimes ignore the age gap again. We go out with older men and younger men, choosing on personality and compatibility rather than some kind of age-equality.

## RELATIONSHIP PATTERNS

Once we have our men, how do our sexual relationships with them progress? Looking for trends, the questionnaire asked, 'Do you have a pattern of emotional relationships developing in a particular way? If so, what is this pattern?', and straight back came the answer that nearly 50 per cent of women consider that there is no pattern. They feel that each relationship is an individual event and shouldn't be categorized. Either that, or during the course of their lives, they feel that they themselves have changed so much that they feel any attempt to track a trend would be meaningless. From the small majority of women who do see a trend, though, there seem to be several typical patterns in sexual partnerships.

First, there are one-night stands. This century, for the first time in women's history, these are a regular and real possibility for us. We tend to have them with an acquaintance, colleague or friend; sex with a complete stranger is far less usual. A typical scenario is to sleep with someone who is part of a group of friends: one evening after a meal or one afternoon after a walk, we end up at home together, and sex simply develops from there. Or we find ourselves in a social situation with someone we know at work. The barriers come down, and, suddenly, professional rapport becomes temporary passion.

*My boss and I went for a drink after work and were talking, getting open and drunk and enjoying ourselves. It was the period in between me and my fiancé splitting up and moving in together. The actual sex happened in town by the bus stop; if we had been warm and comfortable it would not have happened.*

As in this woman's story, the actual event is often based on a need for sex and comfort, often heightened by our having had something to drink or having been without a partner for a while. We usually know while we are having sex that there's going to be no future relationship, and we don't expect there to be. We wake in the morning feeling better for the physical experience or regretful of it, depending on whether it was physically enjoyable and whether we feel emotionally insecure. And we rarely make an attempt to start a relationship or even to see the man again. If we do meet, there's often some embarrassment; if we were friends beforehand, we consider ourselves lucky if we can go back to being friends again.

## BEING CHASED

Next there are sexual relationships where the desire is at first all on the one or the other side. The need can be ours: *'I tend to make the running, but once the chase is over it is boring to me.'* More often the impetus comes from our partner. He immediately wants us, chasing for quite a while before we even agree to go out with him. We often simply don't fancy him at first. We may like him but don't feel lust. But maybe we enjoy being chased; it makes us feel strong and in control. Slowly we're seduced, by the attention, by the effort, by the sheer romanticism of his approach. We start to want him, or we sleep with him because we grow to feel emotionally close to him.

But then, after sex, we fall in love. We are aroused physiologically simply by having had sex, maybe by the man's technique or by the fact that we have had an effect on him. And, more than that, we become involved emotionally because we have been physically intimate with him. But parallel to our falling in love, our partner is beginning to fall out of lust. He is a man who feels passionately about what he cannot have; this is why he chases so insistently, and why he is often so successful in his chasing. Once the chase is over, though, he starts to lose interest. We become intense, insecure, afraid he will leave. He feels trapped. We cling, he pulls away. The tables are turned, and now it is we who are chasing. The relationship ends badly.

*I have a regular pattern in relationships. My partner chases, but then as the relationship continues. I become intense and insecure. Love for me becomes more dependent as sexual relations continue. My partner feels suffocated and eventually walks out.*

A final pattern involves a more equal involvement. It starts slowly with friendship or quickly with instant reciprocal lust. The act of sex makes the relationship deepen – for both partners. Sometimes the security of making love allows the woman to feel relaxed, and so she blossoms. Sometimes both partners start to contact a deep need they have for each other. They spend more and more time together, make love regularly, become more sexually compatible – and so strengthen their relationship. The outlook is good, and such relationships often last a long time.

*Initially I will do anything to please, even things I don't want to do, because I want him to love me. Later when I feel more secure I relax and can be more assertive. Sometimes I feel resentful because I have compromised myself so much, but it's my own fault.*

## SEXUAL BREAKPOINTS

In all our sexual relationships there are a number of commitment break-points. For the pre-pill generation there was often just one such break-point after having sex together: divorce. Now, even after just the first time in bed, we will sometimes know that it's just not working and therefore end the relationship. Of course this can be because of emotional incompatibility, but where the disillusionment is sexual, this is usually because love-making simply wasn't as physically pleasurable as we thought it was going to be. Women describe this in terms of its *'not feeling good ... it just didn't work ... he didn't smell or taste right'.*

We also judge a partner on whether together we reach an acceptable level of pleasure. This isn't just a matter of technique. It's also linked with our past experience and our expectations. For example, a woman who hasn't previously orgasmed will be quite happy with a partner who doesn't help her to move towards climax, whereas a woman who has been used to coming won't. She will describe him as *'selfish'* or *'bad in bed'*, and unless their emotional involvement is very strong will decide that the relationship isn't worth it.

If we continue to sleep with each other after the first few times, and we are in the market for a committed relationship, our next breakpoint is often after several months. In work relationships, however, it tends to be sooner – at about three to five months. This is because the work situation, where we are often very near to our lover, seems to speed up whatever positive or negative emotional movement there is in our relationship. In some situations, we (or our partner) find that working together simply isn't good for our career prospects. Or we see him in all kinds of mood at work and realize fully what we feel about him – either negatively or positively. What is often important, too, is whether colleagues have found out, and, if they have, how they feel about that. Most of them tend to be supportive; many of them don't even mention the affair even though they've noticed it, to leave it time to develop on its own.

But colleagues can try to wreck a relationship. Particularly if we or our partner are already married to other people, our peer group may feel that they have to pressurize us to keep the status quo. *'The manageress didn't like us talking to each other ... No one said anything to my face but it came back through the grapevine that the other woman interpreted that as easy . . . the other directors found out and made our lives hell . . . I had an affair, and my colleagues were not happy; it spoilt any opportunities of friendship within the department.'* The longer a relationship lasts in a work setting, the more positive colleagues are likely to be towards it; they approve of long-term relationships far more than they approve of casual ones.

## CHOOSING COMMITMENT

After a few days or weeks, more usually between several months and two years, we assess our relationship's long-term sexual potential. This often involves making some sort of further formal commitment, such as living together or getting married. Of course a large part of this decision depends on how emotionally involved we are; but an equally large part depends on how our sexual relationship is developing. We make our decision based on three factors, which seem to be remarkably consistent, a sort of 'sex rating'. Respondents say that these are: first, how often they sleep together – a severe drop in frequency with no outside cause such as work pressure to account for it gives pause for thought. Second, are their needs for sex roughly compatible: very differing needs cause problems, but similar ones, even if they result in hardly ever making love, don't matter, as long as they are the same. Third, is what they want in bed compatible? Differing needs here work only where they are complementary and one partner loves doing something that the other partner only likes receiving. If what they like offends a partner, then in the end the relationship is at risk.

There's often a series of sexual breakpoints further on in our relationship. One is the 'seven-year itch', where we've settled into a comfortable and largely satisfactory sexual routine, which then fossilizes into a ritual. One or both of us gets bored, and maybe turns for sex to someone else: *'My sexual pattern is lust, possession, love, dependence, familiarity, boredom, contempt (or just good friends if you are lucky).'*

Another can be when we have children, and the sheer physical stress in our life means that sex becomes rarer and rarer, until we both lose confidence and it is far easier not to sleep together at all. External stresses and life transitions such as redundancy, return to work, menopause, retirement can also all mean a sexual crisis, and we have to reappraise what is happening.

Significantly, neither work nor holiday relationships often seem to lead to a long-term sexual commitment. Holiday romances frequently last only the length of the vacation, can be wonderful but usually end there. Long-term work romances are equally rare. As mentioned before, such relationships tend to peak and die after a very short time anyway: only 15 respondents ended up in a relationship of more than six months with partners they met at work.

Where long-term work liaisons do develop, they tend to be affairs, where one or the other of us is already committed. This means that they will often have a natural tendency to end rather than to develop into further commitment. Where we do find ourselves in a long-term relationship with someone at work, one or the other of us often has to leave the common situation, in order to allow the relationship to develop. And, a warning: most women say that if a work relationship finishes, the kickback is much worse than usual. Having to be so near a former partner every day is very hard to handle.

*It has been absolutely dreadful at work. I can't even look him in the face at the moment, so things are pretty tense. I also tend to put his letters to the bottom of the pile because I can't stand to see his writing.*

## OUR VERDICT ON MEN

So how does our past history leave those of us who are attracted to men feeling about them? When we generalize from our experience, referring to men as a group, then almost without exception we feel disappointed.

Specifically, we feel that while men have a higher sex drive than we do, they often have no idea how to use that drive to the best advantage. Their passion can be relieved by simple, uncomplicated thrusting, so they have no idea what sensuous foreplay can do. They often don't even know that it exists. They like to penetrate and 'get down to it'. They don't really know how to turn us on with kisses, caresses, clitoral touching, oral sex. This whole ignorance is beautifully summed up – with a practical suggestion of how to cure it – by one woman's comment:

*Men grow up knowing nothing about a women's needs, totally ignorant of the clitoris and where to actually find it. Girls grow up thinking that boys know exactly what to do, then say nothing for fearing of upsetting the male ego. Boys should be sexually educated by older experienced women, like those Indian princes who were shown and taught how to please a woman by special harem members. Then these young princes would marry virgins but be able to make their wives happy and satisfied in bed.*

Equally, though we are drawn to men sexually, we also rarely trust them. We see them either as 'babies or bastards'. We consistently feel that men either harass us or withdraw from us; they pressure us to have sex with them, or reject us by no longer wanting it. We feel used, because we feel we give a great deal sexually and receive very little in return. And we don't trust men because we so often feel sexually betrayed by them.

The issue of sexual fidelity is one that creates so much strong emotion that I have devoted a complete chapter (chapter 22) to it, but the pattern is clear. We see men in general as having very little ability or desire to remain faithful. We constantly expect them to deceive us or to leave us.

*Stand up for yourself. There is no need to be a sex slave and lie back and think of England any more. If enough women get more assertive about their sexual position in society, men would have to start changing their attitudes. It is still very much a man's world. But we'll get there!*

## OUR OPTIMISTIC PRESENT

All this seems as if we hate men – all men. But it is significant that when respondents finally come to talk about their current partner, then the whole picture changes. It is as if each past event has made us more hopeless, but that each new relationship tempts us to be hopeful again. Throughout the questionnaire responses, we consistently show what one respondent calls women's *'triumph of optimism over experience'*. There are some sad comments about our current situation – *'I wish I knew that he'd been faithful to me since we last met'* – but most respondents interpret their current relationship as being generally good.

So the man we are with at the moment is described as understanding in bed. He often values foreplay as much as we do if not more. He *'aims to please'*, supports us and gives us permission to find pleasure in the way that works for us. He doesn't simply 'thrust', but spends time arousing us and encouraging us to arouse ourselves. He teaches us and learns from us.

And where there are problems, we often take responsibility for them – sometimes, sadly, to the point of blaming ourselves. So when we say that men have no sexual knowledge, we also say that we should educate them. When our partner doesn't please us in bed, we apologize for nagging him. We take every opportunity to confirm that our partner is doing his best, and to add that maybe we ourselves are not trying hard enough.

Perhaps all this optimism should be treated with suspicion, with an awareness that if our relationships fail, our current partner may well be seen in a new light, judged just as bitterly as those who came before him. But even if that is so, does it really matter? What the survey shows is that however bad our sexual history, we are still optimistic about the future. However disillusioned we are about the men in our past, we are still capable of loving the man in our present – or continuing to search with hope for the right man in our future.

*Now I've found the man I want to spend my life with, I know that not all men are bastards – just the majority of them.*

VITAL STATISTICS

57.5 per cent of women feel good about the idea of having sex with another woman

33.4 per cent of women have had sex with another girl or woman

92.9 per cent of those who have woman-to-woman sex enjoy it

43.4 per cent orgasm the first time

63.9 per cent who have a first woman-to-woman sexual experience haven't repeated it, but 52.6 per cent would like to

# 7. Women in our lives

*I was 22. My partner was about the same age. We worked in a hotel and I seduced her into bed. It was fantastic. I discovered the joys of giving oral sex to a woman. Basically there was a lot of emotion and love. I had orgasms like no man ever gave me. I think now I know I can be totally myself with a woman. I am relaxed. It's just right.*

THE VAST MAJORITY of those who answered the questionnaire aren't sexually involved with women. But some are, many more have been in the past, and a majority say that they would like to be. So though this isn't a book primarily about the lesbian or bisexual experience, it seems appropriate to look at what respondents have experienced and what they feel.

Let's begin with the figures: 38.8 per cent of respondents say that they have never found the idea of sexual contact with a woman appealing. They don't want to try it; it just doesn't feel right: *'I prefer having penis every time.'* Many added a tolerance rider that they feel good about other women trying it, but that they don't want to themselves: *'Women don't interest me sexually; if they did I would give lesbianism a try. It doesn't disgust me; it's just of no interest to me.'* Only five women express their moral objections or their personal distaste, though they do so extremely strongly: *'It seems pathetic . . . grossly disgusting and totally unnatural . . . it does not seem to be the way things were meant to be, in a religious or in a biological sense.'*

But 57.5 per cent of women feel good about the idea of having sex with another woman. This seems a very high proportion, yet another indication that, nowadays, women's attitudes to their sexuality are broadening, developing, allowing of more possibilities. Some of us say we'd like to try woman-to-woman sex simply because we're curious. More usually, we feel that sex with a woman would offer things that we miss in sex with a man: *'understanding . . . consideration . . . comfort . . . a woman knows what another woman needs sexually'*. This woman's comment is typical:

> *I think I would like to try it, just out of curiosity. I think that sex with a woman, even if it is just a one-night stand, would be very loving and there would be a better sense of closeness. I don't know about carrying this desire out. I would have to wait and see what happens. I'd probably chicken out . . . but it depends on the situation, the woman and my state of mind at the time.*

## DREAMS AND FANTASIES

Many of us dream about having woman-to-woman sex, with and without a man present. If these dreams worry us, it's usually because we wonder whether at some deep level we are lesbian – and don't want to be. Many more of us fantasize consciously about sex with another woman or about being part of a threesome. We're a little unclear whether we'd want to start being sexual with the woman – and we're certain that we would want to be sexual with the man – but there is something immensely tempting about the thought of sheer physical pleasure with another sensuous female. Occasionally our fantasies turn into fully sexual ones.

> *We go to her bedroom. She takes off my bikini and begins kissing and caressing my breasts, working her way downwards. By now I am so wet I can hardly wait for her to reach my clitoris, but she makes me wait, promising me that it will be heaven. Finally she puts her finger into my vagina, and she brings me to orgasm – it is so good that I can hardly stand it. When I have recovered, I make love to her very slowly and gently. I am terrified of doing the wrong thing and hurting her or not satisfying her, but she assures me that she loves me and wants what I am doing. Her breasts are big and maternal, and I get such intense*

*pleasure from sucking gently at them that I almost climax again. I remove the rest of her clothing, then I turn around and bring her to orgasm using my tongue on her clitoris. She tastes good and sweet. We spend a lot more time kissing and exploring each other's bodies until even we are satiated.*

What about turning our fantasies into reality? What stops us finding another woman to have sex with? One thing seems to be that we are scared. Just as we feel wary of our first, pre-intercourse experiences, so we are afraid of not knowing what to do with a woman and are wary of making a fool of ourselves: *'I'd feel like a novice.'* We are particularly cautious of making the first move: we don't know where to meet a woman who would want sex with us, how to approach her or what to do next. Just as when we start to go out with men, we need to know the correct etiquette. A lot of women qualified their desire to go out with another woman by saying, *'If it were a friend, it would help.'*

More than this, though, we see sleeping with a woman as an issue of loyalty and fidelity, which blocks us from even trying it. Many respondents spoke of having an affair with a woman as being just as much of a betrayal of our current partner, as having an affair with a man would be. This seems to show that we don't see sex with women as simply an experiment or a game, but as a real possibility, a real commitment, a real threat.

Women often say that their male partners felt good about the possibility of their sleeping with another woman: *'He would not let other men touch me, but women, now that's different. Big turn-on!'* Perhaps men see their partners having sex with a woman as being a fun, physical thing, which would give them (and their partner) pleasure but would essentially not be a 'real' relationship. Women, suspecting that they would get emotionally involved if they had sex with another woman, are more aware of the dangers.

*I have shared this particular fantasy with my husband, as he finds certain female friends of mine very attractive, and he too fantasizes about me making love with other women. He would like to act out this fantasy, but I am very shy about asking any of my friends to join in a threesome, although the idea excites me.*

## EARLY EXPERIENCES

Some 33.4 per cent of women who answered the question say that they have had some kind of sexual experience with another woman. Most of us are children when it happens. We are friends, the same age or nearly, and we use each other to explore sensuality and sexuality. We look and touch. We examine each other's genitals and explore each other's responses. We experiment and practise with each other. But once we become adults, all this doesn't seem to us to count as woman-to-woman sex; many women made it very clear in their answers that what they did wasn't sexual at all but purely exploration. They haven't done anything like it since childhood, and they are concerned that their basic attraction to men might be in question if they even admit to having enjoyed themselves with girls.

*I was very young – about 13 – and my partner was the same age. We touched and looked at each other, we kissed each other. It felt nice, but there were no orgasms. It seemed experimental in retrospect, not really a lesbian relationship.*

For a very few of us as children, there is also passion. We kiss with closed mouths and then with open mouths. We learn to use our tongues. We touch breasts and discover that nipples erect when they are fondled. We touch genitals and discover that what we do on our own can feel just as good when someone else is doing it. We wonder – and find out – what happens if we lick each other down there. We become aroused, climax and teach each other to climax.

By the time we reach adolescence, as explained in chapter 3, the emphasis is on boyfriends, whatever one's true bias. Because of that emphasis on heterosexual love, the amount of woman-to-woman sexual contact in early adolescence is much less than that in childhood. As a result, lesbian respondents often say they are now frustrated that they were socially pressured into thinking they were heterosexual, or that they feel they wasted their adolescent years with boys when they could have been enjoying girls.

Also, there's some unease about the answers of those women who report adolescent experiences. They are becoming aware of their sexuality then. They're starting to orgasm. Whether it is heterosexual or lesbian, they're starting to see that sex can give other people power over them. So it's perhaps not surprising that where reports of childhood girl-to-girl sex are full of gentle, innocent descriptions of touching and kissing, as they reach adolescence the tone changes: '*I was afraid ... I was uneasy ... it got very heavy.*' We are old enough to be seduced by a boy, and we are also old enough to be seduced by another woman. And if the secrecy and guilt around boy-girl sex is worrying, then the emotional pressure around woman-to-woman sex is even more so.

*She initially seduced me, and it got very heavy; I was 14. It involved mutual masturbation, rubbing against each other to orgasm, mutual oral sex and eventually vibrators, a strap-on dildo that was used on me. I enjoyed most of it physically, and I orgasmed quite a lot. But it was enormously confusing, and the pressure of our secret was enormous.*

## ADULT LOVE

By their late teens the tone of women's answers changes again. By now we feel much more confident; we are able to involve our emotions much more fully: *'I was very in love with that woman, whereas I wasn't with my male partners at the time.'* At this age we know what we are doing. We know how to pleasure and be pleasured: we are developing skill in all the ways that any couple arouse each other, such as kissing, hugging, touching, stroking. We are able to tell another woman how we like our breasts touched and how we like to be masturbated. We can often, with no inhibitions, give and receive oral sex. We know how to bring ourselves to orgasm – and so we can use that knowledge to help another woman climax.

And when it comes to having a first sexual experience with a woman, we are able to benefit, in a way that we can't when we have first inter-course, from the fact of similarity. Our first time with a woman is an extension of masturbating ourselves but with the added pleasure of another person and of emotional involvement. We are able to indulge in long foreplay. We get as much clitoral stimulation and oral sex as we need. Women describing these experiences use the words *'exciting . . . wonder-ful . . . we did everything.'* All this adds up to the fact that 92.9 per cent of women who have had sex with another woman say they enjoyed their first time, as opposed to 22 per cent who enjoyed first intercourse, and that 43.4 per cent orgasmed first time, as compared to 5.7 per cent who climaxed when they lost their virginity.

When we are in our late teenage years and in our early twenties, we may also try woman-to-woman sex as part of a threesome. We've had intercourse and feel confident to extend our boundaries. Our male partners often also want to experiment. So we may end up in bed with a male partner and a female friend, or a female friend and her male partner. This kind of encounter – like any threesome – does often end in tears when it challenges, creates or destroys existing relationships. But it may also give us a great deal of pleasure, as we kiss, touch and watch the man make love to both of us. We can enjoy this kind of experience while feeling only the minimum of real passion for the woman involved, because we can, if we need to, simply concentrate on loving the man. And if we find through these threesomes that we do enjoy woman-to woman-sex, we can take it further.

Just a few women say that they have discovered woman-to-woman sex in their thirties and forties. This experience is slightly different again. Here we are making a choice against the background of decades of heterosexual sex. We are rarely simply experimenting, rarely just having fun. We are far more likely to be realizing our true sexuality for the first time, which is both less difficult and more challenging. It is less difficult because, as older women, we may well be more self-confident, far more determined to go for what we want. But it may be more challenging because we have far more commitments to be resolved before we can really be the sexual person we want to be. What do we tell our husband, our children, our parents? How do we disentangle ourselves from a lifetime of heterosexuality if we suddenly find that, underneath, we are lesbian?

## DOING IT AGAIN

Just under half the respondents who say they have had a sexual experience with a woman say they wouldn't repeat it. Not surprisingly, the younger we are when the event happened, the less likely we are to repeat it, and the more likely we are to look back on it as an experimental one-off.

The main reason for not trying again is that in the end it doesn't feel right. We find out that, actually, we're not turned on by women: *'I didn't enjoy it, I didn't repeat it.'* Or, however much we are turned on by women, we are actually more attracted to men and want to follow that route. Sex with men gives many of us more pleasure, and relationships with men give a lot of us more satisfaction – and not just because, as one woman puts it, *'there is still one thing that a woman cannot give – although there are realistic prostheses available.'*

Sometimes, although woman-to-woman sex in general is something we love, the particular relationship we get into just doesn't work for us. We may become disillusioned with our partner, or she becomes disillusioned with us, and we get hurt. We retreat back into heterosexuality and make no attempt to recreate our lesbian relationship with another woman.

*At the time the affair with this woman took place, my brain was very screwed up, and she seemed to offer a gentleness and loving that was completely missing in my life then. I did live with this woman for about a year, but ... she was insanely jealous of me, and she could not come to terms with the fact that I still had the need and desire to go and see my men friends. I walked out of the relationship for ever, about ten years ago. I still refuse to make contact.*

But some of us realize that woman-to-woman sex is something we want. We may realize that we are attracted only to women, or that we are attracted to the two genders and want to sleep with both. The pull for us is a sense of rightness and a great deal of pleasure: *'I had orgasms like no man ever gave me.'* There is a feeling of homecoming, of sensing that, with women, our sexual needs are understood and are fully met, perhaps for the first time. We are the same, and so we know what to do with each other. This isn't to say, of course, that everything is easy; there is the potential for emotional and sexual problems in just as many lesbian and bi-sexual relationships as there are in heterosexual relationships. The important thing is that if we discover that we love other women, and we act on that, we are being true to our own sexuality.

## TOTALLY COMMITTED

Thirteen women who answered the questionnaire consider themselves to be fully lesbian or bisexual. Some of them knew they were not hetero-sexual from an early age and have had come to terms with that in a society that is essentially straight: *'I used to touch breasts with school friends when aged about 11; I recall liking it a lot and feeling that I had to play down how much I liked it.'* Other women were able, at the time they became sexually active in their teens, simply to meet and experiment with both men and women and then allow their real desires gradually to become clear. A third group thought they were fully heterosexual for a long while, married, had children and then, through a single experience, changed their minds and their orientation completely.

Of course these women have the variety of relationships that all women have. Some have casual relationships, others a central relationship with additional partners, others *'extensions of close friendships with mainly straight girlfriends'*. Yet others have strictly monogamous relationships with other women or bisexuals. Four are currently having lesbian relationships, one is a female-to-male transvestite who sleeps with people of all genders. Another woman had only just come out when she completed the questionnaire; she devotes a delightful number of her answers to celebrating her recent realization.

*I found women attractive from the age of 20. But I failed to act on this, believing it to be normal heterosexual behaviour. Then I slept with a lesbian, and it was beautiful. I came out, and I have no wish to sleep with men ever again. I so regret wasting so much time having poor sex and poor relationships with men. My sex life has improved severalfold.*

How different is the sexual experience of those women who are primarily lesbian and those who are primarily heterosexual? The questionnaire itself was aimed largely at embracing the heterosexual experience; nevertheless, it was striking how similar the lesbian experience seems to be to the heterosexual experience emotionally and sensuously, if not in the mechanics of sex.

This may seem like heresy. Of course the emphasis in woman-to-woman sex is away from penetration and towards clitoral stimulation. And, of course, many women commented that sex with another woman was simpler and more cooperative than sex with a man. But when it comes to love, hate and jealousy, the words used in respondents' answers were the same. When it comes to knowing what's wanted in bed, to supporting an inhibited partner or to getting frustrated with a restless one, the experiences were identical. And when it comes to descriptions of love-making, the sheer pleasure of it and the sheer passion, then most of the time it was not clear whether the accounts under analysis came from heterosexual or from lesbian respondents.

## THE LESSON

Having struggled, often painfully, to contact their true sexuality, it isn't surprising that many lesbian or bisexual women feel strongly about gender politics: *'Women form better relationships, and men are OK for procreation and nothing else.'* Now it's not within the remit of this book to explore the issue of whether heterosexuality, sex between two heterosexual women, bisexuality or lesbian sex is the most valid option. What is worthwhile, however, is to look at what woman-to-woman sex offers us in terms of confirming female sexual experience.

The key message, from these respondents who have had sex with women, is that women's instinctive ways of gaining pleasure are valid and effective. What is natural to a woman is effortlessly arousing and endlessly orgasmic. Female sexual knowledge and female ways of arousal – with their emphasis on sensuousness, long foreplay and clitoral stimulation – usually result in climax after climax, whether or not accompanied by penetration. As one woman expresses it: *'Lesbian foreplay goes on and on for hours . . . orgasms happen, and sex goes on.'*

We can tend to forget this. Particularly if, as heterosexual women, we enjoy intercourse because it gives us emotional intimacy with our partner, we can come to regard it as the only way to make love, and we can fail to see the importance of other ways that may also give us pleasure. Or we can buy into society's emphasis on penetration and feel guilty about the pleasures of masturbation and oral sex. Or we can forget that most female orgasms are dependent on particular ways of stimulation, and guilt-trip ourselves if we don't orgasm through thrusting alone.

What woman-to-woman sex offers those who are aroused by it is a lifelong opportunity to fulfil their sexuality and gain pleasure. What it offers those who don't get aroused by it is proof that female ways of gaining pleasure are wonderful. They do lead to pleasure and orgasms. They are just as valid as 'men's ways' are. And surely we can all learn a lot from that.

*I always climax with a woman. Not because I'm gay, because I know I'm not, and not because I'm bisexual, which I obviously am. I think I climax because women are better lovers and know exactly what to do.*

VITAL STATISTICS

93.2 per cent of women would like some part of their body to be different

Only 2.8 per cent have never done anything to change their appearance

22.2 per cent are not comfortable naked in front of anyone

75.7 per cent of women feel negatively during menstruation

16.3 per cent have their strongest sexual appetitite during their period

Just 10 per cent of women say that they are happy with the way they look

# 8. Your body

*I am 5'10" (over 6' in heels) and 14 stone. I have size 9 feet and men's size hands, no tits to speak of and a huge arse. I would very much like a nice new body designed to spec. I want full breasts, long muscly legs, a pert, hard bum, a very long back, curly hair, green eyes. I want to have normal-sized feet and hands, so I can buy shoes and gloves to fit. I want to be only 5'6" tall so I can look up into men's eyes. I want to be 10 stone so I can be swept up into a man's arms and be cuddled. In the past I have dieted and worked out; that lost what tits I had and made my arse stick out even more. It made me feel even more of a man than I do already.*

WHEN WE'RE VERY young, we're at ease with our bodies. We're not really aware of them, simply experiencing them as natural extensions of ourselves. Respondents to the questionnaire constantly say how natural it was, in childhood and adolescence, to contact their own sexuality through our bodies, how easy and natural it felt when they began to discover their capacity for physical pleasure.

But part of learning how to be a girl is being taught how to be aware of how good our bodies look, particularly to others. We grow up believing that how worth while we are depends on how attractive we are. And if, somewhere along the line, we get the message that we are not as attractive as we could be, we feel bad about that. If, as one woman did, we get called Dumbo at school because our ears stick out, we start to feel bad about ourselves. We compare ourselves to society's ideal and find ourselves wanting. In women's responses, the words, *'I'm not perfect ... I know I'm not perfect,'* crop up time after time.

*I tend to swing a lot between liking my body as it is and feeling that I look awful. I feel I have a pretty face, and I've always had no trouble attracting boyfriends. But I hate the fact that I am flat-chested ... well, perhaps hate is too strong a word. I would rather have bigger boobs and a slimmer stomach and bum but wouldn't most women? In general, I think I am all right.*

The end result of this kind of upbringing seems to be that we're never quite at ease with our bodies. Saying this is not new, of course. But now women have more sexual freedom, the survey results might be expected to show more of them as being happier with their physical appearance. Not so at all. If anything, our standards of physical appearance are higher and so, therefore, are our anxiety levels. Just 10 per cent of women say that they are happy with they way they look. All but 2.8 per cent have at some time tried to change their appearance. And 93.2 per cent say that they want to improve some part of their body. A minority say: *'I'm definitely not obsessed with the body beautiful ... I don't feel the need to live up to the ideas set by society on the images of women'* – but even this minority admits to having dieted, exercised and permed their hair.

And even where we do say that we like some part of our body, we seem to preface our comment with an apology, as if it's not really acceptable to be pleased with ourselves: *'I'm reasonably attractive ... I'm fairly attractive.'* During the analysis of the responses, there was no answer that read: *'I'm stunningly beautiful and proud of it.'* What came through instead is that women are dissatisfied with the way they look and are constantly striving for perfection: *'I don't like my physical appearance – does anybody?'*

## HATING OUR SHAPE

The main issue, and the one we get most emotional about, is weight. Almost every respondent is either actively trying to be thinner or unhappily resigned to being the shape she is. Almost every woman makes some comparison, however slight, with the ideal 'shape' of the women shown in the media. This is not the place to go into detail about why the mass media promotes ideals. But the fact is that the sexual revolution seems, if anything, to have made those ideals more visible and conforming to them more vital. We now need to be seen to be beautiful; if we're not, it's almost as if we have no right to be sexual.

The key body areas that women feel they need to change are stomach, thighs and bottom – all areas that make our shape most obviously female. We want our thighs to be slimmer. We say we have a fat gut. We know we have a fat bottom. We believe that we are overweight with a persistence that defies logic: time after time, women say that other people have complimented them, but that they are not 'taken in' by these reassurances: *'I've been told that I have a lovely figure, but I think I could do with losing a few pounds ... I've been told I haven't got a fat bum, but even so.'* Even one of the only two women who claim to be totally happy with her appearance says that she's felt happy, *'since I lost weight, and feel confident'*. This response is typical:

> *I would probably like my stomach a little flatter. I am very fit and muscular and athletic and love my body, but no matter how slim I am, I always have a slightly rounded belly. I know that it's (a) hereditary (b) womanly and that (c) men like women with curves. But I don't like my own little curves. I would rather have a boyish look. In order to get this, my God, have I dieted? I didn't stop from the age of 15 onwards, on and off. I've also tried mega-exercise regimes like running every day, cycling and doing aerobics.*

For in order to be the shape we want to be, we suffer. We exercise. We go on courses of muscle stimulation. We try liposuction. And we diet. Up to 59 per cent of women mention going on a diet at some time in our lives, and most of them admitting to dieting on and off for several years, usually with the rider *'only once successfully ... with little success ... it never works ... I always put it back on again ... I give in and give up.'* One woman, aged 49, says she has been dieting for *'the last forty years'*.

If a diet doesn't work, we usually blame ourselves, saying that we don't keep to it strictly enough, come off it too quickly or *'find cheeseburger and fries too fascinating'*. And the signs of eating disorder creep to the surface: *'I used to have just one cup of coffee with milk for each meal ... I became bulimic, then anorexic and am still battling with this ... I did diet once but went too far and nearly died.'*

## OTHER CHANGES

Our second most worrying issue is our breasts. Many of us want bigger breasts, most want firmer ones. A few women want smaller breasts, and one says she'd like to have *'one of them reduced so that they both match'*. There are a number of comments such as, *'I wish my boobs were more awake'* from women in their thirties, who are presumably longing for the uptilted breasts that are natural in adolescents but are in fact physiologically untypical of more mature women.

We also change our hair: 41 per cent of respondents have it permed, 31 per cent have it coloured, and almost every woman has it cut or restyled. We're not quite so anxiety-ridden about this, though we do tend to indulge when we're dissatisfied with ourselves and our lives – many women comment that they treat themselves to a perm or cut when a relationship ends, for example. But often a change of hairstyle, shape or colour is simply a fun thing to do, so:

*I constantly change my hair. I get bored with just one look. I have had several perms but prefer to make the most of my straight hair now and just change the style through length. I also colour my hair every so often.*

And then we work to alter a multitude of smaller things that we're not happy about. We want to be rid of the dark patches under our eyes, our sticky-out ears, our knock knees. We want perfect vision, clear skin, smaller feet, thinner calves, a toned body, long and beautiful legs, perfect teeth and a tight vagina. To get 'the body beautiful' we have sunbed sessions, teeth capping, full body massages, face lifts, breast implants, ear pinning and plastic surgery. And this is not to count the minor ways in which we groom ourselves: manicure, leg-shaving, eyebrow-plucking, and make-up.

It's not that all these activities are signs of neurosis. We obviously enjoy many of them, revel in them, regard them as a sign of self-love and a way to give ourselves confidence and a new image. But the relentless list of changes, on and on, does give the impression of underlying unhappiness.

*I would like a smaller bum, smaller thighs and toned up, because they wobble too much. So last year I regularly went on a sunbed, did*

*callanetics and swam a lot. I lost about two stone and became under-*
*weight. I wasn't actively dieting; I just couldn't get myself to eat any*
*solid food.*

## GOING NAKED

It's the anxiety about our bodies that largely underlies our wariness about
being naked: 22.2 per cent of respondents are uncomfortable, even in
front of their lovers. This isn't to do with embarrassment or morality, as
it might have been for our grandmothers. Nowadays, our unwillingness
to be naked has far more to do with how we look to others than with any
moral values. The woman who writes *'I am not comfortable naked in front*
*of anyone because I imagine I am too fat. I assume everyone is similar,'* is
correct in her assumption. Almost all of us who admit to being ill at ease
with our nudity give 'being overweight' or 'looking awful' as the reason.

*I can't say I am entirely comfortable being naked in front of people. It's*
*got nothing to do with breasts or genitals. That doesn't bother me, it's*
*more to do with having this God-awful cellulite on my thighs. I would*
*feel uncomfortable about that in front of anyone – from doctor to lover.*

Of the three-quarters of women who are happy to strip, just under
a fifth will only do so in front of a partner. With our partner we feel
accepted and loved. We know that looks are not everything we offer him
– there are our hands, our mouths and our genitals to make up for what
we feel we lack visually.

With other people than our lovers, though, we often feel we are
being judged on appearance alone: *'Even friends can be critical.'* Or we
feel that we are cutting across their taboos: *'If I feel someone else, parti-*
*cularly a female friend, is uncomfortable with my nakedness, then I will*
*cover up.'* We are especially wary in front of men. What messages are we
giving them if we appear naked before them? What messages will they
read into our nudity and will they want to take advantage of it? *'Men take;*
*their arrogance and sexuality creates a one-up situation.'* And even fewer
of us are comfortable in front of the very people who once saw us
completely naked for a great deal of the time – our family. Now we are
adult, incest taboos take over. Out of the 200 women who completed the
questionnaire, only two of them say that they are at ease nude in front of
close relatives.

Despite all these 'ifs and buts', we are reclaiming our nakedness
nowadays. Lots of us say that being naked is natural, that we do it regularly
'whenever the weather permits,' or that we are now more comfortable
with it than we were before: *'My partner helped me feel comfortable with*

*my body; my women friends admire and love my appearance in a giving way.'* Or we've simply become more confident as we've got older.

*Yes, I am now comfortable being naked in front of almost anybody, male or female, apart from possibly my parents, though this wouldn't happen. I have sunbathed naked on foreign beaches and in my own back garden, and I am not worried by communal changing rooms. I might be embarrassed if I was caught naked by a man I suspected was attracted to me, or if I felt I was overweight at the time, or while my stretch marks are still very visible.*

## PRIVATE PARTS

Happily we are also at ease with our genitals. We almost seem to take them for granted – 34 per cent of respondents say they feel totally neutral about them: *'They're OK, they do the job ... They're normal, just part of me ... I never really thought about them ... I can't see them, so who cares?'*

Where we are negative, it's usually not because of embarrassment. Genitals in the abstract, it seems, are fine. If we feel bad about ours, it is (once again) because they specifically are not acceptable when compared to an ideal: *'My vaginal lips are too large ... I haven't enough pubic hair ... I'm too hairy ... I cut my pubic hair as it gets ridiculously long.'* And, more than once, *'since childbirth, my vagina is too wide, and that makes me feel embarrassed.'*

But many of us feel really good about our genitals and as many as 45.1 per cent of respondents think they are *'beautiful'*, both in themselves and in the pleasure they give us. We like to look, we like to explore; we like to use them to the full: *'I feel better about them since I learned to masturbate ... My genitals are wonderful; I love it when my partner really studies them.'*

When it comes to showing our genitals to those who need to see them professionally, we are more at ease than we are appearing naked but not displaying our private parts. We seem delightfully unbothered by professionals examining us. This is partly because *'I see doctors as doctors ... they're doing a job,'* and partly because we feel secure that professionals will not compare us with an ideal in the same way that friends or lovers will. And just under half of the women say that they don't mind whether a male or female doctor gives them an internal examination (compare this to 22.2 per cent who are uncomfortable being seen naked in front of anyone at all).

When it comes to stating a preference, however, four times as many would rather be examined by a female doctor, because *'they are more likely to understand ... my partner would prefer my being examined by a woman ... if it's a handsome male doctor, I feel uncomfortable as I usually have sexual thoughts.'* Where we do prefer men, it seems to be because we feel women are hard-hearted or unfeeling; we see male doctors as more *'gentle ... sensitive ... compassionate'.*

## PERIOD PROBLEMS

In general we feel good about our genitals. But there is one time of the month where we consistently feel bad about what they produce. When asked how they feel about menstruating, women's reactions range from utter rage, *'How do I feel about periods? How do you mean, feel? They're a messy, disgusting waste of time!'* to sad resignation, *'I just accept them. There's nothing else women can do.'*

These reactions are understandable when one reads the list of symptoms that women suffer when they menstruate. In the time leading up to our period many of us have constantly tender breasts, weight gain, nausea, headaches, dizzy spells, greasy hair and spots. Emotionally we feel moody, irritable and depressed, in some cases so badly that we throw things and hit people. When our period starts, we can have stomach cramps so uncomfortable that we always have to take pain-killers, and this pain can be accompanied by vomiting, diarrhoea and backache. The bleeding itself, as well as involving messiness for up to several days, can make us anaemic. Some respondents say that there is only one week out of every four when they are not suffering some of these side-effects of being a woman.

> *I find menstruating a pain, literally and metaphysically. I experience pre-menstrual tension which makes me moody and bloated. I tend to binge on foods such as bread and cereal. During my period I can experience stomach pains – though it is generally the days before my period that I find the most uncomfortable.*

There seem to be few reasons to celebrate menstruation. Only a handful of us saw anything positive about it, and they are those women who link their periods with their potential fertility: *'It tells me I'm not pregnant ... I dread a time it will stop, because I want to get pregnant ... after having anorexia, which stopped my periods, I now see them as a constant reminder of better health.'* Interestingly, there seemed to be no link between women who have had a positive first experience of menstruating and those who now have an easy time of things – or, conversely, between a negative first period and a tendency to get depressed or ill as an adult.

It wouldn't be surprising if because of all this, the last thing we wanted to do when menstruating was to make love. But significantly, it seems that an old taboo – that of not having sex during one's period – is finally dying. Up to 58.8 per cent of women now make love when they menstruate, though some still feel uncomfortable doing so. We are far less inhibited about the intimacy and far less worried about the mess nowadays. Also, 16.3 per cent of respondents feel more sexual during their periods, and, as one woman says, *'it relieves cramps to have an orgasm!'*

Our reasons for not wanting to make love while we are menstruating are both mental and physical. Intercourse can be painful, particularly as the vagina may already be sore from using a tampon. We may bleed so heavily that making a mess is unavoidable. We may feel intruded on and simply not want the emotional intimacy of making love: *'The week of my period is totally private and I don't want to have sex then.'* It is less likely to be our partner who objects, but he may do, feeling that he doesn't want to touch or taste our menstrual blood – and is likely to be more at ease if he is only penetrating us rather than giving oral sex.

## OUR BODIES AND SEX

In general, then, the theme that came from the whole survey was that few women are totally at ease with their bodies. Whether it's our figures in general, our nakedness in particular, our bodies when we exercise or our genitals when we menstruate, there is always some way in which we are dissatisfied. There is always a sense of wanting to improve.

The basic question to ask, it seems, is whether this dissatisfaction affects our sexuality. Our common sense tells us that it must do, that the more at ease we are with our bodies, the more we will enjoy sex. And, throughout their responses, women echo this thought, saying that as they grow happier with their physical appearance, so they can be more uninhibited in bed.

The significant thing, though, is that 'growing happier' rarely seems to mean 'striving to change'. Those of us who work hardest to control figure and looks, those of us who feel that we most fulfil the media ideal through hard work and deprivation aren't necessarily those of us who feel best about our sexuality. In this sense the media response to the sexual revolution has hindered rather than helped our development, by placing much more stress on 'looking right' than 'feeling right'. For the women who report shifts in their ability to achieve passion link this to an increased awareness of their bodies, hardly ever to a dramatic drop in weight or a cosmetic transformation.

This isn't a proven link; the statistical correlation isn't mathematically significant here. The evidence comes far more from comments, hints and asides that emerge throughout women's accounts. And it is certainly not the case that the many women who report caring for their

appearance were necessarily less sexually aware or skilful than those who
do not. But, consistently, respondents' accounts give the impression that
when we strive for a physical ideal we focus our attention away from
passion not towards it — and that better sex is linked more to acceptance
of our bodies than to victory over them.

*I love going on an occasional treat to an all female health club, where
you can enjoy swimming in the nude for the pure sensual pleasure of it.
I love the fact that women of all shapes and sizes can choose to go naked
if they want. This makes me feel far more positive about my own body.
And I have found that the more relaxed and comfortable I am with my
own body, and the more pleasure I take in its sensuality, the more
enjoyable making love becomes.*

VITAL STATISTICS

92.3 per cent of women have masturbated

29.1 per cent masturbate at least once a week, and 3.1 per cent do it daily

Only 1.8 per cent masturbate without clitoral stimulation

95 per cent come when they masturbate

91.8 per cent always come

27.5 per cent have watched another woman masturbate

# 9. Pleasure alone

*I make love to my own body. Sometimes I take off all my clothes and sit cross-legged in the centre of the bed. Sometimes I lie on my back and sometimes on my stomach, sometimes just arching back, sometimes in front of a mirror, sometimes not. Then I start at my head, touching it, massaging my scalp, then moving down my neck and along the tops of my shoulders. I continue on until I have explored every inch of my body. Sometimes I use a vibrator, nothing flash, and sometimes I just use my hands. I never have any set order, it just depends on how I am feeling at the time. I always reach orgasm.*

WE LOVE MASTURBATION. The survey questions that asked about self-pleasuring resulted in the most wonderfully evocative responses. Women describe in delicious detail just what they do to themselves, how they do it, how many times they do it – and how many orgasms they always have. For the vast majority of women answering the questionnaire, masturbation is a real delight.

Some 81 per cent of women masturbate regularly (only 7.7 per cent have never done, and 11.3 per cent have in the past but don't now). If we do masturbate, we don't do it because other forms of sex aren't wonderful, and we don't do it because we have no chance of intercourse. We do it because we like it and because of what it means to us.

> *Masturbation gives me complete autonomy to provide myself with sexual satisfaction whether I'm in a relationship or not. It makes me feel relaxed and happy. It teaches me about my responses to sex and orgasm. I can explore my body and my fantasies and have an ongoing contact with my sexual nature when I'm not in an intimate relationship. An excellent doctor I once spoke to told me that having sex with yourself should be like taking yourself out to dinner – and I agree completely.*

Masturbation feels good. It releases sexual tension. It helps keeps our sexual parts in working order – whether or not they're otherwise being used. Particularly, it allows us to concentrate on ourselves for a while. When they describe masturbation, respondents seem to luxuriate in being able to enjoy themselves alone, physically, mentally and emotionally. They say they can concentrate totally on their own pleasure, without needing to stop and check out their partner's satisfaction. This freedom feels very good. For while pleasing a partner during love-making is wonderful, it's also *'nice to please myself . . . It gives me self-sufficiency, self-awareness, an ability to know my own needs and to satisfy them.'*

Many women also say that masturbation is more than simply pleasure. It is also an expression of our new-found sexual independence, a statement that we aren't dependent on men for release.

> *You're not under pressure to have a boyfriend just because you feel like having sex. . . . Masturbation stops me climbing the walls and grabbing the first man I see!*

> *Masturbation makes me feel powerful, for it is only me who is giving me the pleasure, and I am answerable to no one. The pure knowledge that I can make my own body feel good is wonderful.*

In addition masturbation is the key for many of us to passion and to orgasm with our partners. Most of us have learnt to climax first of all through pleasuring ourselves; masturbation is a way of building our sexual knowledge so that we can teach it to others: *'If you don't know how to turn yourself on, how do you expect a man to know what turns you on?'*

It allows us to know how to guide partners, to tell them what to do. And for some of us, of course, masturbation is the only way to orgasm or, at least, the only dependable way: *'For me it is important as a release, because I have never yet had an orgasm during sex with a man ... it leads to orgasm and intercourse doesn't ... it sometimes leaves me more satisfied than actual intercourse ... it finishes the job!'*

## HOW OFTEN?

Our masturbation frequency varies enormously: *'How often do I masturbate? How horny am I feeling?'* We say that it depends on many factors: whether we're tired, ill, or stressed; what time of the month it is; how confident and buoyant we feel in our lives; how hard we are working; whether we are feeling good about ourselves. And, of course, as mentioned before, on *'how much I'm getting it ... whether my partner is away'*. The trend is to masturbate less when we are getting sex more. Only one woman says that she masturbates more often when she's in a relationship and feeling constantly aroused than when she is free and single, and sex is on the back burner.

To satisfy those who are curious about frequency, though, here are some figures. Only 1.6 per cent of those women who masturbate do it once a year or less. Most masturbate between once a month to once a day: 58.2 per cent admit to regular patterns between these parameters, with a further 20.5 per cent varying within the two extremes. Up to 16.5 per cent masturbate on average once a month, 12.6 per cent on average once a week, 29.1 per cent on average daily – and 3.1 per cent more than once a day. The woman with the highest total, an eyebrow-raising 15 to 20 times a day adds that *'this can last for several days, and then I have a few days clear, or I may masturbate every day for a while.'* As another woman says, *'I get a very tired hand sometimes.'*

## WHERE?

Next time a colleague pops out of the office for a minute, she may well be going to the loo to bring herself off, particularly if she has watched a particularly erotic movie on television last night, and her partner is away. For there seem to be two separate approaches when we choose where to masturbate: the private and the public. In the relaxed privacy of our own home, we do regular, maintenance masturbation. We like doing it in the bedroom, sprawled on a pile of cushions or lying on a bed or sofa, and in the bathroom where both bath and shower provide warmth and wetness. What's important about both these locations is safety. For while kitchen, living-room or landing are occasional possibilities when the house is empty, bedroom and bathroom are still the places where we are most secure and private. They are the places where we can let the barriers down and be privately passionate.

But we also often masturbate in semi-public. When we want danger to add to the excitement, we choose locations with a high-risk factor. So many women report masturbating in the toilet at school or at work, on trains or in aeroplanes. Others spoke of using one hand to drive and the other hand to bring themselves off. And one brave respondent describes how in the early, lustful stages of a relationship, when she saw her lover only once a week, her frustration would drive her to:

> *Bring myself to orgasm under the desk when I was working on reception. I had an 'early warning system' in that I could hear people approaching from down the corridor. Even so I often answered the phone rather breathlessly when it rang in the middle of a particularly arousing session!*

## PREPARATION

Sometimes, *'the urge just appears,'* and we follow it. More often, particularly when we are planning to masturbate at home, we prepare. Many of us speak of rituals, of needing to do things *'one particular way'*. We don't need ritual in order to get pleasure; after all, the orgasm can happen whatever the surroundings. We need it in order to increase pleasure by repeating the actions, thoughts and feelings that we've used before and that remind us of past pleasure. We often spend hours in anticipation, thinking, fantasizing, stimulating ourselves briefly throughout the day, allowing ourselves to become more and more aroused as time goes on. One woman tells of placing oriental balls in her vagina: *'I'll go shopping or do housework with them in, a form of foreplay.'*

We arrange the setting: dim the lights, play soft music, plump up the cushions, light the candles, place a mirror where we can see ourselves fully. We take a preparatory bath or shower, putting on silky underwear. We may read an erotic book or magazine, watch a video. We let our minds wander: *'I think of my partner ... my current boyfriend ... I remember good sex with partners in the past ... I think of my ideal man ... I think of doing it in full view and wonder what people would think.'* The whole sense is of preparing ourselves for a peak experience; we do see self-pleasuring as just as important, if different, as pleasure with a partner.

Then we start to touch ourselves. We don't usually move straight to our genitals, and, if we do, it is only when we are desperate to come very quickly. Just as foreplay is for many women the better part of love-making, so touching our whole bodies can be just as important as coming. Instead we tend to move slowly from top to toe, massaging or stroking as we go:

*'I explore every inch of my body ... If I have had a bath I use baby oil to moisturise my whole body, including my genitals.'* Then we concentrate particularly on favourite erogenous zones: many women mention their bellies, shoulders, and breasts, and one woman speaks of being able to *'suck my own nipples, just the tips'*, while another *'puts pegs on my nipples, for stimulation'*.

## MASTURBATION POSITIONS

Now we move into our particular position. Intercourse has many positions, a menu of possibilities according to what kind of sensation we want and how quickly we want to climax. There's been very little attention paid to masturbation positions, yet each of us seems to have a favourite, or a series of favourites, which we vary according to how aroused we are, what kind or quality of orgasm we want to have and how quickly we want to come. By far the most usual, a sort of 'masturbation missionary position' is lying back with knees up and legs apart, *'as though a partner were on top of me'*. Next favourite is lying on our stomach, with genitals pressed firmly into the bed or sofa, often with a pillow or cushion underneath to rub against. Many of us sit up, cross-legged or on all fours, many kneel with genitals spread, others stand and arch back. We may start with one position and stay there until we come. Or we may switch positions to give different sensations as we stimulate ourselves, taking a final position perhaps to ease over the edge and into orgasm.

> *Generally, not always, I use my vibrator, mostly on my vagina, occasionally in my anus. This is always used after I have begun to rub my clitoris. I lie on my back, but propped up slightly – also after a while I crouch down with my feet on the floor and bounce up and down on my vibrator, again rubbing my clitoris.*

On reading women's descriptions of which position they usually use, it's clear that there is a common pattern. First, because an overwhelming majority of us need to be able to stimulate our clitoris in order to be able to come, the position we take to masturbate has to allow either easy access with our fingers or a suitable surface to push against.

And, second, we all need a particular internal tension that is right for us. It isn't particularly that we need to have something inside our vagina, though a few women do. It isn't even about our vagina's being opened or stretched; though that's sometimes important, many of us also talk about clenching our vaginal muscles tightly together through the position or movement of our legs or buttocks. Rather, it's about the state of tension or relaxation our vaginal muscles need to be in. Some of us need to relax: *'The more I relax into it, the slower and more powerful the contractions when they come.'* Some of us need our muscles squeezed together, so use a 'legs-crossed' position when lying supine or clenched buttocks when lying prone. Others need a large amount of vaginal stretch: for this, we push our legs apart, lie on our back with feet together and knees pressed down, or squat in a way that forces the vaginal walls apart. Many of us enjoy different types of internal tension at different times or even like varying the sensations by alternately squeezing and stretching.

Just 15 per cent of women love feeling something inside them as they masturbate: *'I love to feel the contractions clutching on to something.'* They say that the orgasm they get is much deeper and more satisfying. They place a suitably shaped object in the vagina or anus. Fingers are the favourite – one, two or as many as feels good. Or, they use an object: the range women mention is truly awe-inspiring, from every suitably shaped vegetable on the greengrocer's counter, through dildos and vibrators, to the do-it-yourself variations of felt-tipped pens, candles, roll-on deodorants, aerosol cans and wine bottles: *'I've used everything from the sink plunger to the Hoover handle.'*

*If I masturbate with my vagina or rectum empty, the orgasm from clitoral stimulation alone is very poor, short and shallow. It's the feeling of my vagina being full to bursting that excites me. So I will often insert a large aerosol, and I sometimes insert an object into my rectum at the same time. I don't move this around; I just enjoy the pressure and feeling of fullness. On my clitoris I use my fingers, made wet with vaginal lubrication or saliva, the palm of my hand or a vibrator. More recently I used the head of my electric toothbrush, which is very powerful. I only ever used to be able to masturbate lying on my tummy with my hand working on my clitoris, vagina and anal area, but then using the objects I've described became an extension of that. I now orgasm lying on my back or standing, but only with these helpers.*

## CLITORAL STIMULATION

All but 1.8 per cent of respondents say they use some kind of clitoral stimulation in order to come when they masturbate. Remember that, in biological terms, it's the clitoris that holds the key to orgasm. The clitoris is the sensitive tip (almost like the glans of a penis) of a clitoral system, a wide-ranging network of nerves and blood vessels that make up our genitals. It's this system that gets aroused – whether through direct stimulation of the clitoris, or through the position and action of the penis in the vagina pulling the genitals and so indirectly stimulating the clitoris. (Many experts now say that in order for a woman to climax at all during intercourse there has to be some form of clitoral stimulation; if you're wondering how, in that case, even 1.8 per cent of women manage to orgasm without clitoral stimulation, unfortunately they don't say. It could be that the movements they are making and positions they are assuming give them that stimulation without them realizing it – or it could be that they know something the rest of us don't!)

What sort of clitoral stimulation do we need? We may use direct finger or hand movements; the middle right-hand finger seems to be a favourite. We may add to this some sort of finger stimulation to the vagina. We may mix and match the two as we go.

While most women rely on fingers, many also enjoy the different sensations created by sex toys. We may use vibrators, of various shapes and sizes. We often employ the showerhead to play a stream of water on the clitoris. There were just a few mentions of *an electric toothbrush head against my clitoris, but used over my underwear'*. And pushing genitals against objects, rather than using objects to stimulate the genitals, was another favourite: *'I thrust against a cushion bag . . . pile of clothes . . . the corner of the bed . . . the arm of my couch.'*

## MASTURBATION MOVEMENTS

Many of us use an up-and-down movement when we masturbate. Not surprisingly, this is very like the basic movement men use when they masturbate their penis, rubbing vertically along the clitoris from bottom to top and back again. Some like a side-to-side rubbing or flicking, others a circular movement. The rhythm varies: some of us prefer it regular, others irregular; some slow and light, others fast and heavy. A few stop and start, though most keep going with a regular rhythm. Many bring themselves to the brink and then wait for a few moments, *'masturbating to near orgasm several times before allowing myself to come'*. Some simply squeeze and hold or place two fingers one on each side of the clitoris and move. Many add a 'dipping' movement into the vagina. This not only feels good but also helps us to transfer fluid from vagina to clitoris. It's very easy for the clitoris to get dry and uncomfortable, so many of us also lick our fingers at intervals or add regular doses of baby oil to our genitals to offset dryness.

How long do we take when we masturbate? There is no norm. We vary, and many women say that the time to climax depends on the mood they are in and how quickly they want to come. If aroused, relaxed and in the right situation, some women say that they can come in seconds. But given the time and the opportunity, many of us stretch out the experience, arousing ourselves and then letting the sensations die away again, for hours. Until, eventually, we are ready to orgasm.

*How long I take really depends on the time available. If I am in a hurry
I will just kneel on the floor, maybe in the bathroom, and use my finger
in a circular motion on my clitoris until I orgasm; this usually takes only
a couple of minutes. If I have plenty of time, I will usually remove my
clothing and lie on the bed on my back with my legs open. I put the first
and third fingers of my left hand at either side of my vagina with my
middle finger inserted into it. I use the middle finger of my right hand,
usually wet with saliva or my own juices, to rub my clitoris up and down
until I orgasm. I will usually fantasize as well. This usually takes five
to ten minutes, depending on how long I can keep going without actually
reaching a climax.*

## DO WE ORGASM?

As many as 95 per cent of women orgasm when they masturbate.
Let's repeat that figure: 95 per cent of women orgasm when they
masturbate. And 91.8 per cent always do: *'a glow ... a tingle ... a
release ... an intense pleasure ... always ... every time ... up to 16 times a
session ... it's difficult to hold back sometimes.'* These facts and these
quotes are incredibly optimistic. They suggest that we ourselves know
what to do in order to climax. And if we have that knowledge, it means
that, with courage and cooperation, we should be able to orgasm whenever we want to.

This statement isn't new, of course. The Hite Report, twenty
years ago, revealed that the majority of women are able to orgasm
regularly if they reclaim their knowledge of clitoral stimulation. It pointed
out that only a misunderstanding of biology led us to believe that we
should climax with simple thrusting alone. Sex therapists, for example,
teaching women to orgasm by starting with masturbation, often report
a 100 per cent success rate. So if we learn how to masturbate and
then take the time to develop our skill, we can be assured of orgasms;
it may be a little more difficult to guarantee orgasms with intercourse, but when we ourselves are in control, we can usually reach
climax.

*I remember when I was about 13 lying in bed one night and putting a
finger inside me and waiting for something to happen! I didn't really
know what to do so wasn't impressed when I didn't see stars or anything.
However, aged 20, following five years of non-orgasmic sex, and after
splitting up with my then boyfriend, I tried again, this time just touching
and rubbing. I brought myself to a huge wonderful orgasm and have
never looked back!*

## MASTURBATION DOUBTS

It's sad, then, given this intense and reliable pleasure factor, that our feelings about masturbation are so mixed. For on reading the accounts of women who masturbate – as well as the accounts of the minority of women who don't masturbate at all – there is a sense of negativity. For all our sexual freedom, we can still feel bad about pleasuring ourselves.

First of all, '*it's not as good as real sex, is it?*' Many of us feel that there is a sort of sexual hierarchy, with partner intercourse at the top and masturbation at the bottom, '*masquerading as the real thing*', as one woman puts it. Masturbation still seems to be the Cinderella of sex '*strictly for underprivileged men*'. Intercourse is better because having someone else involved gives added value and a feeling of intimacy. Masturbation, on the other hand, is inferior because, essentially, it's only for us. So we may not masturbate at all: '*You don't need it if you have a good sex life ... my husband keeps me satisfied sexually.*' Or we may masturbate only when we are single, or when our partner is away. Even those women who feel fine about the fact of masturbating often admit that when they have regular sex, they don't feel as justified in masturbating; if our partner is pleasuring us, we shouldn't need to fulfil ourselves.

And we continue to feel guilty about masturbation: '*I enjoy the feeling, although sometimes it is spoiled by guilt; I usually brush that away.*' It's not just that we feel guilty about sex in general – we can love intercourse but feel guilty about pleasuring ourselves. For women are still trapped in the 'loving is giving' belief. We still suspect that we are simply not 'good women' if we enjoy something that does not involve giving, and that, however much we love our partner, we are 'bad women' if we give to ourselves alone.

> *Masturbation makes me feel at one with my body. But it also makes me feel guilty (as if when I die, all the souls of others who are dead now will know exactly what I have done and that it was wrong). But this doesn't stop me masturbating. I see masturbation as more wrong than intercourse when I feel guilty.*

Our guilt can go one step further. If we're bad because we masturbate, the logical conclusion is that we should be punished for it. Now that sounds silly. We don't really believe any longer, as many people used to, that masturbation will make us go blind or give us venereal disease. But a small but significant group of respondents say that they felt that learning to masturbate, with its emphasis on clitoral stimulation, had somehow made them unable to enjoy any love-making that involves penetration:

*'I do wonder whether I have become able to orgasm only through clitoral stimulation because I have masturbated.'* In fact the evidence suggests that this fear is mistaken. The total opposite is true. The more we masturbate and find out about our own bodies, the more we are able to enjoy love-making, including penetrative sex. We're not bad when we masturbate, and we're not being punished.

Masturbation can be wonderful in its own right, can help us develop our instinctive sexual knowledge. So perhaps now may be time finally to change our minds about it. Why shouldn't we see self-pleasuring as complementary to partnership sex rather than inferior to it, as a wonderful way to give love to ourselves rather than a second-class way to keep love from our partners? Could we now be ready to regard it fully and without reservations as a valid alternative, one that isn't simply useful when we have no other option and that isn't just a second-class citizen to real sex?

*Masturbating makes me feel a sexy person, in tune with and aware of my own body. I tend to lie on my bed, but sometimes I will do it anywhere if the mood takes me. I read stories from porn mags, women's fantasy books/stories or make up my own fantasy to turn myself on. I play with my clitoris, sometimes I play with my breasts as well. Sometimes I insert an object, sometimes I watch myself doing it in front of a mirror. I always reach orgasm.*

VITAL STATISTICS

52.3 per cent of women will allow intercourse on a first date

Only 25.6 per cent have pre-set rules about a date and stick to them all the time

69.2 per cent have seduced a man at some time

69.6 per cent think that women are pressured into having sex

# 10. Sexual rules

*I never used to worry about the end of the night when I was younger. If I got a man and we had sex, fine. If I didn't get a man, or only kissed, that was fine too. I met my present boyfriend one and a half years ago, and within an hour we were naked and heaving. I never used to look for sex, although fellas were attracted to me for sex purposes only because I used to dress like a tart, showed a lot of leg and even more naked skin elsewhere. I suppose in a way I did look for sex, although I didn't go out of my way to get it. I guess I was lonely.*

IN THE POST-PILL age, we don't want rules about whether and when to sleep with someone. Some 61.6 per cent of women say that they simply want to follow their instincts where sex is involved: *'I don't set myself rules because that way, I can't break any.'* We want to know that we are sexually free, free to take pleasure when and where it's available. For now that there seem to be hardly any formal sexual rules in society, and that theoretically everything is allowed, we want to take advantage of that.

Of course, ironically, many of us seem to be still rebelling against rules that were given to us informally, as children, rules that still lurk in the back of our minds and worry us. They make us feel resentful, even now we are grown women. So we say almost defiantly that *'if I fancy him, I go for it.'* We are proud of our own self-direction and feel we are striking a blow against our early upbringing.

*No pre-set rules. Yes, I do have sex on the first date. It happens quite often, depending on the man. If he thinks that I will sleep with him, then I don't. I like to surprise them. I like to be in control before sex. If I want to say no, then I will.*

## THE INNER RULES

In fact this isn't quite the whole picture. We may say we don't have rules, but most of us do have internal guidelines, a kind of sexual wisdom that we follow because it feels sensible. Many women, for example, are now wary of sex on a first date, some because of the AIDS epidemic, more because they want to establish a relationship before being intimate. Early sex can lead to being screwed and left, or to being regarded as 'easy', even in this day and age. *'Never have sex with a stranger'* seems to sum it up. And just a few women take this to its ultimate extreme; they say no to any form of sexual contact on a first date: *'I probably wouldn't go much further than a fairly chaste kiss. I prefer no physical contact.'* These women regard a first date as an opportunity to talk, not touch; afterwards, with time to think, they can make their decision and carry it through on the next meeting or the meeting after that.

*I would never have sex on a first date because you could be in danger of being hurt if the boy only wanted sex. A first date is about getting to know someone and seeing if you are compatible. If you just jump straight into bed you could regret it.*

It seemed probable that there would be an age link with 'first date rules', that younger women would be happier to go further earlier, while older women would be more wary. In fact, there is none. The quote above came from an 18 year old, while many women in their thirties and forties say that as they get older, more sure of themselves and of what they want, sex is more likely to happen early in a relationship. Overall, however, both older and younger women are likely to believe in the broad guidelines of trusting our feelings, sleeping with someone when we want to – but being careful and waiting until we're sure.

All this said, where we do want to sleep with a partner, then actually we go ahead whatever our guidelines. So 74 per cent of respondents do have sex whether or not they previously resolved not to. For over a third of the women who clearly state that they have sexual rules, as well as most of the women who say that they have general but flexible inner guidelines, say that when it comes down to it, they often sleep with a partner earlier than they thought they would. Lustful spontaneity wins over logical decision-making, every time.

## BREAKING THE RULES

We give two kinds of reason why we overturn our previous resolutions. The first kind, where our body rules our head, is motivated by how we feel physically. Many women say that they do sleep with men because they've had something to drink; many more put it down to 'sheer passion'. Both influences make us override our mental resolutions. When asked if they regret these sexual U-turns, women write about drink-inspired sex with an undercurrent of embarrassment and quite some shame. It felt wrong at the time, and it continues to feel wrong now. If they have slept with someone through pure lust, this is far less guilt-inspiring, far more romantic, far more acceptable.

The second kind of rule-breaking, which seems to be our heart ruling our head, is all about futures. When we decide that we're not going to sleep with someone on a first date, it's often because we believe that we are therefore more likely to form a long-term relationship. For while most of us wouldn't agree with the comment that, *'At present I would like a husband, and sex on a first date would give a potential partner an impression of me I would prefer they didn't have'*, we would accept that sex early in a relationship doesn't give us time to assess a partner's long-term potential. Also, a man who wants to go to bed on a first date may only be in it for the sex.

But these reasons can easily be forgotten if, during the date, we get clear signals that the relationship is going to last. If we get on really well, seem compatible and are both talking about love or even commitment, then we feel totally justified in overturning the rules and making love. It's as if holding back is only justifiable if it is more likely to get us what we want: if we get a long-term commitment anyway, then why not have the sex as early as possible? Afterwards, it's only if our judgement is wrong, and the relationship ends, that we have any regrets. If the partnership endures, then this justifies our breaking the rules: *'My two main relationships, one of three years and my marriage, both began with us having sex on the first night. And although the first partnership ended, they both worked well and were not affected by this.'*

But, conversely, we may also abandon our sexual guidelines if we sense that this relationship is not going to go further than a first date. Some of us simply want to enjoy a pleasure that we may never have the chance of again. Others convince ourselves that moving the relationship on to a sexual level will make it more likely to last. Whichever, we can just as easily sleep with a man we know we'll never see again as with one that we believe we'll spend a long time with. If we lust after him, then first-night sex may well be worth it, whatever happens in the morning.

## MEN'S RULES

If women are unsure about how and when sex should happen, men are not. Most men, in our experience, expect early sex. Perhaps that expectation isn't as strong as it was even a few years ago: many women in their thirties say that when they were young, and the pill was at its most popular, first-night intercourse was taken for granted whereas now it isn't. And the AIDS epidemic has shifted etiquette so that sex at the end of an evening may now only be possible with forethought and protection. But many women do feel that even now, potential partners at least make a play for sex almost immediately.

*When I was single 24 years ago, yes, sex was on the agenda almost immediately. Since then, I don't know ... except that the only time I've been on holiday alone I was inundated with offers even though I made it clear that I had a partner at home.*

We notice that this expectation is higher if *'you are single ... you are married and out on your own ... if they know you are a lone parent.'* And we resent that *'If you aren't in a relationship, many men believe women are dying for it – whether we are or not doesn't come into it.'*

We are guilty of some inconsistency here. We may resent a partner's expecting sex if we aren't ready. But if everything feels good, the passion is mutual, and the signs are there of a long-term relationship, then we see his not expecting sex as a rejection or as a sign he lacks confidence: *'I think he's a wimp if he makes no move.'* Unbalanced expectation is a problem, while equal eagerness is evidence of 'love at first sight'.

## FEELING PRESSURED?

Does expectation ever turn to pressure? There are very definite views here, with just one woman only saying that she didn't know. Up to 29.6 per cent of respondents are sure that no such problem exists. Largely younger women, they have never felt pressured and believe it is a thing of the past. On the other hand, 69.6 per cent of the women say that pressure does still exist. Most have been on the receiving end, not of any physical threat but of emotional blackmail. They say that men *'will try it on without asking, and will sulk or feel hard done by if they don't get their own way'*, or that a partner can be polite on the first and second date, but that *'the pressure starts to build by the third.'*

Although we do lay the blame on men, most of us believe that whether such pressure succeeds is largely down to the woman. For while many of us have given way to the demands of early boyfriends, and almost all of us say that at some time or another we've regretted having sex, nowadays we largely feel in control. Where we don't, it is because we *'aren't sufficiently sure of ourselves ... are afraid of losing him ... feel guilty at saying no'*. We may also feel that we owe it to our partner to sleep with him.

> *I have agreed to intercourse on a date out of fear of hurting the man's feelings. I felt guilty that I had let him believe it would come to sex and therefore thought I should go through with it. A lot of times, it also seemed easier than to have a lengthy discussion of the why nots.*

There is, within our responses, a practical guide to staying unpressured. First, give clear signs – by word or action – of what is wanted and what isn't: *'Say no and mean no ... make it clear that you want to take things slowly ... make it clear at the beginning of the date.'* Second, don't allow emotional blackmail; stand firm against it from the start, ending the relationship if necessary. Finally, realize that if he does exert emotional pressure, then he's probably not worth the trouble: *'I never did anything I didn't want to do, and I didn't get second calls from men who couldn't accept that. It's frustrating but for the best.'*

## BEING BRIBED?

If some men expect that the way to get us to sleep with them is to 'feel hard done by', others may well believe they will succeed if they wine and dine us. Most women feel that accepting dinner and then having sex with a partner is totally innocent – if we already feel good about sleeping with him: *'It's fine as long as she wants him as much as he wants her.'* When asked if this might not be prostitution, 83 per cent say no, unless the woman was having sex only for what she would receive in return. If passion or emotional feeling were mutual, then there is no question of immorality.

Where we are unsure about this issue, we focus on whether we're entering into a bargain. It is prostitution *'only if she feels she should pay him back ... only if she expects a meal or payment in return for sex'*. Some women pointed out that it's the man's motives that are suspect. If he feels that he's buying sex — or that in return for a gift, a meal or an invitation to an expensive ball, he should expect to be given sex — then it is prostitution in his mind, and he is at fault.

Most, though, say that nowadays they would never accept a gift of dinner anyway, because of the implications: *'If he buys the food, I buy the wine.'* Almost all claimed monetary equality, with just a few saying that they had allowed a partner with whom they were in long-term relationships to buy them dinner and then had made love. Just one woman, very honestly, comments that:

> *I suppose in a way it is a form of prostitution, but I have to admit to having taken money from a guy to get a cab home afterwards. Then I complain that taking money from him made me seem like a whore. But I still always take the money.*

## ARE WE SEDUCED?

The myth is that, given a little alcohol and some good sexual technique, it is possible to persuade a woman into bed against her principles. It is called seduction, and afterwards women are traditionally expected to feel betrayed. By this definition, very few women in the whole survey reckon that they have been seduced.

Many of us feel that we have had sex unwillingly (see chapter 20), but we are certain that we actually knew at the time that we were reluctant and, in many cases, have made that fact more than clear to the man involved. Where we were willing at the time, because of physical passion or emotional need, we don't really see that as seduction. The man's technique may have influenced things, but our lustful response also played a part. He may have left us in the morning, but that is an emotional betrayal, rarely a sign that he sexually manipulated us into bed. It seems as if seduction, in the old sense, is now an outmoded concept.

On the other hand, many of us claim that we have been willingly and consciously seduced by a regular partner who has, by sheer force of personality or sexuality, persuaded us happily into bed.

The first and most important key reason why a partner succeeds has nothing to do with sex. Over and over women say that the biggest turn-on, the most powerful tool that a man can use to persuade is his interest in them: *'Above all, I want him to listen to me ... take a genuine interest in me ... ask me questions ... listen when I talk instead of raving on about himself.'* We need a potential partner not to tell us how wonderful he is but to show us how wonderful he thinks we are. This certainly confirms what we have stressed before, that while simple lust is more than enough reason to go to bed with a partner, sex is twice as attractive for most of us if we feel an emotional connection.

We also almost inevitably respond to a partner's lust. We love being the centre of attention, and not only because it makes us feel good. It also reassures us that we are not just one of a series, that we are special and that our partner is going to want to stay with us. Whether or not that reassurance proves genuine in the long term, in the short term it satisfies: *'I love feeling that he wants to go to bed with me, just me ... if someone shows keenness and desire, it doesn't matter what he does, it works ... being desired is the best aphrodisiac.'*

Finally, though very definitely last on the list, what a partner does can seduce us. Many women mention kissing and caressing as the keys at this stage: *'He has to be a good kisser ... I can be happily seduced by a kiss on the neck, a nibble on my ear, a single touch.'* This parallels our early experiences in sex, when we loved boyfriends to kiss us even when we weren't happy to go further. As then, we are taking things step by step, and kissing is a way of gathering information. On a purely biological level, it allows us to check out whether, close to, he feels, smells and tastes 'right'. It also shows us a man's sexual approach, whether or not it's compatible with ours, whether he is gentle and sensitive or eager and thrusting. A man needs to show us what it will be like to sleep with him; then we can begin to judge whether we want that experience.

> *He teased me outside my knickers and then slipped his hand inside my knickers and touched me – by which stage I was very wet. Then he put his fingers in both of our mouths as we kissed. This was such a turn-on because I quickly realized that this partner had few limits to adventure sexually. I wanted to be with him, and he very easily seduced me.*

## WHEN WE SEDUCE

The picture in general then about sexual rules is that, nowadays, we are in charge; we not only have our guidelines but we also break them when instinct demands or a partner tempts us. Finally, though, what happens when the tables are turned? What happens if we, not our partner, does the seducing?

As many as 69.2 per cent of respondents reckon that they have, at some time, seduced a man. Those who haven't done it, regret that: *'No, I haven't. Pity,'* or admit that they would if they only knew where to start. Those who have seduced say that they did it simply because they wanted to: they took the decision into their own hands completely and made things happen. The impression is that such behaviour is something new, a result of increased sexual freedom.

Why do we seduce? Those who did it just for the sex felt a need and went out to get someone, almost anyone, to meet that need: *'I was living in a sexless marriage and the only way I could get sexual satisfaction was to deliberately seduce someone.'*

But very few of us do it for the purely physical pleasure – and we believe that because of this, we're different from men. Far more of us seduce for psychological reasons. Some of us are bored and need a challenge. Some of us want power over men and feel that arousing them is a way to control them: *'I like making men know they want me but letting them think they've done all the work. It's a game to me, and it's funny to stand back and look at what I've done.'*

Or we may seduce in order to start a relationship then urge it on. We want to get together with a particular man, and he doesn't seem to be taking the initiative. So we do more than simply encourage his moves – we make the moves ourselves. We make our suggestions very plain, we actively persuade rather than simply respond. Like men, we even use alcohol to oil the mechanisms: *'I waited until he'd had a drink so he wouldn't be shy.'* And we give attention, use body language, pay compliments in a very active way and assertive way. Then we suggest sex or simply move in.

> *I seduced my current partner when we were away on a course together because I've fancied him for years, and this was too good a chance to miss. I talked to him, flirted with him, laughed at all his jokes, then invited him to my room for coffee and a chat. He took the hint and took over. I didn't expect us to fall so deeply in love though.*

## THE KICKBACK

If we seduce, afterwards we often feel a mixture of excitement and guilt. The impression we give is that because seduction is commonly done for power as well as for pleasure, we do sometimes get an emotional kickback. Many women said that *'after an initial feeling of self-congratulation, I later wished I hadn't done it.'* Others said that they'd seduced when younger but wouldn't do it now.

> *Yes, I used to regularly seduce an ex-boyfriend when he was going out with someone else. I did it in order to keep a hold on him, to prevent the bonds of honesty and trust forming between him and his girlfriend and to get one over on her.*

For the fact is that our experience of being the seducer is much the same as our experience of being seduced: it's fine when both are willing and the experience is pleasurable. Otherwise it leaves a nasty taste in the mouth.

This fact highlights a theme that actually runs throughout every response on sexual rules and that, in fact, seems to underpin our practising the 'new morality'. It's this. Where, in the heat of the moment, we follow our innate sense of what is right, then whether or not our partner is expecting us to sleep with him, is seducing us or even being himself seduced, the outcome is generally good. We don't regret it afterwards. And this is true whether or not we are keeping or breaking the sexual guidelines that we have worked out in advance. It is true whether we rush into sex or say no to it.

But when things don't feel right — when we know at the time that our actions are wrongly motivated — then it all goes wrong. Whether or not we are keeping to our own formal rules, we regret what we do. And we regret what we don't do. Later we blame ourselves for our actions — or for our failure to act. And, in the end, all the excitement and sexual pleasure mean nothing; all our self-righteous holding back and waiting seem pointless.

*I knew at the time it wasn't right ... but I went ahead anyway. The sex was good but I felt so bad about myself in the morning that I went off sex for months. Serves me right, I suppose!*

VITAL STATISTICS

78.7 per cent of women believe that they are more frank than men about sex

52.3 per cent find it easy to ask verbally for what they want in bed

24.1 per cent would not be honest with their partners about their sexual history

36.8 per cent feel bad when their partner talks about his sexual history

# 11. Sexual communication

*We have discussed previous partners and experiences with each other, but I must admit I have not always told him everything. I would not lie, but I feel embarrassed about many of the things in my past and would not want to risk my current relationship. Also, I don't want my husband to think he is inexperienced in comparison to me; I have had more sexual partners than him. In fact, as far as I am concerned, he is the best lover I have ever had, but I can't risk it.*

EVERY WOMAN WHO answered the questionnaire expresses, somewhere in her responses, a need to communicate with her partner. We thrive on talking, on being able to say what we want and show what we need, on being heard, on receiving feed-back. So do we communicate fully about sex? If so, how do we do it? If not, what stops us?

In general the picture looks bright; we're more than satisfied with the way we communicate with our partner. As many as 80.5 per cent of respondents feel that their partner talks to them about sex openly and at length and listens to what they have to say. They feel their partner values sexual communication as much as they do – and they say that they simply wouldn't stay in a relationship with a partner who didn't.

*I am much more open these days to discuss sex and my sexuality with whoever will listen. I would have problems now with a relationship where myself and my partner did not discuss sex.*

So only 14.8 per cent of women say that there are problems in their sexual communication. It seemed likely that any such difficulties would be caused by a simple unwillingness by our partners to communicate, a kind of mass male refusal to talk. In fact, only one or two women say that this is the root of their particular partnership problem: *'He doesn't like talking . . . he watches television,'* although many others feel that men in general are less communicative than women and are more prone to *'brag . . . embellish the truth . . . exaggerate . . . boast'.*

But those of us who have problems with partnership communication say that they are far more due to the fact that, over the course of our relationship, what we talk about has become so negative and critical that, now, we simply don't do it. We may be afraid of what we feel about our partners, and so we don't speak out: *'I would be so critical of his performance that I can't say anything to him . . . I am often on the attack when I discuss sex with him . . . It's my fault; I am frightened of hurting him, and I don't love him.'* We may be afraid of our partners' reactions: *'He gets upset so we don't bother talking . . . I am afraid of what he'll say or do . . . He might leave.'* We may be afraid we may hurt our partner:

*The problem is that after the hard time we've had with his industrial injury, I find him totally unapproachable. If I said to him that I wanted to make love more often he would just turn it around against himself and probably shout about my being a sex maniac or something.*

*My partner and I don't talk openly. A lot of things are left unsaid, particularly how I feel about his physical appearance; I don't want to hurt his feelings. Even when we talk about my occasional lack of interest and arousal, I lie and tend to blame myself rather than him. My problem is that, firstly, I want to keep some of my feelings about my own sexuality to myself and that, secondly, I don't know how to tell him what I really feel about him at the present. I am hoping that he will come to take more pride in his appearance through my giving subtle hints rather than heavy-handed criticism.*

## ASKING AND GETTING

When it comes to asking for what they want during sex, over three-quarters of respondents feel they do it well. They often put down their success to being with a partner who is receptive and makes it easy for them to ask: *'I ask, he complies. No problem.'*

But the main reason that we get what we want is that we ourselves feel good about asking. For, happily, women do now seem to have a great deal of self-confidence in the way we make our requests in bed. We may believe that it's our responsibility to ask. Or we may have an experienced partner, who finds our requests a turn-on. We may feel that asking makes us a better lover: and so it does – a self-fulfilling prophecy.

We also seem able to overcome any blocks we may have about asking by doing it in a particular way. The best option seems to be asking 'in advance', over the phone, when we are in the car, or any time when we're not actually having sex. That doesn't interrupt the flow or suggest any criticism of our partner's performance: *'After, or before the act, I find it easier to say general things – "I want you to talk dirty" or "Can you do it really hard tonight?" or "I want to be tender and loving this time."'*

If we do ask at the time, we often use a sort of running commentary on what feels good, to guide our partner in making the right moves: *'I say, "up a bit, down a bit, left a bit ... do that again ... carry on, don't stop",'* or we use a particular tone of voice, allow our noises and groans to indicate pleasure, talk dirty, or *'simply whisper'*.

For most women doing rather than telling works well. This is particularly so for those of us for whom asking is either still too scary or too disruptive to love-making. We kiss and touch. We snuggle up or move away. We guide his hand. We place his hand over ours so that he can feel what to do. We edge ourselves into the relevant position or take the lead in moving us both to a good configuration: *'I grab his buttocks to control the pace, or thrust myself upwards while he thrusts down.'* As time goes by we develop a body-language code that allows us to show him just what feels good.

Just a few of us said that we add to these lines of communication by actual demonstration. We show our partner what to do by masturbating while they watch. Fewer of us still say that we watch our partner masturbating *'to see if I can learn'*. It's significant that we don't find such demonstrations completely easy; masturbating to teach does seem to be a risky option – or maybe it feels uninvolved because we are doing while our partner is on the sidelines, watching. But those who do it find that they learn a great deal.

## FEAR OF ASKING

Despite the fact that most of us feel fine about asking for what we want in bed, 15.2 per cent of women are still wary of doing so. They may be wary of their partner's response; he feels threatened by their asking: *'My husband sees it as criticism so I just put up with it.'* Or he just isn't motivated to change what he's doing: *'I ask, but it's a waste of time ... I've told him the way but he doesn't use it.'* Or their partner isn't too experienced or is rather inhibited.

Also, there's a more widespread fear, the fear of 'what people might think'. This fear isn't of our particular partner's reaction but is linked with some message that we've received in the past, probably from our upbringing, some *'inbuilt prudery that stops me being as adventurous as I would like to be'.* We may feel that if we ask for what we want, the critical 'people in our head' will think we're somehow oversexed. Every time we think of asking, we seem to hear their negative comments clearly and pull back. Whenever or whatever we feel like suggesting, we see their shocked faces and stay quiet.

There may also be a subplot to our not asking for pleasure. We may not actually want our partners to know just what to do. If they do, they may be able to arouse us, without fail, every time. It might mean that they would be able to send us out of control. They might gain too much power over us. When asked if they told their partners any foolproof ways to please them, 32.8 per cent of the women said no. And many of these women didn't want to tell their partners exactly how to turn them on because that would hand over just too much power: *'My partner is not aware that I have a foolproof way to be turned on, and so he does not exploit it.'*

## REVEALING THE PAST

Talking about sex in the past rather than sex in the present is a lot more difficult for us. Over half the women in the survey aren't able to talk fully about past partners with their current partners. If they do, they feel they can't be honest about what has really happened.

Mainly we feel uncomfortable about sex we have had before. It's strange: society has over the past thirty years enabled, supported and encouraged women to be sexually active and free. Yet many of us still feel guilty, whatever our generation and whatever our actual partner score. We feel guilty largely about the numbers of partners we have had (however big or small that number is). And we also feel guilty about what we have done with those partners sexually, and how much we have enjoyed that. Once again a lot of our bad feeling is tied up with sex that we didn't want to have, or sex that we regret: but we seem unable really to believe that simply regretting will wipe the slate clean. So instead we feel guilty.

> *I have spoken about my sexual past, but only because he asked. I haven't told him about all my partners as I don't want him to think I am a slut. I don't feel I have been, as my partners span a lot of years, but just saying how many I've had sounds awful, especially as I was married at the time. I now realize I was searching for what was missing in my life.*

Even if we believe that he loves us, we often think that our current partner will feel negatively about our past. And so we think that confiding everything will risk our relationship – particularly if it is a new one: *'I'll tell him, but not yet; we're not secure enough to weather it.'* The idea of sexually experienced woman as whore still lingers on; society still has a hangover from pre-pill times that a woman with a past is a woman who doesn't deserve love.

We also believe that our partner may be jealous. He will think about us with other partners and feel bad. He will feel put down if we've had more partners than he has. Even worse, he will worry about performance or about size: *'Most men need to check that they are the biggest so far.'*

## WANTING TO TALK

Perhaps the saddest thing about all this is that we want to confide in our partner. We want to tell him everything; almost, we want to be forgiven. But telling everything is too risky a step, and 57.2 per cent of the women in our survey won't take it.

> *It would be nice in some ways to unburden myself fully and have no secrets, but once one finds out personal things about someone, it cannot help but affect how this is perceived.*

In contrast, the 42.8 per cent of women who are totally open either feel that they have nothing to hide or, more likely, that they want more than anything to be totally honest with their partner: *'We never hide anything from each other.'* It seems to be important to us that everything is known. We may well be careful to tell the truth in a tactful way, and we may hold back on negative details about past lovers so as not to put ourselves or them in a bad light. But we don't conceal the number of partners, and we are truthful about the facts when challenged.

> *If he asks about previous sexual partners I'd tell him, but I wouldn't give details. I'd be honest and tell him the number of partners. My current*

*partner sometimes asks about his brother's performance in comparison to his, but I won't discuss that openly because I don't feel it's right to.*

*I have nothing to hide. But there is a right and wrong way to be open. I have had an experience where I got the feeling a partner was flaunting his ex-girlfriends at me. This is offensive, and I wouldn't put anyone else in this position.*

## WHEN BEING TOLD HURTS

It seems that many of our reasons for telling or not telling a partner about our past sex stem from how we would feel if the positions were reversed – or how we have felt when the positions were reversed. For whereas only 67 per cent of women will tell their partner anything about their past sex lives (with fewer than this number being totally open), 77.4 per cent of women have heard from their partner about their past sex lives. Our partners tend to be more up front with us than we are with them. And many of us don't like it.

Some of us have never been told, never asked or never listened to the answers. We feel we know ourselves well enough to know that we simply couldn't cope: *'No, I have never been told, but if I was I would be pretty pissed off, as I am an extremely jealous person.'* Maybe we also feel that it is the present that matters, and that raking up the past is pointless. And, also, we may feel that men's accounts of the past may not be all that accurate.

*I don't like to hear much about partners' past history. I do like to know how much they've slept around and so on, for my own protection. But men often lie, so it's a waste of time hearing about their past sexual activities.*

Some 36.8 per cent of women say that they have suffered emotionally because their partner has been open about their past: *'I felt sad, unhappy, devastated.'* And even if we tell ourselves that we want to hear it all, the main thing we feel is jealous. We compare ourselves to past conquests, draw parallels between what our partner did with them, and what he does with us, worry about whether other women were better than we are.

*Yes, my boyfriend told me, and whenever I think about it, I feel deeply sick with jealousy. I have a very good imagination, and I cannot bear it when I let myself think about it. But I just have to know everything, despite the way it hurts and makes my stomach turn over.*

Up to 40.6 per cent of women feel good about having been told about their partners' past and would want to be told in future. We are proud of the bond with our partner that allows us to do this: *'I know everything there is to know about my husband's past ... I'm pleased my partner has been honest with me.'* And we are able to see past relationships as somehow separate from the relationship we are having here and now; consequently, they are unimportant: *'I'm not jealous. ... He didn't know me then.'*

## TWO-WAY COMMUNICATION

Not surprisingly, these know-everything women's reasons dovetail with the reasons that the tell-everything women have: they want to be totally honest; they see openness and sincerity as vital parts of their relationship. By contrast, the tell-nothing women are often those who do not want to be told. For a theme that in the end emerges throughout the entire questionnaire is that for many couples, openness or secrecy are completely reciprocal.

It seems that we often have the same beliefs as our partners about the importance and relevance of communication. Whether we are communicating about what our sexual preferences are, about what we want in bed or about sexual history, both we and our partners very often hold the same kind of judgements – one way or another. So those of us who are uneasy about our past are more likely to feel bad about learning all the details of our partner's sexual history. Those of us who are at ease with our own past are more likely to be accepting of those of our partner.

It is unclear whether we instinctively get together with men who feel and think the same way as we do – or whether we and they pick up these attitudes from each other. However it happens, though, how much we are prepared to tell is always directly with how much we are happy to hear. And vice versa.

> *I know I'd be jealous to hear of his previous sexual experiences. It's my willy, and I like to think I'm the only one who's used it. And know he thinks the same way as he's got a jealous nature.*

VITAL STATISTICS

60.7 per cent of women make love once or more a week

53.8 per cent have a particular time of day they prefer when making love

43.5 per cent prefer to make love indoors, 23.4 per cent outdoors

Only 2.4 per cent say their favourite setting for sex is a car

# 12. Setting the scene

*A good meal and music are enjoyable. Dancing, both slow and fast, makes me feel like making love. Also, I like being somewhere with a crowd that includes my partner, but spending much of that time apart. The occasional looks and glances between us turns me on.*

SCENE-SETTING GIVES sex its flavour. When we do it, where we do it, how we lead up to doing it: these are all factors that make each act of love special. So those parts of the questionnaire that ask about the time, the place, the preliminaries, the first move – all these evoked answers that show our initiative, our imagination, and our individuality.

First of all, when do we make love? We don't like feeling that there is any pattern. The very word makes our hackles rise. If we are living together – and many of us are – we want particularly to feel that we have the freedom to make love whenever we want to or, rather, whenever work, children and other commitments allow. And we are wary of losing spontaneity by creating any kind of regular ritual, which may make sex less meaningful: *'I think routines are bad for caring relationships.'* Instead, we like to think of ourselves as passionate enough to abandon all plans if we feel like having sex: *'My partner calls me Martini girl – any time, any place, anywhere.'*

There are no regular days set aside for sex. We usually make love in the evening or during the night, but we do make love in the day when the need arises mutually. It all depends, as far as the amount of love-making is concerned, on how we are feeling at that particular time.

Where we do have a specific day set aside for sex, we make it clear that that's due to external circumstances. The days we make love are perhaps the days we meet our partner or, *'I'm a shift worker, so the only time I catch up with him is at the weekend.'* Despite our hatred of patterns, in fact, there is a common thread: weekends are the most usual time for making love. We go out on those nights, and celebration leads to sex; we don't have to get up in the morning, so we lie in and make love.

When it comes to timing, we do have favourites; somehow preferring a particular time doesn't seem as negative as only making love on a particular day. And many of us feel that our bodies have an arousal cycle that peaks between certain hours. We may prefer mornings because we are more aroused, sensitive and responsive. We may prefer the evening because that allows us to relax, spend as long as we like having sex and then *'fall asleep in each other's arms'*. And we seem to be remarkably compatible with our partners over timing: there were only a few rueful comments that *'I like the night-time, he prefers the morning.'*

## THE TIME

How often do we make love? There was a feeling of slight insecurity at this question: Are we doing it often enough? Are we doing it too much? And are we perhaps being compared to other women and how often they do it? The sexual revolution does seem to have made issues such as this more emotionally fraught; there is more of an element of competition than there was before. The answers to the question of 'How often?' actually show a consistently even spread, with almost the same number of women – 7-8 per cent – making love about once a month and about once a day. The vast majority make love once or more a week, and the others follow variations on a theme, making love at different frequencies at different times.

If our love-making is regular and weekly, this usually indicates that we have a stable, long-term relationship. We're married or living together. Alternatively, either we or our lover are married, and so we can only meet once a week. (In this situation, however, we do seem to get regular passionate sex with our lover, whereas our husband often gets lukewarm love-making or none at all.)

Women who make love once a month are often slightly older, in their thirties or forties. In the current jargon, they are DILS (double-income-low-sex) couples. Almost all have been married for more than ten years. They feel secure in their relationships, if a little unhappy at the outside factors that consistently come between them and a more regular sex life. They report tiredness, late shifts, stress, visitors, children and a day-to-day routine that is just too busy. They don't feel that the quality of their sex life is a problem, though it may be a disappointment; it is certainly just a spin-off from a busy life and a live-in relationship.

At the other end of the spectrum, those in the 'once or more a day' contingent are mostly in late teens and early twenties. They have been with their partner for a very short time, and passion is still new and exciting. Youth gives them raging hormones – and new and exciting relationships. They and their partner don't live together, and so when they do meet, they need to make up for lost time: *'We make love every day – sometimes more than once. We would both like to make love more often, but, unfortunately, we have to go to work.'*

There is a group of women whose love-making patterns vary. They may have sex hardly at all for several weeks, and then suddenly have several days of almost constant love-making. Some are separated from their partners for long periods of time: she is a student, and they meet one weekend out of four; her partner lives out of town or is in the army. Some, like the once a monthers, are married with children; their lives fluctuate between times when they are constantly busy, caring for their families, and times when, on holiday and without the children, they can turn their attention completely to rediscovering sex.

Sometimes on holiday they may make love between two and three times a night, every night of the week. And sometimes at home they make love twice in a night, two or three times a week, or once at night and once in the morning for a few days. Then sometimes they only make love once a week or once a fortnight. Usually tiredness gets in the way of making love more often; they suffer from pressures of work and pressures of home, children especially.

## THE PLACE

When it comes to where we make love, we like tradition. Most of us choose the bedroom on a regular basis, *'where it is comfortable and warm ... because we have children and so experiments are limited.'* But almost all of us have made love elsewhere, usually indoors at home – the living room, where our favourite setting is in front of an open fire, the kitchen, over the dining-room table, or in the shower or bath:

> *I like the bathroom, with all its different fixtures to drape over ... nooks to squeeze into ... the extra tension of trying to grip slippery surfaces ... at the end, instead of dropping off to sleep, I like sliding into a hot bath.*

Those of us who have the privacy to do so have also made love at work. This usually happens at the start of a relationship when lust overcomes inhibitions, and respondents give examples of sex in a variety of professional settings ranging from the office to a cupboard, a lift and a loading bay. Medical settings seem to be particularly popular, including a doctor's surgery, a dentist's chair (with the dentist), a dental-department darkroom (while waiting for the X-rays to develop), on the floor of an ambulance crew room and actually on a hospital trolley.

*My husband was in hospital for a long period. I went to visit when he was almost better, and we nipped into one of the patient bathrooms and had a screw and a bath together. This was one of the most exciting and quite frightening experiences of my life. I was on tenterhooks all the time wondering how long it would be before somebody wanted the bathroom, or the nurses came looking for my husband.*

Quite a few of us have had sex in a car, though usually in our teenage days. This seems to be the most unpopular venue with only 2.4 per cent choosing it as a favourite. Cars also seems to be the place where on-lookers are most likely to catch us, as a lorry pulls up, a double-decker bus drives by, or a woman walks past and peers in through the sun-roof. Variations on the car theme include *'an ambulance ... the back of a van while someone else was driving ... over the bonnet of a car ... on the reclining seats of a Daimler in a garage ... in a Mini, which was very difficult and ruined the shock absorbers'.*

Outdoor venues are extremely popular: woods and beaches top the list, but other locations include *'a hayloft ... a tent ... up a mountain ... in the sea ... the garden ... a cornfield ... on a motorbike ... in a graveyard ... on a football pitch ... down a cave ... on a park bench (though we got stopped by a policeman)'.*

But by far the favourite and the most exciting venues for sex are the truly public ones. Risk of being caught seems to be an extremely effective aphrodisiac, and so we make love *'at a bus stop ... at 3 p.m. in a crowded car park ... the first-class toilet on an Intercity train ... in the college grounds with my students in close proximity ... in the changing rooms of a local department store ... in a telephone box'*, and surely the most unusual one ever, *'at Buckingham Palace, in a bedroom, with his feet up against the door to stop anyone coming in'!*

## WHO INITIATES?

Women are no longer happy simply agreeing to a partner's wish for sex. Nearly three-quarters of them now reckon they share equally with their

partners the role of making the first move – and only 12.2 per cent say
that they never do so. We seem to have claimed an essential equality in
bed that allows us to both be seducer and seduced, and this is true whatever age we are and whatever our previous sexual experiences.

*Initiating sex is quite equally balanced. Both of us knows what the other
one wants and when they want it or not. I quite frequently make the
first move and then lead all the way through the sexual act. My partner
is happy with this, and I think he quite enjoys it when I dominate sex.*

We share the initiative because both we and our men want that. It
makes us feel that we are an equal partnership. We're more likely to make
the first move when we've settled down into a relationship and feel secure
in it, and also more likely when we've been aroused by some external
stimulus, such as a book or a film. We dress provocatively, knowing that
this will send a signal to our partner. We make sure that there's good food
and wine, to get him in the mood. We talk dirty, kiss him, touch him up.
Or, maybe, we just ask.

Taking the lead is usually easy: our partners respond well. They love
us to lead, either simply because it shows we desire them, or because they
like not having to do the work all the time. They find it *'exciting . . . a turn-
on . . . loves it . . . I do not think any of my partners have felt threatened
when I have taken the leading role.'* They lie back and enjoy having less
responsibility for making sex work than perhaps is often the case.

There does seem to be an essential difference between what we do
to initiate sex with partners and what they might do to make the same
suggestion to us. Their challenge is to arouse us. We rarely have to do
this – our task is only to get ourselves in the mood for sex and then show
them that we are. We may act and take the initiative, but we rarely have
to persuade. In this sense, in many ways we do seem have an easier time
than our male partners.

Very few women complain that they had to try hard, apart from one
woman who says that, *'He was so uninterested in sex that I would
frequently have to unzip his pants, get him aroused, then sit on him – even
if he did laugh.'* Where there is a negative response, or where our partner
always insists on taking the lead, that's usually because it cuts across his
idea of male and female roles. Initiating sex is what he should do, agreeing
to it is what we – or any decent woman – should do. So, if we suggest
sex, he's either appalled or threatened; he withdraws emotionally or
simply cannot perform: *'One of my boyfriends commented that he thought
a girl was easy if she initiated sex!'* We get the message and don't attempt
to take the lead again. Some of us are relieved and happy about that

because we find leading to be a strain, though rather more of us are frustrated and feel criticized and devalued.

## WORKING UP TO IT...

So, now, we are almost ready to make love: the time is right, and we know it's going to happen. How do we put in place those final, essential details? When asked what preliminaries we liked, only a few women said none, and even some of those respondents added that that was only true when *a straightforward urgent bang*' is what's needed: *'The only preliminary I need is to see my partner driving up in his car. I like it best when he grabs me as he comes in the door.'*

Some of us begin preparing for sex hours or even days before the act. We play sport or dance to arouse ourselves, spend time talking and laughing with a partner or in a group. Being with other people, catching each other's eye, knowing something is going to happen but holding back: all these make sex even more exciting when it finally happens: *'It's great to fancy each other all night and hold out on the moment.'* To make things worse − or better − if we are going out, perhaps we leave off the underwear, and *'find it very enjoyable that my husband knows I've nothing on under my dress, especially if we're in a crowded place'*.

We also love to create the right setting for love-making. If it's indoors − most of us still prefer to make love at home − we love sensual luxury: soft pillows, fluffy rugs, cushions, incense and no distractions, a warm bath filled with bubbles. Most of us like a dim light or candles, so we can see each other during sex. But some prefer darkness, often because we are wary of a partner seeing our body, or because we don't want to see his: *'I don't like looking at my husband's bald head.'*

Just under half of us like to play music, *'slow ... romantic ... soulful ... bassy'*. We may look at sexy magazines and videos, though, if so, we prefer the sex to be set in the context of not only a loving relationship but also a thought-through scenario. Porn that is short on plot, with just a few set scenes as an excuse for instant thrusting, leaves us cold.

*The only film I can recall really turning me on was one about an American college lecturer who had left her husband and become emotionally and sexually involved with another girl. The scenes of love-making were not just explicit but incredibly tender and beautiful and made me feel very excited. They had the same effect on my husband, and we had a very successful night after seeing this film.*

We often talk. Only one or two women say that words aren't subtle enough, and that silence and eye contact is the best way. Others talk romantically or talk dirty *'the ruder the better'*, particularly describing what we are going to do with each other: *'Sitting in the pub, face to face, talking dirty is a real turn-on for both of us.'* We fantasize or get our partner to tell fantasies for us (see chapter 18). The words and the thoughts create arousal long before we touch.

A meal and alcohol is the classic prelude to sex – but in fact many of us don't like making love on a full stomach and hate having sex when even slightly the worse for drink. Instead we prefer snacks and just a little wine or champagne to boost our confidence and help us relax. (Just a few women mention that certain 'illegal substances' were useful for this too.) One woman recommends *'prawns and cider, a wonderfully stimulating combination. It sounds a little strange, but works wonders for the sexual machinery – well, it does for mine!'* And, often, we'll merge eating and drinking into love-making itself, by moving from one to the other with some overlap. We may pass bits from one mouth to another with a kiss, sup wine from each other's belly buttons or spread food over each other and lick it off.

And, of course, sooner or later, we slide over the threshold into actual love-making. We look, we reach out for each other, we kiss. We move into the next stage, foreplay. The scene setting is over, and the action is about to begin.

*I enjoy a lot of things. It depends what mood I am in and where we are. Sexy talk, bathing, food. We'll start eating (messy food is best). We get it on our fingers, so we lick and suck it off and in the end we are eating it off each other's body and drinking wine from each other's mouth. Actually, I enjoy anything. I just like sex and all that goes with it.*

VITAL STATISTICS

72.6 per cent of women think that foreplay is as or more important than intercourse

27.8 per cent are not happy with the foreplay they get

71.4 per cent of women reckon that their partners give foreplay willingly

51.9 per cent of women have masturbated in front of their partners and enjoyed it

# 13. Getting aroused

*Foreplay? Lots of kissing all over both partners'
bodies… touching, licking, hugging, undressing,
gentle gnawing, talking, stroking, stimulating
nipples and genitals with mouths, hands,
masturbation, sighing and groaning, hands through
hair, massage, looking, teasing, complimenting.
I like foreplay to last until I feel like intercourse or
really want to orgasm (not the same thing), and this
can vary from minutes to hours.*

THIS CHAPTER WAS meant to be a lead-in to the chapter on
intercourse, a kind of taster to the central core of the book about
penetrative sex. In fact, having read women's accounts of foreplay and analysed the results of their responses, it became vital
to re-think the focus. For what women are saying about foreplay
is very different to what the textbooks often say.

The fact is this: 72.6 per cent of women think that foreplay is as
important or more important than intercourse. However much we enjoy
penetration – and we do, very much – foreplay is just as vital for nearly
three-quarters of women. We want both, but if we had to choose, we might
well choose foreplay.

This was astounding but not surprising – astounding because in
every account of sex that we read, factual and fictional, the peak of love-

making is always presented as intercourse. Foreplay has been seen as just that, play before the serious business of penetration. We have concentrated our minds and our bodies on intercourse itself, relied on cultural, medical and religious messages about its importance. For many thousands of years, we have accepted that, because penetration is needed to make babies, it is the key act. It is only now that baby-making has been largely taken out of the equation that we are free to expand our options.

On the other hand, it's not surprising that we should like foreplay so much, because it is so enjoyable. Those who love it speak of the *'enhanced feeling . . . totally different . . . so arousing . . . stimulating and unrestricting . . . leaves me feeling elated'*. It allows us to express our relationship, to move with our partner, using our whole bodies to please him, showing tenderness and affection.

Not only does foreplay show the love we feel for each other but it can also create it: *'Foreplay dictates how I feel about my partner.'* And while most of us want intercourse as a sign of our togetherness and our love, foreplay gives *'the tenderness and affection that actual intercourse doesn't necessarily involve'*.

*Foreplay is more important to me than intercourse because it's more emotional than just penetration. You are taking the time to explore each other's bodies and that in itself shows a deeper level of desire and feelings than sex. I hate the feeling that someone is just 'homing in' on that one area between your legs as if that will be enough to turn you on. I could quite happily spend an hour just kissing and caressing my boyfriend, but if I had to have penetrative sex for an hour I'd probably end up very sore!*

Also, most of us need foreplay in order to get aroused: *'It's essential to get the juices going,'* as one woman says. Many of us need it in order to even allow penetration, most need it if we are to orgasm. The vast majority of us, most of the time, don't, like men, need only penetration or penetration-like acts in order to come. We stimulate passion by using the whole of our bodies, and the whole of our bodies need stimulating if we are to feel passion.

## NO FOREPLAY NEEDED

All this isn't true for all of us. Just three women say that they never need foreplay. Others say that there are occasions when they don't need it. These answers seem to be clearly linked with how quickly and how strongly we get aroused. If we are already excited, from some other external stimulation or from our own internal thoughts and fantasies, then foreplay is less important. If we are feeling the strong emotions of joy, anger or even grief, then we need foreplay less (though fear diminishes arousal, so the more anxious we are, the more foreplay we need). It is as if in these situations, our bodies take over. We want penetration now, without any physical preparation, without waiting for the confirmation of a relationship link, without needing affection.

If we are both aware that we want sex urgently and do not need foreplay, we will just go ahead with intercourse. We tend to refer to this as screwing rather than making love and recognize that we both enjoy a quick screw occasionally: *'I am happy with the amount of foreplay we have; I still think the most important part is being willing and ready mentally, and he can always tell, if, on the odd occasion, I still just go along with it for his sake. He avoids this.'*

One particular theme here is especially significant. If we initiate intercourse, then often we *'don't need much foreplay . . . just the thought of sex is enough.'* If we are aroused enough to initiate sex then we may well be mentally and physically ready for intercourse, and want it now, without waiting. Yet there is also an undercurrent here of a reason that is less physical and more psychological – that if we are in control, we are more aroused. As mentioned before, the more anxious we are, the less passionate we become. It seems logical, therefore, that the reverse is true. The more relaxed and confident we are because we feel in control of the sexual process, the more passionate we can be – making foreplay before intercourse less necessary.

## PARTNERS AND FOREPLAY

Unsurprisingly men consistently seem slightly less interested in foreplay than we are. Biologically that's not surprising, for penetrative acts are often the way men most easily and most naturally get aroused and climax. So whereas only 2.2 per cent of women think foreplay isn't important at all, 8.7 per cent of men feel this; whereas 11.9 per cent of women think foreplay less important than intercourse, the figure for men is 31.3 per cent; and whereas 34.8 per cent of women think foreplay more important than intercourse, only 13.9 per cent of men do so.

When men disregard foreplay completely, women have a variety of responses. If we ourselves feel that foreplay is not too important, then there seems to be sexual compatibility and no bad feeling. But if we love foreplay, and our partner sees it as irrelevant, then we view their attitude as sad, denying themselves real pleasure in sensuous kissing and caressing. We also feel it is unfair on us: *'He's not bothered how I feel as long as he gets what he wants . . . they prefer getting their leg over to getting in the mood.'*

Where a man does feel good about foreplay, it is often for the same reasons as women do: *'It helps him be totally aroused.'* He loves cuddles and kissing, stroking and touching, as a physical pleasure in itself as well as a way to reaffirm the relationship. And there's also a strong feeling from respondents that men value foreplay simply because it gives pleasure to women. It allows us to get aroused – and that makes them aroused: *'The more I am turned on, the more he is turned on.'* Men like to see us passionate; it spurs them on. And, significantly, many women report that their partners increasingly value foreplay, as if now that sex itself is becoming more equal, they are beginning to appreciate the sensuous side of love-making and to demand it more.

> *I think that foreplay is as equally important to my partner as it is to me. He loves to know that he's turning me on, either through things that he's doing or things I'm doing to him. I think if we didn't spend any time on foreplay he would feel as dissatisfied as I would.*

## WHAT DO WE DO?

There is no pattern, no set routine of what to do first and what to do next in foreplay. We hate the very thought: *'If I found myself following a pattern, I wouldn't be very pleased ... I had a long-term partner for a time, and we settled into a routine very quickly, which I did not like.'* We like to see ourselves being spontaneous and responsive, *'moulding ourselves to each other's ways'*, adapting *'according to our moods and needs at the time'*. We are sure that this is the way to keep interest and lust alive in our relationship, and we try hard not to get into a rut.

But, we do have a sexual repertoire, a series of moves on which we can call, some favourites, some kept for special occasions. We like to involve all our senses, and use the whole of our body. We like to surprise.

The starting-point is often to kiss. We like *'long slow kisses ... without the rest of our bodies touching ... (a nuzzle from a day-old beard is always welcome)'*. Then we move on to caressing, hands wandering all over, perhaps a massage, perhaps simply stroking, *'but not in any continuous pattern so I never know where he will touch me next'*. We may talk dirty as we move; if not, we certainly breathe heavily, moan or whimper. The sound itself turns us both on. Fairly soon we will undress, a little or a lot.

> *We start by touching each other with our clothes on, then we start taking each other's clothes off. My boyfriend enjoys it if I stand behind him and kiss his back and shoulders while I undo his jeans and feel his legs and genitals. I enjoy lying on my stomach and having him kiss my back and shoulders and touching my sides gently.*

Then we'll explore each other's bodies with hands and with mouths, stroking, teasing, licking, sucking, biting, smacking, scratching, *'generally paying attention to all the other areas of each other's bodies that get missed out during intercourse'*. We taste and smell each other, *'looking for buttons and pushing those buttons in new order for varying lengths of time, a sort of Morse code through sight, touch, smell, sound, and taste'*.

Our partner pays attention to us: *'Sucks my nipples and licks his way down my body to my genitals'*. He licks everywhere, bites or rubs or simply strokes. He clutches our hair, pulls us to him, wets his fingers and reaches down between our legs. He touches our clitoris lightly or heavily, keeping a steady rhythm or alternating so we have to wait. He inserts one or two fingers inside our vagina, holding still or moving slightly while his other hand continues to stimulate. He gives us oral sex (see chapter 14) until we're aroused and moist and on the point of coming.

We in return kiss his ears, stroke his inner thigh, play with and suck his nipples, rub his penis, play with his balls: *'I give him a massage, starting with his feet, working up to his neck with no genital contact. Then I will rub my breasts on him. Then I massage his backside, his balls, the skin in between and his anus. Then put my finger inside his anus and rub his prostate ... I have fondled the balls and stroked the penis with my feet, so inspired and articulate.'*

## MUTUAL MASTURBATION

Sometimes we move on to masturbating each other. We lie side by side and reach down to each other, or kneel over and under each other in the classic 'sixty-nine' configuration. We say that in this position, the rhythm is difficult to coordinate but has the added bonus of feeling our own pleasure while seeing our partner's response.

*My partner and I usually begin with long slow kisses. We remove each other's clothing (unless we are already in bed, i.e. Saturday/Sunday mornings), and we use our hands to caress each other. My partner usually sucks my nipples and licks his way down my body to my genitals. He then uses his tongue and his fingers simultaneously to bring me to orgasm. When I have orgasmed, I usually turn him on to his back and use my tongue on his penis and testicles until he is very aroused or until he has orgasmed.*

Sometimes we masturbate in front of our partner. This is still something of a sexual risk for us; we feel it's embarrassing, something that a partner will be shocked by. Or, we have doubts about masturbation itself and think it's not as loving as completely mutual sex. Those of us who do love it use it to arouse ourselves even further – or do it because our partner loves to see us bring ourselves off. Almost always he joins in, sometimes taking over completely, more usually lending a hand. He will hold, kiss, play with our breasts as we stimulate our clitoris, hold our genitals open for us, put his fingers or a vibrator inside us while we touch ourselves. He'll talk dirty to us or urge us on; he'll sometimes tell us to stop and wait on his 'permission'. He'll hold us, when we eventually climax, until we come to.

> *My present boyfriend asks me to masturbate myself, or he'll move my hand down to my genitals. I feel sexy when he is watching me, he'll touch my breasts or kiss them while I am masturbating, or he will tease my bum with his finger. He always holds me closely and tells me it's his most favourite sexual thing. I always get aroused. I always orgasm and always enjoy it.*

More often our partner will masturbate in front of us – 71.5 per cent of men do, as against 58.6 per cent of women. We actually have a problem with this, one of the very few times that we don't completely like what our partner does. We can be wary, feel that it's all too *'aggressive and urgent'*, get *'amused . . . shy . . . embarrassed'*, or feel *'horrid . . . usurped . . . unwanted'*. For whereas masturbating ourselves makes us feel guilty that we're not involving our partner, watching him masturbate can make us feel uninvolved and so rejected.

> *If a partner masturbates in front of me I tend not to take any notice. It doesn't really bother me. I'm just glad they don't expect me to satisfy them every time they get aroused and can content themselves without putting any pressure on me.*

If we do love watching our partner masturbate, it's because we feel *'happy that he is happy'*. We can stand back and allow him to enjoy the pleasure without feeling threatened, and we can ourselves get turned on by his arousal: *'I could tell he enjoyed it and that excited me . . . It shows that he is in touch with his body and that turned me on . . . I love watching partners masturbate. It makes them look so boyish and innocent, as though I'm looking at them without them knowing.'*

We often help by talking dirty, kissing and licking him, sucking his nipples, stroking his inner thighs and testicles, or by placing our hands over his hands while he moves, with *'my finger up his arse-hole'*. And when he comes we hold him, and perhaps let him ejaculate over our breasts or our stomach.

*I love watching my partner masturbate. I am fascinated by that organ
appearing and disappearing in his hand, and I love it when the head
peeps out of the foreskin. I also love the way his balls move and tighten,
though they are too sensitive to touch, which I love doing. When he
tosses in front of me, I feel as though he trusts me to share a good, private
thing. I sometimes assist him by a lick on his penis head or penis eye,
or by placing my hand under his near the root of his penis and following
his rhythm. I may stop him and suck him off, or just smooth his velvety
tip of his penis head, another incredible turn-on for me. At other times,
I rub my body on to his or push my breasts in his face or his spare hand.
He seems to like these things. At least, he hasn't complained yet.*

We and our partner often get so aroused when the other is masturbating that we join in. Women often report pleasuring themselves to
climax along with their partners, though slightly more said the reverse:
*'My partner asked me to masturbate myself. As I was doing it, he was
getting aroused so he started to masturbate himself, and we both climaxed
together.'*

## THE FOOLPROOF WAY

Of all the techniques we use in foreplay, what works best? In answer
to the question, Is there a foolproof way to get you aroused? 67.1 per
cent of women said that, yes, there was. And it is significant that many
of these techniques aren't physical at all but mental. Foreplay begins
in the mind. Spontaneous compliments excite us. Imagining what sex
will be like turns us on. Risky sex – the thought of being found out –
is a favourite. And many of us say that talking about what we are going
to do with our partner, or being told by our partner what he is going
to do to us, is guaranteed to arouse.

Fantasies (see chapter 18) are essential too: *'My partner makes up
fantasies for me, usually involving other women.'* Other mental foreplay
techniques involve seeing a partner in sexy clothes such as boxer shorts,
watching *'bouncing bottoms on the telly'*, seeing soft-core porn on video or
in magazines, or *'making me wait long enough (a week), then telephoning
me numerous times on the day he's coming, so that I'm incredibly excited
in anticipation'*.

Physically we love the more obvious ways of arousal: having our
breasts touched, having our clitoris touched outside or inside our panties,
*'having a man's head up my knickers always turns me on'*. But, though
when we are in the mood, sudden or energetic sexual moves can turn us
on, most foolproof ways are based on tenderness and gentleness, and they
involve parts of the body very far removed from our genitals. It's as if, not

surprisingly, 'being jumped' is never as guaranteed a turn-on as gentle persuasion – a single touch, on arm or hand, a gentle kiss on the ear. The back of the neck emerged as the surprise erogenous zone here, with many women mentioning that they always respond strongly to having it touched, massaged, kissed or licked: *'I like to have my back caressed and the back of my neck kissed and breathed on. It sends shivers down my spine when it's like a cold breeze on the back of my neck.'* Equally, making us wait is always certain to arouse:

> *The foolproof way to turn me on is for me to be laid down nude on the bed and for my partner to sit at my feet. He then slowly opens my legs and kisses his way up to my genitals. I am usually at the point of orgasm before he reaches my genitals. I do not believe that he knows that this method is foolproof, and I have not told him because I do not want him to use this method each time. Alternatively, perhaps he does know, and he doesn't use this method each time but prefers variety.*

## IS FOREPLAY GOOD ENOUGH?

It all sounds wonderful. But the final question we must ask is whether foreplay is satisfactory. We love it – but are we getting it in the way we want?

Those of us who really aren't happy about foreplay either don't get it at all, or our partners give it unwillingly. Some 15.1 per cent of women feel that men do it either because they've heard they should – younger men are particularly criticized for this – or because they have to in order to penetrate. What is done is done speedily and inadequately, unspontaneously and only if we ask: *'Often he doesn't touch me at all and then asks if I'm ready, which of course I'm not. I feel hurt and angry at his selfishness.'*

Most of us are generally happy with the foreplay we receive but do still want improvements. What our partner does may not be quite right. Only a few of us comment on this – most are able to tell or show our partners what to do (see chapter 11) – but it can still be a problem.

> *I love foreplay. I like to be touched all over and kissed, stroked. My boyfriend rubs his penis on me, and it does turn me on but not enough to prepare me for penetration. In the end the only way I can really turn myself on is by giving him oral sex. He never does this to me, however.*

Secondly, and far more typically, what our partner does may not last long enough. He may have a short sexual attention-span and like to move on to intercourse well before we are ready. So we often encourage him to cut foreplay short when we would actually like it to last longer. Ironically, as our relationship develops, and we both become more secure, he often feels he doesn't need to try as hard and then foreplay *'slowly wanes as time goes by'*. In fact, for most women, it's not time to move on from foreplay until *'we both want to have intercourse so much that we feel like bursting'*.

The end judgement on foreplay, however, is positive. Partners do seem to have learnt over the years that it does matter. So most women are becoming increasingly happy with what we have and how much we have. We feel good about our ability to give and receive, to use our imaginations and to arouse our partner. We feel good about our partner's attitude, his approach and his technique. We feel good about our mutual ability to please each other, making foreplay more and more become *'after play . . . and during play'*.

*I could fill pages trying to explain how three fingers placed over my pudenda and held at the perfect pressure for the right length of time will suspend time, or the sight and sound of my partner when I've tweaked a nerve in him will, in itself, strike a chord of pleasure in me. For me, play is the root word of foreplay.*

VITAL STATISTICS

57.9 per cent of women like giving oral sex

37.3 per cent are always happy for their partner to come in their mouth

88.8 per cent like receiving oral sex

77.3 per cent come through oral sex

73.2 per cent of men like giving oral sex and give it whether asked or not

# 14. Giving and receiving oral sex

*Yes, yes, yes! Giving oral sex is the ultimate power. It adds a bit of 'naughty'; new partners are always freaked out by my enthusiasm. I have control and when in love, it is the most intimate thing to let my man fuck my mouth.*

WE FEEL THAT oral sex is one of the most special things we can do with a partner. It's probably because of this that the questions about oral sex created some of the strongest and most positive responses in the survey – and, at the same time, some of the most definite judgements against casual usage. Both when giving and receiving, we are willing and happy to do oral sex only with those we most love. We may have intercourse with someone we don't know, but we'll rarely have oral sex.

When it comes to giving oral sex, we like the basics. We like the smell of our partner's body, the sensation of our mouth against his (or her) genitals, the movement as we lick and suck. More than this, we like what oral sex does for our partner and what that means. We love to give him pleasure, to allow him to lie back and enjoy without having to act.

We see oral sex as showing as much love for him as having intercourse – perhaps more, because giving oral sex seems more outrageous and is so much more intimate.

We also like the power we have when we give oral sex. Women say that they feel more control during this than during any other form of love-making, as our partner lies back and surrenders to us: *'I like having the power to bring him from a limp penis right up to orgasm ... The look of pleasure on a partner's face is wonderful. It also makes me feel in control, which I like.'*

## NOT GIVING IT

Some of us don't give oral sex at all. It's the physical act that puts us off. We don't like the thought of having a man's genitals in our mouth. We are *'frightened he will come in my mouth ... frightened he will take a leak'*. Sometimes a past experience of unwilling oral sex has traumatized us – several women say they were made to do it when assaulted. Many of us have tried it, didn't like it and now won't do it. We get uncomfortable giving oral sex, and our neck hurts. We find the whole act boring and *'don't like the view'*. We feel nauseous from the action, the smell, the taste: *'It makes me feel sick having something so far inside my mouth.'*

We sometimes say no to particular people. Many of us, for example, can't imagine giving oral sex to a casual partner – only 10 per cent of women say yes consistently. That's not only down to fear of disease but also because we need to love before we can even consider doing it: *'I find this too intimate to share with just anyone.'*

We may be wary of oral sex because we're unsure of what we're doing. Just as when we were young, we worried that we weren't kissing correctly, now we worry that we're not giving oral sex properly. And, particularly with a new or very experienced partner, we may quite simply be afraid of doing it wrong. We feel we can't ask for tuition – after all, we're supposed to be knowledgeable – and are wary of hurting, not pleasing or simply looking like a fool. In fact, every partner likes something different, and so the only way is to start from scratch with each new one and learn what he likes. Because of this, just as when we were young, many women say that an understanding partner allowed them to relax enough to begin learning, gain confidence and start to enjoy themselves.

*I do it naturally now with my current partner as he was so patient and caring when we began. I never had been able to before. It used to frighten me as I felt under pressure.*

*Yes, I have oral sex with my current partner which I found unacceptable with previous ones. He was just so patient and didn't make me gag. He lets me lead and never pushes or forces me – so I now enjoy oral sex.*

If we are usually happy to give oral sex, we can say no sometimes for purely erotic reasons: *'I know he'll last longer . . . I like it to be a treat . . . I want to do something different.'* But even the most enthusiastic of us also say no when we have our off days, when we are tired, feeling ill or emotionally down. And we will also say no if for some reason our partner doesn't smell good. He may be ill or *'hasn't had a bath that day; I'll always say no unless he goes and has a wash.'* It seems to matter to those of us who enjoy oral sex that we can say no if we want to; we need to feel that we have power over our own mouths as much as over our own genitals.

We don't feel good about saying no, however. Almost half of the respondents admit to guilt feelings when they refuse oral sex, mainly because they somehow feel they are letting their partner down, refusing him intimacy and pleasure. They feel that they don't have the right to refuse when it is something their partner wants and enjoys. So they may well override their objections and agree – almost 10 per cent of women always do.

## GIVING ORAL SEX

When we do give oral sex, for most of us it involves pleasuring our partner's whole body: *'In my opinion, oral sex should be given to every part of the body.'* So we won't usually focus directly and immediately on his genitals. Instead, we'll start on his chest or stomach, or at an extremity like his mouth, hands or feet. We'll work our way down or up slowly, teasing, licking, biting. We may let our partner wonder whether we are going to go the whole way. We focus on his nipples, maybe pause at his navel, or nibble gradually up the inside of his thigh. We sometimes combine this with a finger in his anus or lick his bottom. There is sometimes a tension here: we take our time and linger, while he may want us to hurry, push our head towards his genitals or urge us on. For while our partner may want us to move straight to his genitals, we like to pleasure in the way we would want to be pleasured, slowly, sensitively and with attention to detail: *'First, I tease. I like to start at his stomach and kiss and bite, heading downwards and making him squirm, wondering, Is she going to?'*

When we reach a partner's genitals, often we stop once again to make him wait. We may nibble his pubic hair, cup his balls in one hand or suck them, one after the other. With the penis, there seem to be two separate main strategies. Either we plunge straight in, putting his penis directly

into our mouths quite deeply so that he gets all the sensation at once. Or
we may tease, with firm strokes of our tongue along the underside, playing
with the head of the penis, kissing, brushing our lips across the top, licking
and nibbling with the foreskin rolled back. Or we do first one, then – *just
as he is getting used to it'* – we do the other.

*To start with, I run my tongue along his penis and, as a friend told me,
treat it like an ice cream. Then I cover it with my mouth. He likes me
to run my teeth gently around the top, then I place a firm grip around
his penis with my lips.*

Once we've taken the penis in our mouth, we usually also use our
fingers to encircle it: *'I push it in and out with my hand wrapped round
it . . . use my hand on the stem rhythmically going up and down . . . simulate
the in- and out- movements of intercourse with my mouth.'* At the same time,
our mouth is sucking, and our tongue is working; we flick it over his glans,
press it into the hole at the head of his penis, wiggle it round the sensitive
area under the head. We suck hard with each in-and-out movement or
gently bite *'with my teeth covered by my lips . . . to make him gasp'.* Our
hands continue to urge him up and down or keep fondling his balls.

*I'll alternate – going up and down the shaft with my tongue, teasing the
ridge, then sucking the head hard, trying to gauge what he likes best.
When he really starts thrusting, I try to follow his rhythm, sucking
quite hard.*

*I take the head of his penis in my mouth, flicking my tongue all over it
rapidly. Then slowly, just as he is getting used to this, I take his entire
penis in my mouth right down to the back of my throat. I move up and
down like this, continuing to flick my tongue over his glans. I also take
his testicles into my mouth to caress and suck.*

*I usually start by licking the penis down to the base of the shaft. Then
I spend some time kissing and licking the top, rolling back the foreskin
with my fingers. Then I take the penis in my mouth sucking up and
down. I sometimes lick at the base of the penis, around the testicles and
around the base of the testicles.*

## TO COME OR NOT?

All the time we are gauging how close our partner is to coming. Perhaps
his erection rises that bit more, or we can feel his semen beginning to
pump. His movements are getting wilder and his voice louder. We need

to decide whether to allow him to climax – and, if he does, whether to allow him to come in our mouth.

Some of us are not happy with the thought. Of women who give oral sex 16.7 per cent won't give it to climax at all. They don't like it or anything about it: *'It makes my flesh creep.'* They feel pressured and under threat at either the thought or the reality of a man's body fluids in their mouth. They're happy to please him and allow him to feel the sensations, but nothing further.

If we are happy for our partner to come, then we still may not let him come in our mouth: *'I'd be sick and that would spoil everything.'* Often we find our own ways round the problem: *'I try to discreetly spit it out in tissue . . . I take off my mouth at the last minute and fool him by letting it run back out of my mouth down his penis. He is too content to notice.'*

Of the women who do give oral sex – and that includes 50 per cent of women from time to time – the majority do it primarily because their partner wants it. They feel positive about it because it is a signal of real intimacy, because they feel they are offering their partner a very real gift. But we almost all hate the reality of our partner's climaxing in our mouth. It feels weird, it smells funny, and it tastes bad: *'I now can't eat parsnip soup since it is a vivid reminder.'* Only a few women say they are really turned on by swallowing their partner's come, and only one says, *'When he does come I make sure I get every last drop in my mouth.'*

From the answers women give to the questionnaire, not liking a partner to come in our mouth doesn't seem to be any kind of rejection. Most women simply don't like swallowing body fluids, in the same way as they wouldn't want to drink a partner's urine or blood.

Some women suggest that liking or disliking semen is linked with how much love they feel for a partner. This isn't a universal belief; many of the women who say that they don't like giving oral sex do like other kinds of very intimate sex with their partner. And some women who don't like it say that they still do it because they love their partner and want to give him pleasure. But more than one woman does admit that she hated oral sex until she met someone she loved, whose smell and the taste was acceptable. Others say that they started to dislike oral sex with a partner when the relationship started to break down. And still others draw a distinction between oral sex with one partner and another. So maybe there is a link between love and willingness to give oral sex.

*I don't enjoy giving oral sex to my husband as I don't love him. I love my lover and feel it's another natural part of sex. It's a very personal type of sex to me; loving the person means giving and doing everything to every part of their body.*

## RECEIVING ORAL SEX

We are occasionally unhappy about giving oral sex. But we are over-whelmingly enthusiastic about receiving it. Only 9 per cent of women don't like it. This is often because they are older women who are slightly ill at ease with the whole thought of oral sex or more usually because *'he doesn't do it properly'*.

The rest of women who receive it *'love it ... adore it ... always'*. They get real emotional closeness from the intimacy of the act. They feel loved and wanted when it's happening. And compared to many sexual acts, where the actual physical pleasure is limited or not guaranteed, and it's the emotional meaning of the act that makes it worthwhile, oral sex is almost always pleasurable. Women can lie back and simply enjoy the sensations, often completely secure in the knowledge that they will come.

It is a significant fact that when describing how they themselves give oral sex, women know exactly what's happening. They give a detailed account of the proceedings. But when it comes to describing what their partner does when giving oral sex, they are fairly reticent. Are they simply so overcome by passion that they cannot remember? Perhaps they are unable to tell what is being done when they are on the receiving end.

Most of us, as when we are giving oral sex, think of the term as meaning that attention is paid to the whole body: *'Do my neck, ears, ribcage and tummy count as oral sex, too?'* They do indeed. So when we receive, we love our partner to cover our entire skin with tiny kisses, nibbles, licks and bites. We particularly like attention paid to our sensitive bits, the backs of our knees, inside our elbows and ear lobes. And we are happy if our partner takes a long time, lingering round the edges before homing in to the centre of our body.

A lot of women mention food as an delightful added extra to oral sex. Jam, yoghurt and ice cream seem to be enjoyed, though by far the favourites were chocolate and cream: *'Having chocolate sauce licked off me slowly was the most exciting thing I have ever done ... We had a fight with spray whipped cream, rubbed it all over each other and licked it off. We made love standing up in front of a mirror still dripping in cream and then showered.'*

## TO THE GENITALS

Next our partner may move on to our breasts and nipples. Interestingly, very few women mention these specifically, but those who do say they enjoy having them licked, sucked, nuzzled and occasionally gently bitten.

And so to our genitals. It's good if our partner approaches them slowly, making us wait, moving carefully down our stomach or up along our thighs. His hands can help, stroking and rubbing, while mouth and tongue arouse us gently. Perhaps our partner moves us on to our stomach, kissing our buttocks (tonguing the anus isn't really liked). Perhaps he turns us on our back, holds our vagina open and starts licking our clitoris and vagina.

> *He swings me round so my legs are hanging over the edge of the bed. Then he'll get down on the floor and put my legs over his shoulders to raise my hips, open me up with his hands and away he goes. He will use one or two fingers as well. He will lick my thighs and stomach, sometimes my bum; he does it differently each time.*

Our genitals are incredibly sensitive, so many women suggest guidelines or make pleas to partners. Be gentle and sensitive: *'It has to be gently done for proper enjoyment ... sometimes he gets carried away and it hurts.'* On the other hand, too gentle can be equally misguided: *'Sometimes I'd like to tell him to lick me hard and to lap it up like a dog does with water.'* Or ask us to explain exactly which other particular movement or stimulation works for us. And remember that what we like often changes in mid-session.

But if a partner is aware of what might irritate, then anything goes. Licking the clitoris seems to be the most popular, with kisses and nibbles a close second. Bites work when applied to the bottom – but not to the clitoris, at least not without going very gently. Other movements that seem to work are *'tickling the entrance to my vaginal passage with his tongue ... with tongue inside my vagina ... moving his tongue in and out of my vagina ... stimulating my clitoris by flicking it ... holding my vulva apart and surrounding my clitoris with his mouth ... moving his fingers in and out of my vagina'.*

If we like our vagina stretched, perhaps he inserts his fingers or a dildo there while his tongue keeps working. Or, *'sometimes, we use ice-cubes on each other in conjunction with our tongues, which we both find an incredible turn-on.'*

## DO WE COME?

We often do come when receiving oral sex. Not nearly as frequently as when we masturbate and not quite as frequently as through intercourse. But over three-quarters of women come through oral sex, and many of those who do say it is the sole way they have to climax: *'There's only one way that succeeds every time and that's oral sex.'*

If we don't come it's often not because we can't but because we choose not to. Quite a few women say, *'I don't want to ... I don't wish to orgasm this way,'* but they don't explain why. Sometimes it feels better to orgasm through intercourse, so we hold off or move to penetration before we climax. Certainly there are partners who agree with this: *'I orgasm through oral sex every time he allows me to, but sometimes he won't let me and prefers me to come during intercourse.'* One of the few specific reasons women give for not orgasming during oral sex is this one, though it's probably not typical!

> *I do not usually orgasm with oral sex. To reach an orgasm I need to use all my lower body muscles and to squeeze my thighs together. Since I am a fitness fanatic and have muscles, it is impossible to orgasm in this way. My partner's brains would end up on the ceiling.*

Those of us who do come during oral sex are universally in favour of it: *'I orgasm almost every time. I rarely fail to go over the top this way. It's the only real way to orgasm as far as I am concerned.'* Where it works for us, it not only gives guaranteed orgasms but also more of them: one woman says she comes regularly *'every three to five minutes'* if her partner keeps going. And, of course, oral sex is also useful as an arouser, a preparation for intercourse. We can come through it without risking our partner's erection and so make ourselves moist and receptive for penetration.

## PARTNERS' FEELINGS

The only fly in the oral sex ointment is that we tend to believe that partners dislike giving it. Those women who are wary of oral sex – as well as some who used to be wary and now like it – talk of their belief that men resent being asked to lick them off, hate the smell and get bored. Often we have past experiences to confirm our fears.

> *I can't let go enough. This was a taboo area with my ex-husband. He said it smelt and disliked doing it, so I still have the feeling that the partner must do it, not enjoying himself.*

> *I have to ask. He doesn't really enjoy it. He doesn't like it much due to me being hairy; I would have to shave and then ask.*

The statistics, though, seem to suggest that most women's fears are groundless. Only 7.3 per cent of partners seem positively unhappy to give oral sex. The rest not only seem to regard it as special and 'naughty' but they also enjoy the practicalities of doing it, and they don't worry about odour or boredom.

*In the past I have always been embarrassed and worried what I would look like and smell like. Also that the man is doing it out of duty because I sucked his cock. But my present partner really enjoys it – and now so do I.*

Men's enthusiasm may be because they like to be close to us, to breathe in our smell and taste in the same way as we like to experience them at close quarters when we give oral sex: *'He loves to have my perfume all over his face.'* Or it may be because they love to see us so turned on: *'One of my partners said it was worth it just for my expression.'* Whatever their reasons, most men love giving oral sex.

In fact, a final and very strong theme emerges from the questions on oral sex, and it is this. Embarrassingly, men are far more enthusiastic about giving oral sex than women are: 73.2 per cent of them will give it whether asked or not, compared with only 57.9 per cent of women: *'I adore having oral sex done to me. I don't enjoy doing it very much; I find it boring.'*

There are probably sound, practical reasons for this. Male and female physiology does differ, and men don't have to worry that we will spurt semen in their mouths. Equally, this is not to say we should give oral sex where we don't want to. But, nevertheless, there does seem to be a reticence on our part about the whole issue. Perhaps in the future, with experience and confidence, such reticence on our part will die away. But, in the meantime, when we're giving out the medals for sexual willingness, we ought to remember that men are often more amenable than women in this respect – and give credit where credit is due!

*I love having oral sex done to me. I love the sensation of my boyfriend's lips and tongue enveloping my vaginal area and feeling the wetness of his saliva and my juices mixing. I prefer it when it's a bit slower and softer, especially if his stubble is coming through, although a hot passionate tonguing is always a turn-on. My boyfriend would go down on me anytime, I never have to ask, and I think it's one of his favourite parts of our love-making.*

VITAL STATISTICS

25 per cent of women usually make love more than once in a session

94.7 per cent enjoy intercourse

88.3 per cent experiment with different positions in intercourse

69.8 per cent feel uncomfortable during intercourse at some point

79.2 per cent come through intercourse, though not always

# 15. Intercourse

*Yes, I do enjoy intercourse. I like the excitement of kissing and touching each other, the feeling of my boyfriend getting harder and how that feels inside me. I love the wetness and the fit of our bodies and feeling his body crushed against mine. I just love the overall closeness of intercourse, feeling his body surround me and fill me up. It's as if we are one thing, and I don't want to let go of him when I feel like that.*

WHEN WE TALK about intercourse what we talk about is closeness. The questionnaire answers used that word again and again. We feel intercourse is: *'The closest you can get to someone ... the merging with each other ... the intimate sharing ... a feeling of completeness ... only my child will have that sort of closeness'.* We like the passion of intercourse, the way we both move together towards climax. We like the physical and emotional abandonment, the trust we have when our partner is thrusting. And we enjoy the fact that our partner can come inside us and the *'feeling of achievement'* that gives. As many as 94.7 per cent of women who have intercourse love it.

It isn't only what intercourse means to us that we love. We also love the sensations it brings us: *'It reaches parts of me that other acts cannot reach.'* The first feeling of entry arouses us, the movement and sensation of intercourse give us pleasure. We also love watching our partner's face and body move *'in ways only I can see'*. If we do come through penetration, then the intimacy of it makes us feel very different from when we come in any other way; and, whether or not we come, the experience of feeling our partner ejaculate inside us is totally unique.

*I love it! I love the feeling it gives me of being satisfied, feeling good about myself, feeling healthy and complete. I love the whole process of intercourse from the first subtle signs to the culmination of orgasm.*

We think of intercourse as really beginning at the point where foreplay moves into penetration. Having both become aroused through kisses, cuddles, touching, stroking, and masturbation with hand and tongue, he penetrates us. Some women report a definite shift in sexual awareness as that happens, a kind of refocusing of sensation. Sometimes it is completely pleasurable, at other times, it can can be quite painful; whichever, the refocusing does signal a different stage in love-making. We feel instantly closer, we often take a deep breath and feel ourselves relax.

*When he penetrates me it makes my whole body tingle. I can also feel his penis hitting the walls of my vagina, which gives me a feeling of pleasure but pain.*

## WHICH POSITION?

There's usually a moment of adjustment, as we both get used to the new situation. We feel him hardening inside us, and we love how that feels. We've often chosen a position that suits us, or we shift into one. What we like varies, according to what pleases us physically and what mood we are in. The key issue is usually depth: how deep does any particular position allow our partner's penis to go. But other factors are important, too. How much do we want to move, and how much do we want to leave the movement to him; how much control do we want to have; how much opportunity to stimulate our clitoris do we need; how much do we want to lie face to face, kiss and talk? We will choose one position, then another or have one preferred position for a few weeks and then switch to another favourite.

*I like many different positions, usually doing all of them during love-making. I like it laying down if I am tired and let the man do the work, or if I am full of energy I will go on top and do different positions.*

Our favourite position is still the missionary; that fact is so much of a cliché that some women even apologize in their answers for choosing it. The missionary position allows deep penetration and forceful sex on his part; several women mention enhancing this by spreading their legs wide or getting the internal tension they want by pushing their legs together or clenching their vagina. The position also allows us to relax; women who like it seem to be happy to let their partners set the pace and to follow that, losing themselves in sensation without needing to control. And, of course, it allows us to be face to face with our partner, watching, smiling, kissing, licking.

*My favourite position is the missionary. I like the rhythm to start off slowly so I can feel every movement; then slowly but surely the movements get faster and more intense.*

*In the missionary position, lift your bended legs as high as possible, as near to his ears as you can get them and clench your vagina in, as if he's in a vice. Once he's in, don't let him out until you want him out.*

Our second favourite position, for many of the same reasons, is with the woman on top, sitting or kneeling. This also allows us deep penetration but turns the tables in terms of control. This time it is our partner who can relax; we in turn can set the pace and the depth, by moving up and down in our own way. Again, we can see our partner, again we can smile or talk.

Other positions are mentioned far less often. They give us novelty and make a change, but only a few of them are our favourites. Laying curled up together with rear penetration; on the edge of a table or bed, with him standing or kneeling on the floor; standing up against the wall, 'slow and erotic'. All these give us different sensations and different kinds of pleasure.

*I have no definite favourite but enjoy one position for a couple of weeks before having a favourite another. At the moment the best one is with me on my back and my partner kneeling. The depth of penetration is deeper, and he can pull me on to him by my shoulders. I don't dislike any positions; they just go in and out of favour.*

*I would never be judgemental or recommend anything, but the sexual position that my partner and I mostly use is brilliant. It was recommended by the Association for People with Disabilities and Sexual Problems, and it's for people with an arthritic condition. It involves me being on my back with my legs over his shoulders. It means I don't put any pressure on my hips, knees or back joints; it also means we often have simultaneous mega-orgasms.*

## DISLIKED POSITIONS

Where we object to an intercourse position, the reason is usually that it is uncomfortable or embarrassing. We really don't like any position where we look silly or feel awkward and hate anything that is uncomfortable and distracts us from what we are doing. (We also don't like anal sex – but more of that later, in chapter 19.)

Some of us dislike being on top because of the sensations it gives and also because we may feel too open and vulnerable, sitting up and exposed. Somehow, for some of us, it doesn't feel as close as the face-to-face intimacy of the missionary position: *'It feels uncomfortable ... difficult to achieve friction ... hurts my back and backache is a real passion killer ... I feel as if he is scrutinizing my reactions ... my ex-husband used to laugh at my boobs bouncing, and I've never got over that.'*

But the real no-no of vaginal sexual positions is doggie-style, rear entry while we are kneeling or on all fours. We hate it not so much because it isn't pleasurable – some of us say it is, though others say that it hurts our womb. We hate the position mainly because it feels depersonalized. The fact that we can't see our partner's face, and that he is entering us from behind, gives it a peculiarly anonymous feel, removing any sense of relationship. And because the whole value of intercourse to most of us is that element of closeness, we find this position *'degrading ... I feel I am being manipulated ... humiliating ... hate the lack of contact ... not a loving position ... makes me feel cheap and unloved ... undignified ... feels vulnerable ... my body likes doggy but my head says it's animalistic'.*

## MOVEMENT AND RHYTHM

Where positions are concerned, we have distinct loves and hates. With intercourse movements, speeds and rhythms, it's not so clear cut. Most of us don't really dislike anything, except perhaps very hard pumping when we're not in the mood: *'Too quick, speedy fucking leaves me cold.'*

We do, however, seem to fall into two distinct groups when it comes to the kind of movement we prefer, though we can easily accept and even get aroused by, any other type of action. The first group loves thrusting movements, long or shallow, slow and sensitive, rough and hard *'thrusting...pumping... quite fast'.* Just as the key factor when we choose position is the depth it allows, so the key factor when we are moving is often how deep the thrust is: the deeper the better for most of us.

The second group prefers a kind of writhing movement, 'a rhythmic grinding ... I grind my groin around in circles on his penis.' The difference is not only in the motion, which is circular rather than direct, but also in the speed, which tends to be a lot slower and more sensuous.

In general the speed we like when making love varies according to the mood we're in: 'Fast and hard ... slow and sexual ... sometimes I want slow loving and other times I want a fast kick.' Many women say that just after penetration they prefer slow movement, but that they then like it to build up to a peak as they get more aroused.

A constant rhythm seemed to be what most women both expect and like – so much so that most of us don't refer to the issue. Two women, however, make a special mention of liking an irregular rhythm: 'I was with a bloke who had an unusual rhythm, which was very nice – he went in slow and out fast ... the rhythm needs to be slightly irregular, stopping and starting until the very end. This bit is vital.'

While we are having sex, all the time we can add in other things to build the passion. We love to look at our partner, keep eye contact and watch his arousal. We are slightly more wary of his looking at us, particularly if we are not too secure about our body image. We may both want to look at ourselves 'in the wardrobe mirror'. We may speak to each other, words of love or simply talking dirty. We can touch with hands, rub with legs and arms: 'I just like to get my hands on him.' We can kiss and lick, nibble, blow and bite in the same way, if with a little less freedom of movement, than during foreplay. Our partner can stimulate our breasts, our bottoms, our clitoris. We can reach down and stroke his balls, lick his nipples or scratch our nails down his back.

## DO WE EXPERIMENT?

We love to experiment during intercourse. Only 7.8 per cent of women say they never do so. The rest love to try new things, mostly spontaneously and usually with great success. The key seems to be not to worry about whether experiments work – and to be happy to go back to tried and tested solutions if something new disappoints us.

The few couples who don't experiment at all feel bad about that. Some blame themselves for their lack of bravery or their inhibition. More often they blame their partner for not cooperating: 'I've tried to make him do more positions but it's impossible ... My recent partner didn't like other positions; he often lost his erection because I tried to cajole him into trying.' And just one or two of us seem quite despairing about it: 'Why bother with new positions ... I never feel anything whichever position we're in.'

But these women are in a minority; most of us experiment a great deal. Sometimes it's we who instigate the experimentation. We feel good about that because our partners are happy with it, and we are proud of ourselves for our inventiveness. Where our partners alone instigate, we blame ourselves for not participating, explaining that: *'I'm not that inventive ... I'm basically shy,'* though some women say that they have started to suggest things as they have *'lost fear and anxiety'.* Usually we feel that taking the initiative is a mutual thing, a sign of our equal partnership. We may read about a position or see it on a video or film and suggest it to our partner; the decision whether to try it is shared, and the experiment is put into practice next time we're in bed. Or it's all spontaneous: *'We both seem to have the same idea at the same time, grin and go for it.'*

Most women have intercourse just once in a session. Either their partner finds that enough and can't get aroused again, or they are satisfied by the single act. Just 25 per cent of respondents usually have intercourse more than once each time; they and their partner are young, often in their late teens or early twenties, and they're in a new relationship or one where they don't see their partner for long periods. When they do meet, they make up for lost time: the highest figure mentioned for heterosexual sex was *'nine times in a day',* the highest for woman-to-woman sex *'eight times'* though many respondents comment that, *'I don't count, I just enjoy.'*

## WHAT HELPS US COME?

Up to 79.2 per cent of women climax through intercourse. It's a good average, an optimistic figure that shows what pleasure intercourse gives us. But let's be really clear. If we do orgasm, it isn't usually just through thrusting, the no-hands method, as it's called. With penetration, we often need to lie, move or touch ourselves in a particular way in order to get aroused enough to orgasm.

About a third of women who do climax through intercourse get the stimulation they need from the positions they use during intercourse. Many choose the missionary position for this: *'I truly believe that the missionary position, boring as the image may be, is the best position for orgasm.'* One or two say that lying face down allows the penis *'to hit the right spot'.* Some say that *'closing my legs completely and crossing my ankles'* allows the proper stimulation, perhaps by putting pressure on the clitoris from each side. Others recommend clenching their buttocks and thrusting upwards with each thrust, moving the pelvis in tiny, tight circles.

It may be that the movement of the penis against our clitoris on its outward movement is what is needed: some women report that this happened naturally, given the angle of their partner's penis or that *'he'll come right out of me to rub my clitoris with his penis before penetrating me again.'* Or it may be just general stimulation from our partner's body rather than his penis that does the trick. Again, many women recommend the missionary position, particularly with our legs on his shoulders, or *'me on top with my legs inside my partner's legs, so that my clitoris is rubbed by his pubic bone'*.

A majority of respondents, about two-thirds, need specific clitoral stimulation in order to come. To be precise, they need to use their fingers, partner's fingers or some kind of sex toy. So positions that allow 'plenty of access' are best. Any woman-on-top or rear-entry positions seem to provide this, while the missionary position, while not quite as good, allows us to slide our hands down between our bodies. We can then finger ourselves, letting our rhythm blend with our partner's rhythm as he thrusts, to bring ourselves to orgasm.

## PROBLEMS?

Do we have any difficulties with intercourse? Or is our experience of it always wonderful? Firstly, when it comes to orgasm, 20.8 per cent never climax through intercourse and only 16 per cent do always. (Compare this with the 5 per cent who never come when they masturbate, with most of the remaining 95 per cent reporting that they always climax.) It's a low ratio, though, in fact, higher than reported in many earlier sex surveys – hopefully a sign that increasingly we know and can ask for what we want in bed. Also, only a few women report being dissatisfied with this orgasm rate, despite its being so far removed from the rate they can gain when alone. So, in all honesty, lack of orgasm through intercourse isn't the main problem that women report.

However, the questionnaire asked, 'Do you get more or less excited the longer intercourse goes on?' Now, because we love intercourse so much, it might be expected that the response 'more excited' would occur in almost every case. The answer, however, was very different. Only 31.3 per cent of women say that they get more excited the longer intercourse goes on, 38.3 per cent that they get less excited, 3.5 per cent that they get neither less nor more excited, and 26.1 per cent that it varies. This means that up to half of all women consistently get less aroused as intercourse continues. (Imagine what life would be like if two-thirds of men always lost their erection while they were having sex!)

Why this amazing loss of arousal? Was it simply lack of comfort? Some 69.8 per cent of women said that at some time or another, they were uncomfortable during intercourse. As it continues, they suffer cramp, get muscle strain from being in one position too long, feel sore from lying on a hard surface. Some positions are painful, particularly rear-entry ones where the womb is being nudged. And as thrusting goes on, women say that their vagina may become sore, particularly if they are using condoms and are irritated by the lubricant.

But surely it isn't just discomfort that makes for less aroused during intercourse? If so, are we to presume that the 31.3 per cent of women who get more excited with intercourse never lie on hard surfaces or use condoms? It's more likely that they do do these things — but that their increasing arousal anaesthetizes them to discomfort. If women feel uncomfortable to distraction during intercourse, surely it's that they don't get sufficiently aroused to ignore the problems?

## WHY DO WE LOVE IT?

So why do we often fail to get aroused during intercourse? And, secondly, why do we, nevertheless, like it so much?

The answer to the first question hinges on the fact we've referred to before: penetration of itself isn't usually what directly creates arousal. Most of us need particular positions, movements or external stimulation to 'reach the right parts'. We often know instinctively what these are — most of us have discovered a lot about our needs through masturbation. But the sense that comes through clearly in the survey is that sometimes we still don't feel able during intercourse to do what works for us sexually. We don't feel able to delay penetration until we are feeling aroused enough to benefit from it. We follow our partner's positions or movements, whether or not they work for us. We don't feel able to touch our clitoris or ask our partner to do so. The result is that for some of us all the time, and for most of us just occasionally, intercourse is a sexual non-event.

The reason that despite this, we still like intercourse so much is because it is very rarely an emotional non-event. The fact remains that intercourse is ultimately satisfying on other levels than the purely physical. And here we come full circle and remind ourselves of the initial theme of this chapter — that we love intercourse because it is not simply the physiological pleasure alone that makes it so special. Intercourse is a unique experience in combining a whole range of mental, emotional and physical factors. It gives us unity with our partner. It is a mutual form of love-making. It allows us to give pleasure as well as to receive it. And for that reason, whatever the drawbacks of intercourse, it will continue to be the highpoint of partnership sex for heterosexual women. Even if it isn't always the peak of pleasure.

> Yes, I love the unity, the deep intimacy, the closeness between two people. Physically I like the actual penetration part, the wholeness and entirety of that moment of full penetration, that feeling of interlocking and oneness, completeness. It is probably more the idea than the act. It never has lead to orgasm, but that's not to say that it never will. I don't enjoy any sexual activity more than intercourse.

VITAL STATISTICS

55.6 per cent of women say orgasms with their partner aren't important to them

3.7 per cent never orgasm, 26.5 per cent do all the time

53.1 per cent find it easy to orgasm

Over 93 per cent of women cannot orgasm just through penetration

87.5 per cent have different kinds of orgasm

60 per cent have multiple orgasms

# 16. Orgasm

*What does an orgasm feel like? How many pages have I got? It is like waves of pleasure crashing over me from head to toe. With each wave I get intense pleasure around my clitoris and inside me; the feelings are all over my body but particularly there. I see colours and sometimes a dark void with colours at the other side. These waves wash over me six or seven times.*

THE EVIDENCE FROM the survey is quite clear. Women have the potential to orgasm from early in our sexual lives, and more and more of us are fulfilling that potential. We may learn to orgasm quite spontaneously, when we are really only children. We touch ourselves, maybe accidentally, maybe taught by a girlfriend or inspired by a magazine article. We find the feeling good and carry on.

If we are very young, we may have to wait a few years before we climax, though the earliest account of an orgasm from a woman in this survey is actually at 4 years old. But as they entered puberty and sexual maturity, many women say they orgasmed the very first time they tried it, and the rest report orgasm fairly soon after. It's easy and spontaneous. They are *'surprised ... delighted'*, but in some ways they take it for granted. It's natural, after all.

It's only if our parents find us masturbating and scold that we may have any problem at all with orgasming by ourselves in our early years. If this does happen, we don't lose the knack of masturbation, but we might put it on hold for a few years and rediscover it when we are older.

## ADOLESCENT MASTURBATION

With adolescence comes partners. Some of us learn to orgasm for the first time when puberty and boyfriends combine to make it happen. It's usually through manual sex rather than oral that we first learn, simply because 'fingering' is much more common with adolescents than oral sex is. Being taught to orgasm by a partner may not be quite as reliable or as easy as learning on our own, however. For in these early relationships, we often let our partners take the lead; they know less about female anatomy and female sexuality than we do, so our chances of orgasming with them are much reduced. It is only if we are lucky that our boyfriend will know what to do, or that together we will be able to explore the possibilities.

*I first orgasmed when I was 18. My ex-fiancé and myself were lying on the settee in our home. I was lying on him, and he started kissing and touching my neck, shoulders and breasts until I had to beg him. Then he started on my clitoris, and I orgasmed within minutes.*

Another group of us learn to orgasm only after we start to have intercourse. The first experience of sex itself isn't, as explained in chapter 4, the best time to aim for a first orgasm. Only 5.7 per cent of women did orgasm during the event, and all of these had done so before and were experienced in mutual masturbation. But once we start having intercourse regularly, we may get the right sort of stimulation simply through trial, error and experience. And if we try oral sex after we have slept together, this can also be the turning-point. We learn to orgasm through that and then develop our ability to orgasm in other ways.

*I had my first orgasm about two years ago. It was when I was having an affair with an older man. I was tied up at the time on the bed, he was stimulating my clitoris and had a finger up my bum.*

*I first had what I recognized as an orgasm at age 22 with my husband playing with my clitoris. It was the first time I had been able to allow someone to carry on playing with me for long enough; usually I used to*

*stop them as my clitoris felt too sensitive. I had never come in this way*
*before, and my immediate reaction was to cry. I had waited for it for so*
*long. I wrote a letter to a magazine about it which was published.*

It could be that childbirth is the turning-point: quite a few of us link
starting to climax with having a child: *'Especially since childbirth, orgasms*
*have thankfully become the norm.'* Or it could be that we need to break
away from a single partner and start learning and experimenting before
we can really contact our potential: many of us say that we didn't orgasm
with a husband but during an affair or once divorced, and that with older,
more experienced partners, climaxing followed naturally.

*I had my first orgasm at 36 years old. I was having an affair with a*
*very sexually enlightened doctor whose gentle but erotic touch brought*
*me to my first orgasm. Violins played!*

## WHO ORGASMS?

Of all the women in the survey, only seven (3.7 per cent) never orgasm.
The rest do so rarely (3.7 per cent), occasionally (11.1 per cent), frequently (40.2 per cent), always (26.5 per cent) and variably (14.8 per
cent). In other words most respondents orgasm regularly and almost all
of them do at some time or another.

We orgasm in a variety of ways. By far the most reliable is to masturbate ourselves; 95 per cent of survey respondents can orgasm that way.
They write about these orgasms as being easy, quick, controllable and
endless; they can have dozens if they want to. With our partner, we orgasm
through masturbation by hand and mouth, much less reliably but again
quite easily. Some of us use a vibrator, with or without our partner.
Intercourse gives a good rate of orgasm only as long as we include some
form of extra stimulation through position, movement or by direct
touching. Most of us, when making love with our partner include more
than one of these elements in order to climax.

*While performing oral sex, my boyfriend would use his fingers inside*
*and outside my vagina, on and around my clitoris and to stroke my inner*
*thigh. I would either orgasm during this, and then we would have sex,*
*or he would take me to the point of orgasm then penetrate me, and*
*I could orgasm. Or, we would have intercourse first without orgasm, then*
*move to oral sex as explained and back to penetration and orgasm. If,*
*however, we had less oral sex and more penetration, he could bring me*
*to orgasm by rubbing my clitoris while penetrating me.*

In general women in this survey find orgasming throughout intercourse fairly easy, though it always depends on several factors: how we are feeling at the time, whether our relationship is going well, and exactly what we are doing in bed. Those of us who do find it easy have a common outlook – we experience full concentration on what is happening physically in our bodies, with no 'wandering minds' or emotional disruption. Whether this is because our level of arousal is so high that our minds can't wander, or whether it is because we can keep our minds focused and so enhance our sensations, it is not clear. But that is the pattern.

Also, those women who come easily through intercourse seem to have actual physical strategies for increasing our arousal. They use them in a relaxed way, without guilt-tripping themselves about having to come naturally and spontaneously 'through love alone'. They recommend long foreplay to begin with, watching a sexy film, going easy on the alcohol – 'coming is fairly easy when sober and impossible when drunk!' – and using a vibrator. Time and again, respondents mention knowing exactly what they need in terms of position, movement or added help by hand – and they are not afraid to ask for that.

> I orgasm in the missionary position, with him lying on top, using a very hard, long, slow, thrusting movement. I close my legs around his penis and rest his testicles inside my outer lips; I really squeeze, with all my muscles. I can only come if he uses one hand to rub my clitoris and the other under my buttocks touching my anus. Therefore I take his full weight, and he is penetrating very hard, while stimulating my clitoris and anal area. Like this I come very deeply and it lasts for ages.

## KINDS OF ORGASM

Some 82.5 per cent of women say that they have different kinds of orgasm. They almost all draw a distinction between orgasms gained through clitoral stimulation alone and those that involve penetration. But there's a very wide variety of descriptions of the two kinds – many at total variance with each other. Some feel that an orgasm gained through clitoral stimulation alone is more direct and powerful, others that a penetrative orgasm gives a more widespread effect.

> I have two different types of orgasms. Orgasm from clitoris stimulation is usually shorter but more intense, while orgasm from penetration is not so intense but softer and longer, with the feeling extending throughout my body, especially in my legs.

Many women draw a distinction between a purely genital and an all-body orgasm – the latter affecting more than just the clitoris and vagina. The way to create an all-body orgasm varies from respondent to respondent: some use a particular type of stimulation; others combine stimulation in vagina and clitoris; others say that they can only create it through self-masturbation; yet others need intercourse with clitoral stimulation.

*My orgasms vary between what I term a pussy come and a body come. When I masturbate by rubbing my legs I experience a pussy come; that's rhythmic throbbing of the vaginal walls and a hot feeling of release. The strongest sense of orgasm I can only achieve lying on my back by masturbation or oral sex. Then my toes start tingling and curling, and my whole body begins to vibrate. At the moment of orgasm, I tend to bring my head up, and my whole body seems to have contractions, felt most strongly in my pelvis. After a very strong orgasm I find it difficult to move for two or three minutes.*

There is a widespread feeling that combining penetration and direct clitoral stimulation is the best of both worlds: *'I get a lot of pleasure from having a man inside me, and if my clitoris is also being stimulated it sends me into a different sphere in my brain.'* And just one or two women say that they can get an orgasm from pressing the G spot just inside their vagina; the resulting sensation is like *'heat spreading through my body that takes my breath away'*. (Other women, incidentally, say they don't believe in the G spot, or if that there is one then they haven't got it!)

Timing seems to matter too. If we wait a long time to orgasm, either because we choose to or because our partner himself holds back, then the climax is more powerful: *'If I approach climax then slow down and reach a plateau of feeling, the orgasm comes from deeper inside the body ... If my partner takes me to the brink of orgasm and then stops and does it again, when I eventually orgasm, it's very intense.'* The experience of being 'held back' by a partner was one a number of women report: some felt it was teasing, others saw it as extremely powerful foreplay: *'I feel like screaming, and he just smiles because he knows what's going on.'*

What about multiple orgasms? If we don't have them, we may say that we don't believe in them: *'I don't think they exist – but good luck to those who say they have them.'* If we do have them – and 60 per cent of women say they do – then we describe one long, repeating orgasm that is both extended and intense: *'Strange ... everything is alive ... sometimes it's so intense that I can't handle it.'* There seems to be no pattern as to when or why these multiple climaxes happen, except that *'feeling very loving towards a partner'* seems to help.

*I have multiple orgasms frequently. The intensity varies depending on how the orgasm is reached. Sometimes it is so intense I can't handle it. I have had to ask my boyfriend not to make me come so often. I suppose I am very lucky.*

## WHAT DOES IT FEEL LIKE?

Women answering the questionnaire give some wonderfully poetic descriptions of their orgasms. Significantly, those who preface their accounts by saying that they cannot possibly describe their orgasms are often the ones who describe it most emotionally and erotically.

*Now I've never put this into words: A euphoric explosion! The best feeling ever. It engulfs my whole body and contains so much strength. I am often very weak afterwards. It's inexorable.*

An orgasm can last a few seconds, or 'for ever' – the most specific description given said that the respondent's orgasm lasts precisely eight seconds! The feeling usually starts in the genitals – though just a few women describe it as beginning in their feet. Then it builds, either focusing around the clitoris more and more intensely until it is *'almost a pain'*, concentrating in the vagina, which starts to *'contract ... pulse ... pump ... like a fist opening and closing in my vulva'*, or affecting the whole body with *'ripples of pleasure outwards in all directions'*. It may culminate in a peak, or it may simply plateau out in a sustained level of sensation that then declines slowly. The sensation can be *'like sneezing, if that makes sense'*. It often feels like an explosion – many women use that term. We may tingle or go light. We may feel all our muscles tighten and contract, or we may feel totally numb. We liken the sensation to an electric shock, a *'volcano, slowly grumbling and moaning until it eventually erupts with pleasure and relief'*, or *'waves on an ocean'*. The most unusual description given was, *'I feel slim.'*

At the time of orgasm our whole body exerts itself. Our heart may pound, our skin feel hot, our ears ring. We may have pins and needles, an all-over flush, a red rash, a blush. Our breathing stops, or we take gulps of air – *'in case regular breathing stops the pleasure'*. Many of us feel as if we are about to lose consciousness.

*It begins with a burning sensation in the soles of my feet, then a mounting heat in my body. Then I 'black out' for a second, feel a kind of explosion and then a sense of warmth and well being.*

And we feel superb: *'Wonderful ... happy ... no problems ... I don't care ... nothing else matters for those few moments'*. Body, mind and emotions come together, and *'It feels as if nothing else will ever be so perfect.'*

## WHAT DOES IT LOOK LIKE?

As many as 91.3 per cent of women say that they show external signs when they come. We seem to follow two common patterns. Either we go rigid and very still: *'I freeze up.'* Or we *'shiver ... shake ... go into spasm ... arch my back ... give unrestrained pelvic thrusts'*. We may gain amazing strength, hanging on to a partner if we are with him when we come, clamping our legs around him, scratching, digging our nails into back or backside. We may throw our partner off us, or simply *'collapse with a huge sigh of relief ... go all limp on him'*.

And we make noise. Almost every women who describes her orgasm mentions the sound she makes. We scream, we shout, we moan. We make noises at the back of the throat. We shout our partner's name, we tell him we love him, we shout obscenities and blasphemies and past partner's names. Some women say they have tried to keep silent: *'I bite my thumb to quieten myself down,'* and some add that: *'My boyfriend said, "Let it out, I want to hear you" – so now I do.'*

With all this activity going on, our partner usually knows that we've come. We don't think very highly of the very few partners who don't notice, or who think they do and who are wrong. This woman's comment is one of the more tolerant, as she takes the responsibility upon herself for his lack of knowledge.

> *My partner does not really know when I have orgasmed because sometimes he says he thinks I've orgasmed, and I haven't and vice versa. Sometimes when I have orgasmed, and he doesn't think I have, he is quite surprised.*

More often we are proud of our clear signals, and there is a general tone of gleeful laughter when we talk about whether our partner has spotted them or not: *'He can usually tell: I shake and have a tendency to collapse in a heap ... I scream and shout, stop breathing for about ten seconds and claw his back ... Yes, he knows. The whole neighbourhood knows!'*

## AFTERWARDS

After our orgasm we may totally relax and fall asleep. Or we may stay awake but feel weak and peaceful. Interestingly very few women report the reaction that some men get, of feeling enlivened and energetic. Rather, we feel vulnerable. We cry and *'become very pathetic after an orgasm, needing hugs and kisses'*. And we need to protect ourselves, often literally. The woman who says, *'I immediately feel as if I want to curl up around my vagina and keep it safe and protected. Does that sound weird?!'* is quite typical. Many report that immediately after orgasm, their genitals are sore, fragile and can't be touched. Some simply can't carry on love-making at all.

The vast majority of us, however, after a short time, are ready for another orgasm. While most of us don't necessarily go for two climaxes in one session, 80.5 per cent of women say they can. We can bring ourselves off several times in succession. We may have an orgasm through foreplay with our partner, then another during intercourse. Whether we do or not all depends on the circumstances — how relaxed we are, how much time there is available, whether our partner's state of arousal means that he can move from masturbation to intercourse.

*It depends on how well I can control my body at that particular time. I use my buttocks, thighs and calf muscles to control my orgasms, so I have many small ones until I decide to let go and have a huge one. I am immediately ready to start again.*

## IF WE MISS COMING

Sometimes we move towards orgasm and then don't quite reach it. (The issue of those of us who don't orgasm at all is covered in chapter 21.) This is most likely to happen during intercourse, rarely during masturbation. Sometimes something intrudes from outside, *'I hear the baby cry or think of something that happened during the day,'* and this cuts across our physical concentration and simply cuts off the potential climax. More often there's some internal pressure: *'When I am ill ... overtired ... anxious ... stressed ... after my period ... trying too hard'*. We feel the arousal building, and then suddenly our mind takes over, and the excitement dies away. Sometimes our partner does something disturbing, either without realizing or through sheer ignorance of what we need. Either he *'changes tactics'*, shifting position or rhythm without checking out whether it is working for us. Or he comes first and simply withdraws, leaving us *'feeling just the same as before intercourse'*.

When this happens 79.2 per cent of women feel bad. The 20 per cent who feel fine seem to have a particular approach to the issue, based on the knowledge that they will come next time they make love. If they know they can have an orgasm when they want to, then missing one occasionally isn't a problem. So they just say lightly that *'things like that happen ... it doesn't take long to get over it ... it'll be all the better next time'* and feel genuinely accepting of the problem. We may feel bad, but we reason it out for ourselves.

Those of us who feel bad about not reaching orgasm either have no secure basis of reliable orgasms or tend to have a very strong physical reaction to not coming. This reaction also creates strong emotions in us: *'My vagina throbs . . . I feel like bursting into tears . . . It sent me barmy, and it only ever happened once.'* We tend to blame ourselves sometimes, feeling we've created a crisis – or feeling that by coming so irregularly we are a sexual failure overall. More often we blame our partners, feeling a rush of anger against them immediately and a grumbling resentment afterward. We want our partners to know what to do, to touch us the right way, to be able to bring us to orgasm reliably. They can't, and we resent it, on top of feeling bad about ourselves: *'I feel very let down by myself, but I take it out on him.'*

On the other hand some partners seem to be very supportive of our orgasms – almost too supportive on occasions. So while many women love the fact that their partner wants them to come, *'I think it's more important to him that I reach orgasm than any other partner I've had. That's one of the reasons our sex life is so good,'* other women feel oppressed by their partner's concern. They feel that men nowadays see female orgasms as a proof of male sexuality and so pressure women to climax.

## TAKING ACTION

Those of us who recover emotionally best after a failure to climax are those of us who make sure that we have an orgasm with our partner as soon as possible after the missing one. *'My partner always masturbates me afterwards; I can only describe this as wonderful.'* Originally a few of us feel wary about our partner's doing this until we are reassured that he feels neither guilty nor threatened: *'I felt embarrassed and guilty at first, but once I realized my partner did not mind at all, I felt quite relaxed and happy about it.'* And while for some the intimacy of coming by hand or mouth does seem to be *'second best'* to coming during intercourse, for others, who make masturbating the end of a good session or even the start of another one, it is an integral and wonderful part of love-making.

It's not nearly as good to masturbate alone if partnership sex fails to provide an orgasm. We tend to do that when a partner is unaware that we haven't come and would be threatened by knowing. We wait until he's not around, or we pop to the loo and do it there. Doing this feels very different from masturbating with our partner's support. We feel guilty and furtive, *'unsexy, as if it's out of labour I do it, not love or even lust'.* We are very angry at our partner, *'cheated, tense, let down, disappointed, frustrated and unloved'.* The common thought is: *'He should have known.'*

## FAKING IT

Another time when we tend to feel 'he should have known' is when we fake orgasm. Yet we fake it so well that perhaps it's unfair to expect our partners to know. The significant thing is that we almost always claim that we fake in order to protect our partners — but underneath we'd really like them to second-guess us and for our selfless action not actually to work.

Some 43.5 per cent of women have never faked it. They are outraged at the thought: *'Certainly not ... never!!'* They want to create *'an honest and good sexual relationship'* not one based on lies. Or they reckon that if they do fake, then in the end it's their own fault if the man never learns what makes them come.

*No, there is no point in pretending that a man has made you come if he hasn't. My orgasm is as important as his and more so than his ego. He could do the same moves again next time, thinking it was what I enjoyed.*

Where we do fake — and over half of women do — we almost all feel that we are doing it because of our partners. We want to please, *'to make him feel secure ... to give him confidence ... to help him come ... to keep him happy'*. Our partners seem to worry if we don't come, perhaps because they have been told so often in the media that we should: *'He used to ask me all the time if I'd orgasmed ... I didn't mind not coming, but he did ... I wanted to make him stop fussing.'* Some of us also fake orgasm in order to bring intercourse to an end: we're not in the mood, we're tired, we feel stupid because we can't come, or *'the sex was really crap but I didn't want to hurt their feelings by telling them this.'* Just one woman says wryly that she only fakes *'when we have visitors'.*

We don't feel good about faking. Of those women who do it, 92 per cent feel that they shouldn't have or shouldn't have to. We feel that our partners should know when we orgasm or not and should either support us to climax or shouldn't be so insecure that they need us to. We resent what we see as the emotional blackmail that results in our having to fake it — though as we get older, we become more able to resist the pressure, and, in general, tend to fake climax less and less.

*I faked it with my ex-husband for about 18 months before we were married. I felt stupid at not being able to come and thought he would feel let down if I didn't. I was eventually able to admit I was faking, and he was very supportive.*

*I have faked orgasm, mainly because the men I have been with expected*

*me to orgasm. When I didn't they got upset, so it was easier to say I had.*
*Nowadays I tend not to fake it, because there's no point.*

## HOW IMPORTANT ARE ORGASMS?

We love orgasms and get frustrated when we don't have them. We describe
them at length and with great enjoyment. We revel in every aspect of
them. But where do they stand in the grand scale of things?

The first thing to say is that we do have an orgasmic hierarchy. We've
been brought up to think that sex in a loving relationship is best, and
from that it's a simple step to believing that the best orgasm is a shared
orgasm. We've also read and often believed all the sex experts who over
the years have told us that vaginal orgasms are more loving, more inte-
grated and more mature. And we've bought in to the male way of
achieving orgasm through penetration alone. So, almost subconsciously,
we have a tendency to feel that solo masturbation orgasms are at the
bottom of the hierarchy. Orgasms through mutual masturbation or oral
sex come next, because they are shared. Orgasm through penetration plus
hand to clitoris stimulation are next. Orgasms through intercourse alone
are the most worthwhile.

We give lots of reasons for preferring orgasms with our partner. It
isn't just that we believe that they are morally or ethically better. Whether
they occur through intercourse or not, 50.5 per cent of women definitely
prefer them (as opposed to 6.8 per cent who prefer orgasms alone).
We like shared climaxes because they feel close and intimate, because
they are part of making love. They are emotionally more satisfying.

And they are physically better. Being with our partner means that
we have more orgasm options: mutual masturbation; penetration; penetration with masturbation, and oral sex, which as one woman quite
correctly points out, *'unfortunately I can't do for myself'*. And with a
partner orgasms *'last longer ... are more intense ... happen in multiples
... are trembling and uncontrollable'*.

*Sexual penetration leading to orgasm is entirely different from any other*
*kind. I can orgasm then via my clitoris or my vagina walls or ecstatically,*
*through both. On the whole, penetration produces orgasm via my vagina*
*only, although it has happened a couple of times through my clitoris,*
*together with the other type of orgasm, if separately from it. I have also*
*masturbated myself during intercourse, again ecstatically. Orgasm*
*during intercourse is more lasting and satisfying. It is like a waterfall*
*rising to a peak only to crash down and overwhelm me. I have sometimes*
*quite literally fainted through orgasm, cried and clawed my husband's*
*back to bits. I've bitten him and screamed the house down.*

Partnership orgasms are wonderful – and our believing that is totally understandable. But the idea of an orgasmic hierarchy is worrying. Firstly, it leads to guilt about masturbation, which is an excellent (and seemingly very reliable) way of having pleasure and developing our pleasure potential: *'It's easier to come when you are alone because you know how to do it. It's more difficult for men to get the trick.'* Happily most of us don't stop masturbating – but because of the orgasm hierarchy, some of us do feel guilty.

Secondly, by believing that intercourse orgasms are more worth while than any other sort – a kind of penetrative snobbery – we put ourselves in a total double bind. For the vast majority (if not all, according to some researchers) of women don't have orgasms just through the act of being penetrated by a penis. We need a blend of position, movement and clitoral stimulation. And if we think intercourse orgasms are more valuable than masturbatory ones, it's a simple but treacherous step to believing that penetration is good, anything else is bad, and that extra stimulation during intercourse is a sign that we are somehow not a 'real woman'. We believe that simple thrusting should do it and then think we are lacking in some way when it doesn't; we fight shy of getting what we need during intercourse and then feel guilty when we don't come.

## THE RIGHT TO ORGASM

There is a final significant point here. Why is it that, given that over half of women prefer partnership orgasms, 55.6 per cent also say that it doesn't matter whether they have an orgasm with their partner or not? There seems to be a contradiction here; are partnership orgasms significant or aren't they? One explanation is that when it comes to relationships, we believe orgasms to be less important than other things – and we want to be seen to believe that. We want to feel that we value other things more – company, affection, love – and that pure physical pleasure is less crucial to our relationship.

There is, however, possibly another reason for the seeming contradiction, and it's this. For many women, partnership orgasms are unreliable. As mentioned earlier, we may miss out on them, occasionally or always, through intercourse. We may not feel able to take them through mutual masturbation or oral sex. And if, for us, orgasm isn't always available when we are with our partner, we have two choices. Firstly, to insist, assert, demand. Secondly, to convince ourselves that in fact, our orgasms aren't important, and that if they don't happen, that's fine.

A number of comments from women who come rarely or not at all through intercourse seem to back up the suspicion that we tend to choose the second option. These women say that they are disappointed about the unreliability of their orgasms, but that they have, in very much the way I have just described, come to terms with their situation: *'I have learnt to accept what I get and enjoy it . . . I used to think not being able to orgasm during intercourse was a problem, but I have stopped worrying about it . . . I understand that most women don't climax during sex so there's no point in getting help.'*

The survey statistics tell the same story. Women who don't orgasm with their partners are less likely to say that partnership orgasms are vital – they seem resigned to the way things are. It is the women who do climax in partnership situations who say they are important and get upset if they don't have them. The bottom line is that if we don't get orgasms we justify this to ourselves and accept it. Only if we do get orgasms do we allow ourselves the luxury of allowing them to matter.

This is not to say that we should do what we all too often criticize men for doing: make the orgasm the be all and end all of sex. Of course, love and affection, cuddles and snuggles are important, and if we lose sight of this fact, we lose something very valuable indeed. But it is worth speculating whether if, in the end, we were to think of partnership orgasms as being just as vital as partnership affection, we would be more likely to get both. The attitude that wanting to climax during sex is some-how selfish is surely now outmoded? There's nothing wrong with having orgasms. There's nothing wrong with holding out for them, with arranging our love-making so we get them, with teaching our partners to give them or with masturbating ourselves during intercourse until we come. It doesn't detract from our loving if we, like our partners, have an orgasm every time. So why not have our cake and eat it?

*I used to be very upset and worried that I couldn't orgasm with my partner. I used to think that although I enjoyed our love-making, I was slightly frigid. Then I had an orgasm with an older more experienced man during a short holiday affair. Since then I have became more relaxed about my body, and now orgasms are the norm.*

VITAL STATISTICS

87.1 per cent of women have failed to use contraception at least once

21.1 per cent of women say that their choice of contraception interferes with love-making

22.5 per cent have had an STD

99.2 per cent say that they are aware of STD and AIDS

35.3 per cent say they are at risk of having HIV infection

53.6 per cent say they have changed their sexual behaviour because of AIDS

# 17. Taking precautions

*I'm aware of the risks, but I've had two partners where I've slept with them within a week of knowing them and haven't used a condom.*
*It's crossed my mind, but I'm more concerned about pregnancy than AIDS. I know that's a wrong attitude.*

SEX IS WONDERFUL, but nowadays it's also dangerous. Throughout their answers, and particularly in response to those questions that focus on contraception and sexual problems, women who've responded to the survey write with awareness and conscious fear of the need for safety and protection.

Our first and most basic concern is actually to avoid getting pregnant. Even before we lose our virginity, before first intercourse, we try to be careful. Some of us make sure that the boy doesn't climax, others that, if he does, we keep the sperm well away from the vagina. Only a few *'do everything except penetration'* and in hindsight say they were *'lucky to get away with it'*.

Just a few of the younger women in the survey begin using contraception when the petting starts to *'get very heavy'* but before intercourse itself. If we do, we are often in a steady relationship with our partner, the kind of relationship where we can talk about sex and about the need for contraception: we agree that as he is ejaculating, there is a slight risk, and we start to use condoms. Parallel to this, knowing that intercourse is just a few steps away, we get ourselves put on the pill. Very few women say that they had their parents' formal blessing for this; it is more usual to go to the doctor or the family-planning clinic confidentially.

The pattern of contraception when we actually lose our virginity is clear. Those of us who lose it at an earlier age, on the spur of the moment, with a casual partner, or in something of a pressured situation, are part of the alarming 38.9 per cent who don't use protection at all. In this situation it's usually the boy who takes the initiative, and despite the fact that he is more experienced, he often doesn't suggest contraception, and the girl just goes along with that. Many of us realize what's happening and quite rightly, we panic.

*I was so frightened of getting pregnant that all I could do was mentally scream, 'Get it out of me! I don't want a baby!'*

*The first time wasn't planned, so we didn't use contraception. We did after that, but it was too late. I was pregnant the very first time, as I'd always known I would be.*

Couples who have only known each other a short while, or who don't really discuss whether or not they will sleep together, tend to use condoms – a spur-of-the-moment method for a spur-of-the-moment decision. Some older women, though, comment that when they lost their virginity, condoms *'weren't really fashionable'*, and a much higher number of them than of younger women fall into the no-contraception category.

Not surprisingly the pill is the method of forward planning. It's used by those of us who have had a number of relationships that involved mutual masturbation and who have known for a while that intercourse is imminent; by couples who are both virgins, and who have planned and waited for the right time; and by the sexual decision-makers, couples who have talked it through and decided to postpone sex for a while until they're really ready.

## CONTRACEPTION NOW

After we've begun to have intercourse, most of us do start using contraception regularly. Those of us who are on the pill stay on it, those who are using condoms continue to use them until we settle into a permanent relationship or unless taking the pill doesn't agree with us. In general, of course, it is we rather than our male partners who take responsibility for contraception: more 'female decision' methods of contraception are mentioned in women's responses than 'male decision' methods.

Almost all of us feel happy about our knowledge of contraception and our ability to use it. But there is an undercurrent of dissatisfaction at the fact of contraception – that it should be necessary at all. And there were specific whinges about particular forms of protection. No method seems to be universally applauded, and they all have their problems.

> *I've tried all forms of contraception, none of which agreed with me. The pill made me ill and warped my personality, made me horrible for ten years. Sheaths made me sore. The cap and spermicide gave me thrush. The coil nearly killed me by causing anaphylactic shock twice. Sponges were quite good, but in the end I decided to go and get sterilised.*

When they answered the questionnaire, 17 per cent of the women weren't using contraception. This is mainly because they weren't in a sexual partnership and didn't need to do so (although many women who aren't in a sexual partnership do carry on taking the pill, just in case). Another contingent has stopped using contraception because they want to get pregnant, about half a dozen because they have passed the menopause, and just one said she'd never found a satisfactory method.

Just a handful of women are using what we might call 'minority' methods: the coil and the diaphragm. These seem to have a range of differing problems of their own. The diaphragm is *'messy... fiddly... unspontaneous'*; the coil doesn't need any forethought, but *'I'm sure it caused my thrush.'* With both methods oral sex is less attractive because of the need to use spermicide.

Those who have opted for sterilization – or whose partners have opted for vasectomy – tend, not surprisingly, to be in the older age group. These are the methods of choice for couples who have had their family and want to opt out completely. They seem to give almost complete peace of mind and have no reported side-effects, though one woman says that: *'I still worry sometimes about how effective sterilization is, but we can't do any more than this.'* In fact, though, some of us do do more: even where we have been sterilized, we may still use condoms if we are wary of AIDS.

## FAVOURITE METHODS

Most of us who are sexually active use either the pill or condoms. If we are on the pill, we're usually in a permanent relationship, where we want sex often, spontaneously and without fuss. We're happy to take responsibility for regularly taking it, and it can also control our periods. We feel relaxed with the pill and commonly like it. Where we do worry, it's partly to do with the here-and-now side-effects and partly our long-term fears. We report a number of classic symptoms, including weight gain, depression, thrush, cystitis, loss of desire — and unexpected pregnancy, though thankfully only in one case. Long term, we are wary of flooding our bodies with hormones and of the horrors that we've heard they might create.

But those who are on the pill, even though they expressed worries, rarely said they were going to come off it — or not yet. Our attitude seems to be that the pill is so convenient that we are happy to accept a slight future risk in exchange for the many current benefits. A half-sister to the pill, hormonal injections, is mentioned by only one woman, who found the side-effects as bad and felt trapped by the long-term nature of the method.

Condoms are far and away the method that creates the strongest negative feelings in respondents. If we're using them, we've usually tried other means and have only come back to using condoms because these other methods give us negative symptoms. Or we are younger women who aren't in a steady relationship and don't want the side-effects of the pill when we aren't having regular sex. Or we're using other contraceptive methods but want to protect ourselves against sexually transmitted diseases (STDs) when having sex with new partners We may feel safer using condoms, think they are more ecological than other methods or like the fact of not having to pump chemicals into our bodies.

*We use condoms every time we have sex. I am happy about my knowledge of the contraception we use, and if I was to consider changing I would find out about the other options. I did consider going on the pill for a while but I wasn't happy about the possible side-effects. I have never had sex without condoms, so I don't really know if this affects sex at all.*

On the other hand, most of us, even those who use them, dislike condoms intensely. As far as safety is concerned, they aren't fully reliable: they roll off, they burst. Also, we don't like stopping to put them on, as that makes love-making lose momentum. We don't feel as close to our partner when we wear them during intercourse; we prefer feeling his sperm inside us. Maybe our partner *'dislikes condoms because he is circumcised and therefore already less sensitive'*. Maybe we are allergic to them. And, after sex, we can't just lie there but have to *'see to them'*; if we don't, we often end up lying on a wet patch.

The final judgement then on protection is that no one method gives us total satisfaction. And it can be even worse if our partner adds to our problems. In general in fact, most women say that they take responsibility for contraception, while their partner simply agrees or supports; just a few partners rise to the challenge and have a vasectomy. But just a few male partners disagree with our choice of contraception, and where they do, they can pressure us emotionally or undermine our using protection. Some dislike using condoms or object to our using the coil or the cap because they can feel it. Others either try to persuade us to go on the pill because it allows spontaneity or to come off it because they feel it's dangerous.

> *I'm not thrilled about using condoms. But he's said he wouldn't allow me to keep a baby if I happened to fall pregnant, so we use them. My partner wants me to go back on the injection, but I get very angry at this and usually tell him to fuck off. It's my body.*

## SEXUALLY TRANSMITTED DISEASES (STDs)

When it comes to protection against disease rather than protection against pregnancy, we also seem to be very aware. Younger women learn about STDs at school, although then they often don't take them seriously.

> *Sexually transmitted diseases were discussed at school as a kind of joke, so I was aware of them at about the age of 14. I didn't know the full horrors of these diseases then, though, just the basics.*

Older women have seen the issue of STDs highlighted by the AIDS epidemic and have often made it their business to find out about other sexually transmitted diseases through reading and talking with others. Some of us have found out through lectures at work, being a blood donor or through knowing people who are HIV positive. Unsurprisingly, considering the publicity surrounding it and the prognosis given to those with HIV, most women when answering this set of questions target AIDS as the key problem and seem to think that other sexually transmitted conditions aren't nearly as important or dangerous.

Only a quarter of women have actually had a sexually transmitted disease. Those who have escaped disease seem relieved and grateful but somewhat angry at the very suggestion that they might have ever caught anything. Those who have been infected mention thrush, vaginal warts, herpes, crabs, chlamydia, gonorrhoea, *'unspecified something or other'* and cervical cancer (which, incidentally, can be caused by a number of factors and is not therefore, strictly speaking, a sexually transmitted disease). In response to all these problems, we feel a range of negative emotions, few of them seemingly linked to the type of disease but only to how severe it is and to how it affects our relationship. Respondents say they feel *'dirty . . . scared . . . ashamed . . . pissed off . . . devastated . . . mainly upset at the treatment . . . was I manic! I drove my doctor mad!'*

As these comments show, we blame ourselves strongly for catching such diseases. Yet when it comes to partners who might have transmitted them, we actually seem much less upset. We seem to see the link as being irrelevant if the disease has been caught by a partner in the past, before he knew us. We're only furious when a current partner has caught something through being unfaithful, and then it is mainly the infidelity that hurts. And we're only furious at a past partner where the disease we caught from him directly affects a current relationship.

> *I got crabs once! I was utterly horrified. However, within two hours of realizing what they were, I'd been to the chemist and got the appropriate lotion and all were gone, never to return. I waited for my boyfriend to mention something, but he never did. I hadn't been with anyone else, so I assumed it must have been his being unfaithful. However, he never got them! When I eventually asked him what he'd been up to he was stunned! Didn't know a thing about it. I was unconvinced until I found out that a friend had got them from a bed rather than a person. I'd just got back from two weeks of doing gigs on a boat, sleeping in a very 'slept in' bunk bed. I can only assume that's where the little blighters came from. Since then, I've always slept in my sleeping bag!*

## HIV AND AIDS

Over a third of the women in the survey feel that they might be at risk of becoming HIV positive. They think this because they believe that everyone is: *'All people, ages, races, male or female are at risk . . . so everyone is at risk; condoms split.'* Some also reckon that their particular sexual history means there might be a problem. They may have had previous unprotected sex: older women who comment that they had casual affairs before HIV was discovered are aware of this. Or they are sleeping with someone who has unprotected sex. Or they or their partners are at risk professionally: *'My husband has clients who are HIV positive; he was involved in a case where an HIV positive sufferer deliberately bit another person and a policeman, both of whom have now tested positive.'*

Of the two-thirds of women who don't feel they're at risk, some have only had one partner who is a virgin, and some have had the HIV test and only then had unprotected sex. Others say that they always use condoms, or that they insist that a new partner has the test.

*I don't regard myself as at risk now. When I was younger, before it came to light, yes I was at risk, and I had an AIDS test, which was negative. I've had three partners in the past six and a half years: two of them had AIDS tests, and one had been celibate for four years. If I do have a new partner I always use a condom.*

Just over half of respondents, 53.6 per cent, are trying to change their sexual behaviour. They are doing this particularly in response to the AIDS crisis, though they are also conscious of possible risks from STDs in general. So they are now far more wary of sleeping with 'casual' partners. They use condoms rigorously, even when they're on the pill or have been sterilized, they insist on partners cooperating with this. They take the test or insist that their partner does. They aim at having more long-term faithful relationships, and react strongly if their partner does sleep around. As many as 99.2 per cent of women reckon that they are fully aware of the risks of becoming HIV positive.

## ARE WE AT RISK – OF PREGNANCY?

But are we? Over both contraception and STDs, we consistently say that we feel competent, aware and in control. And it would be comforting to think that we are right. But the evidence is a little more ambiguous than that.

When it comes to contraception, 87.1 per cent of respondents say that at some time, they've had sex without protection. When we disregard those who made love unprotected because they wanted to get pregnant, the figure drops to 83 per cent. Some have gone unprotected because of partner pressure: *'My partner refused to use contraception or insisted on having sex when we didn't have any protection available.'* Some have had sex under the mistaken impression that it was safe: *'He meant to withdraw but he had an orgasm.'* They realize in hindsight how unwise they have been: *'It's scary . . . never again . . . it still sends shivers down my spine . . . I must have been mad.'* But they've still done it: it's almost as if, now that society has given women sexual freedom because of the high contraceptive reliability of the pill, we take that freedom regardless of whether we are using contraception or not. And the possible results are all too obvious:

*I have always had sex without contraceptive aids. Both husbands practised coitus interruptus – their decision – and I had four children,*

*three before the age of 21 and one at 41 when I thought my husband*
*was no longer capable!*

The effects are almost always physically and mentally traumatic.
Nearly a third of women have had terminated pregnancies because of not
using contraception, and the most positive word used in any woman's
account of termination was 'relieved'. They feel *'sad ... depressed ...*
*regretful ... guilty... angry at myself ... angry at my partner... sexually*
*dead ... ashamed and stupid'.* And although for most the decision to have
a termination was the *'best decision I could make at the time',* nevertheless
the short- and long-term after-effects are often devastating:

> *I had an abortion about six months ago because of taking risks with*
> *contraception, because of my partner and the situation I was in at the*
> *time. It was the most devastating, traumatic, painful thing that has ever*
> *happened to me. I am still very affected by it and still feel terrible grief*
> *over the loss of a baby who was very real to me. It has changed my life*
> *and although I am healing, I feel I will never forget and will never be the*
> *same again. I feel very wary of getting involved again because the*
> *slightest bit of emotion I feel for someone will bring forth all the pain*
> *and sadness I feel at terminating my baby's life. I don't feel ready*
> *for another sexual relationship yet, and I won't ever take risks with*
> *contraception again or allow myself to be manipulated again.*

## ARE WE AT RISK – OF DISEASE?

When it comes to sex without protection against the HIV virus, accounts
are if anything even more horrifying because they reveal not only
ignorance but also a tendency to allow lust to overcome caution. A high
99.2 per cent of respondents say that they are fully aware of the problems,
and 64.7 per cent claim not to be at risk. But the questionnaire answers
show that we are still doing some incredibly dangerous things. More of us
than we think are having unsafe sex, as this comment shows.

> *With my present partner I allow him to enter me before ejaculation*
> *without a condom, and enjoy the fact that I know he can't climax at*
> *that time, and I will only allow him to reach for a condom when I am*
> *nearing orgasm also.*

Also, many still equate sexual risk with sleeping with a partner we
don't know well. We say that we wouldn't sleep with someone casually or
would insist on wearing a condom for a one-night stand. But many go on
to say that once they have known a partner for a few weeks, they are

happy to have sex without condoms, and that having a committed relationship with a partner removes the risks: *'I insist on using a condom the first time with a new partner ... once I have been with a boyfriend for a few months I go on the pill.'*

The problem is that these approaches totally ignores the fact of AIDS; neatly summed up by one respondent, this is that *'you don't have sex with just one person; if they haven't taken precautions, then effectively you are having sex with their entire history of partners'*. In other words, knowing someone and having a relationship with them doesn't mean that they or you are safe if either of you has ever, in your lives, had unprotected sex. And as we know, 83 per cent of women have.

In addition, even if we understand the risks, we often go ahead and take them: *'I often don't use condoms in the heat of the moment ... I had an AIDS test before embarking on my last serious relationship but have since had sex without a condom with two partners ... I am at risk but this doesn't alter my behaviour.'*

There is no explanation of why we put ourselves in danger like this. Perhaps we haven't really become aware of what the risks really are. Or, maybe, as many women comment, we are as aware as we can be – but, in the heat of the moment, the pull of lust is greater than the fear of death.

But let's not be too pessimistic. Many women who answered the questionnaire obviously aren't in any danger. Many more have realized the risks and are taking appropriate action. And possibly, in the end, those who are taking risks will realize that doing so is not worth it.

*I read all the papers, then see the statistics, then look at my daughter. No bonk is worth leaving her motherless.*

VITAL STATISTICS

76.9 per cent of women have sexual dreams

59.1 per cent of women fantasize during love-making

71.8 per cent of women enjoy and are turned on by some porn magazines and videos

60 per cent tell their partners about their fantasies

33.6 per cent of women act out their fantasies with a partner

# 18. Dreams and fantasies

*This is my fantasy: to have a line of about six men all lined up, armed and ready for action, and then for them each to have sex with me until they come inside me, one by one. Then to have a female play with me, make me come and to feel all that amount of sperm shook out of me. I have seen this done on a video, and it really turned me on, and I never forgot it.*

SEX ISN'T ONLY about our bodies. Many sexually aware women nowadays use mental stimulation in order to get turned on in the first place, in order to stay aroused, in order to enjoy making love fully. The questionnaire sections that asked about dreams and fantasies brought forth an incredibly rich vein of long and deliciously detailed answers.

Let's start with sexual dreams. They happen more rarely than fantasies, but they aren't as controllable. When we have them and remember them, which 76.9 per cent of women do, our conscious mind isn't able to filter out those things about which we feel inhibited or wary. So dreams are frightening. They bring up much stronger, more threatening feelings than fantasies do.

These may be very distressing indeed, real nightmares occasionally, with women 'having sex with people I don't want to have sex with ... with someone I wouldn't dream of making love to'. We are not only upset because of the emotions these dreams bring up of terror and hatred, 'aggression and passion', which often leave us shaking and sweating as we wake. We are also disturbed that we should ever have these dreams – particularly if they are about having sex with someone we hate or someone who is unacceptable to our conscience. If we do, for example, dream erotically about our father or our best friend's partner, that makes us wonder about our subconscious desires and doubt ourselves.

## EROTIC DREAMS

Despite all this, many of us find our sexual dreams erotic. The things we dream about may well be almost identical to the disturbing dreams just described, but our reaction to them is totally different; we get turned on instead of frightened. We dream about what we want, what we can't have, what we are afraid to have: hardly anyone dreams about their present lover, except perhaps at the very beginning or end of a relationship, when we're not quite sure we can have him. We dream of sex with forbidden people: 'I often dream about my boss, or once even my brother. We are always just about to have full sex.' We dream about having sex with women 'myself and another woman about to seduce a young, very good-looking girl'. Perhaps we dream about sex with strangers, acquaintances, pop stars or sports personalities. We dream about an ideal lover or a perfect mate.

> I was in a small darkened room and before me was a man having a shower. He was bathed in golden light, he was tall, naked, heavily built (and perfectly haired for me). I walked to him, and the emotions of the dream were so powerful I can still feel them. This was so very right; there was a great feeling of belonging. The two of us belonged together. We held each other in the shower, and slowly and effortlessly we sexually moulded, made love and became one. It was profoundly loving and intensely pleasurable. But his face was shrouded in shadow. I know his body but not his identity. I live in hopes of finding this true lover of mine in my lifetime.

We also often dream about being sexually dominated, being gently and passionately raped. However threatening that fact is to the feminist part of us, however much we are sexual decision-makers, we do dream about these things, and we do enjoy our dreams. And, equally, whether heterosexual or lesbian, we often dream about being sexually in charge: *'I have erotic dreams very regularly, and nine times out of ten I am being very domineering and forcing men to fuck me or perform oral sex on me . . . in many of my dreams I am a man fucking a woman.'* Or we dream about someone we want and cannot have, because we have split up, because he doesn't love us – or, as in the case of this woman, because our husband has died: *'I've had dreams when my husband appeared, and we felt differently towards each other, and we made love. My feelings were very strong, and I woke up thinking he was alive and that we were just separated.'*

## ARE DREAMS ACCEPTABLE?

In general we feel good about erotic dreams. However, unless we are already interested in dream interpretation, we don't particularly concern ourselves about their deep meaning or worrying implications. We admit that dreaming about unacceptable people is part of human nature, and we enjoy the feelings they arouse. And these dreams are often very arousing. We can get very turned on in a dream by an action or an event that wouldn't arouse us in real life. We can be excited by vague and undefined images, or by the kind of illogical sequence of events that dreams often contain. We feel *'really on fire . . . shaking . . . wet between the legs'*, and we may, in our sleep, add to the pleasure physically by touching ourselves: *'My husband says he knows when I'm dreaming sexually because I moan with pleasure and masturbate while asleep.'* Often, we climax in our dreams or wake up in the middle of an orgasm. And then we carry around with us the erotic feeling for the rest of the day. Some of us even reproduce the feeling in later dreams.

> *My dreams are usually very very dark, and I rarely ever see the man. The oldest one I remember had me crawling on a street along the curb in a thick fog, very damp. A dark figure approached, and I very slowly rolled on to my back and stretched out. I didn't feel penetration as such, but I felt the same inside as if I had. In fact I'd never had intercourse before the dream. I liked the dream, the way it felt, and I enjoyed remembering it. I have had similar ones ever since.*

We don't usually carry our dreams with us into real life. Very few of the women in the survey speak of discussing their dreams, enacting them or building in the concepts and images from them into their sexual foreplay. It is as if dreams are too uncontrollable, sufficiently outside their everyday experience, that they would feel uneasy trying to recreate them with their lovers. The emotions they raise are often too strong, and even where they are a turn-on and delightful, they are often sufficiently taboo not to be explored in the full light of day. Except, of course, where we have precognitive dreams, as this woman reports doing:

*I had hurt my back and was sleeping on my bedroom floor on my quilt. Just as I was waking, I dreamt a very real dream, that a man I wanted to make love to me was naked and came under my quilt and made love to me as I lay there. I held his body and remembered the feel of his small prick inside me and even the smell of his heavy body. About a week later, I met him and walked with him in some woods. We fondled each other and kissed, and his smell, his chest and belly and prick were exactly as in my dream. I already knew his body. We made love on later occasions, and he truly was the same as my dream.*

## FANTASIES

Fantasies are much more under our control than dreams, much more what we consciously want. Hence we utilize them more often and with far more awareness to enhance our sex lives. There is a remarkable consistency in the accounts of their sexual fantasies between what women are happy to fantasize about and what is acceptable to them in real life. This isn't to say, of course, that fantasies are truly realistic: we almost always adapt them so that they are safe and don't include any awkward or embarrassing bits such as those that occur in any normal human sexual relationship. We have total freedom, in our fantasies, to idealize: *'In reality the men wouldn't be irresistibly handsome and intelligent, and all I need to get excited.'* Nor is there any real danger that we might put our fantasies into action; hardly any of us do: *'I'd see red if I saw it happening in real life.'* Fantasies are simply what we would want to happen if only we could create the world. We can't, so our fantasies stay unrealized – mental images designed to turn us on.

Where we don't fantasize, we usually don't say that we are ashamed or wary of what we might imagine. Instead, we consistently give as our reason for not fantasizing the fact that we want to concentrate on reality: *'I don't have fantasies ... I enjoy the real world ... It sounds boring I know, but I am totally content with what I have and don't feel that I need fantasies.'*

The 59.1 per cent of women who do use fantasy disagree with this viewpoint. They say that they fantasize not in order to make up for a sex life that is poor but to enhance the excellent sex life they already have. They use it to arouse themselves during the day as they work; to prepare them for love-making later on. They often fantasize as they masturbate, using the sexual freedom of pleasing only themselves to indulge their minds as well as their bodies. They fantasize as part of foreplay, maybe sharing ideas with their partner over the phone before meeting, or over dinner before going to bed. They may mentally replay their fantasies as they make love, though some women don't do this because: *'I find it difficult to hold on to a fantasy during sex ... I just enjoy the person ... I like to think about and concentrate on what we are doing and how it feels.'* There is a sense in which it is disloyal to think about anything else but their partner when they are making love with them.

Used properly, though, we feel our fantasies are good for us. They allow us to explore possibilities that would be just too risky in real life: *'In reality, I wouldn't go in any car alone with three men, because it would end in rape.'* Fantasies can give us mentally the sexual stimulation that we are lacking physically and so help us get aroused in bed. They are good for our relationship because they help us to be mentally intimate with our partner. They make us feel powerful and in control. Above all, they turn us on: everyone who fantasized said that it increased their arousal, and several women say that they needed fantasy to tip them over the edge to orgasm.

## TYPES OF FANTASY

We gather our sexual images from many sources as we grow up. We see and hear people who arouse us. We catch glimpses of photos or films. We read books and make our own mental pictures. Significantly, although we do sometimes watch porn films or read porn magazines and then fantasize about the contents, we are more likely to take an idea from a non-sexual source and develop this into a sexual one. Unsurprisingly, younger women report a greater variety of fantasy images than older women, as if they have explored a richer vein of sexual possibilities through their lives. But all of us have favourites or at any rate typical themes that we go back to again and again.

*My favourite fantasies always involve people lusting after me, men whom everyone else wants. Both my previous partners were extremely popular with women, so there's something I like about having sexual power over men who hold sexual power over others. It's about being the one who gets the cream, but more than that, I have to be the one the cream lusts over.*

Perhaps the most basic fantasy is to imagine ourselves making love in an unusual setting. These are often romantic but, as with all fantasies, unlikely or out of our reach: '*A log cabin with the snow falling . . . a castle with fourposter bed . . . the Taj Mahal by moonlight . . . a glass-built room in the middle of the high street so that we could see out but no one could see in.*' Fantasies may be risky and impossible – often illegal – usually because they involve being seen or caught: '*On top of a fire engine . . . on the top of a double decker bus . . . in the lobby of Lloyd's bank.*' Interestingly, some people's fantasies are not nearly so risky as other people's reality, as described in chapter 19!

Many of us have fantasies about being with a different partner, though if we start to fantasize seriously about someone available, then this isn't so much arousing as a cause for concern and possibly preventative action. So we usually think about a sufficiently unlikely or outrageous partner so that we don't feel we're being disloyal and imagine: '*being taken by a muscular bronzed stable boy over a saddle . . . the window cleaner opening the window, climbing in, ripping off his clothes*'. This mental change of partner allows us to contact all the arousal of surprise and novelty – while still remaining in control.

We also often fantasize about women. Even those respondents who say they have never seriously considered a lesbian relationship find something fascinating about the thought of woman-to-woman sex with its overtones of forbidden pleasure. 'Straight' respondents tend to imagine another woman as part of a threesome, or '*with a man watching us*', while lesbian respondents often say that they imagine several women, watching and taking part.

*My favourite fantasy is being held down by two gorgeous women who want to make love to me. Maybe it will come true one day. I still occasionally fantasize about men but would never go back to them – it's weird.*

## MORE FANTASIES

Another favourite theme is forced sex. We imagine being overcome or being made to have pleasure: very few respondents actually said they wanted to be raped or feel pain, though one woman writes: '*He would tie me to the bed with chains so tight that I would be bleeding, then he would just totally make love to me for hours on end.*' More usual were accounts of '*being suspended somehow in a dark, warm room and being touched all over . . . being blindfolded . . . being a sex slave*'. We seem to be a little guilty about this kind of fantasy, not so much about the sex but more about the domination aspects. We feel that we shouldn't, even in our thoughts, accept the idea of women as submissive. So though many women do seem to recognize clearly the distinction between awful reality and the safe controlled forced sex of their fantasies, they squirm a little as they write their accounts of them.

We're not nearly so embarrassed about those fantasies where women are dominant. Many of us like to be *'women on top'* in our minds, semi-raping our partner, tying him up, whipping him and forcing him to undergo man-to-man sex. We feel unworried by this because we see it as so removed from what we could do in reality, whereas male-female violence is a fact of life.

*My favourite fantasy is that I force my partner to be a love slave to two men. I have a picture in my head of my partner on all fours with a lead around his neck, being held by a man in front. I force my partner to perform oral sex on this man by whipping him. I then tell the other man to go behind my partner and have anal sex with him. The man grabs my partner's thighs and does this quite roughly. To show that my partner is grateful to the two men and to me for finding them, he is forced to make love to me and comes almost immediately. I never usually get beyond that scene.*

By far our most common fantasy, though, is of taking part in group sex. Because it is an alien concept, to us as well as to our partners, we seem to find it irresistible, though far fewer of us would want to do it in real life – and hardly anyone fantasizes about a partner doing it. We love the thought of multiple sensation; of being overcome by so much pleasure that we cannot resist; of being unable to choose (or sometimes even know) which partner has us next: *'I fantasize of having sex with a man and about six others standing there naked watching, waiting their turn.'*

## SHARING FANTASIES

When it comes actually to sharing our fantasies, some of us are wary. We like to keep our special images private, because we feel they will be spoilt if someone else knows. We want to keep them for private masturbation. Or, more often, we think our partner will disapprove or be embarrassed. We feel about our fantasies much the same as we do about our past sex lives – that we should be ashamed of them: *'He would go spare if he heard any of these things ... if he could read my mind, he would be completely disgusted.'*

Those of us who do share our imaginings say that we do it for arousal and to build trust and closeness with our partner. We may talk about our fantasies as we have them, using them as a prelude to love-making. We can also use them as an instant 'distanced-turn on' to get our partner aroused where there's no possibility of partnership sex, during phone calls or over a restaurant meal. Sharing fantasies in the car is another favourite, possibly to the accompaniment of masturbation, with the excitement of knowing that we can only go so far and no further: *'My husband talks to me about things he would like to do to me and what he would like me to do to him while we are driving along in the car.'*

We also often choose to do the ultimate – to act out our fantasies. It feels as if the watershed is sharing them; once the silence is broken, many couples are able to go further and act them out. The only reasons some women give for not doing so are that *'there's no way they will be as good as the fantasy,'* and *'it is very difficult to find people to share our interests.'* But if we are keen – and our partners are almost always willing and enthusiastic – then many of us do seem to be able to recreate very effectively in reality the arousal we feel in our fantasies.

Of course, as mentioned before, this only applies to some fantasies, the ones that can successfully be translated into real life – though where they can't, we adapt what we fantasize about. We tone down the rape so that our partner simply holds us down; we adapt the thought of having group sex so that it is our partner who plays more than one role.

Many of our scenarios are straightforward sex, where our lover acts out our fantasy of being made love to in a special way. One blindfolds the other then *'arouses them in whatever way they can think of'*, we have oral sex in unusual places, murmur special words to each other while having sex.

> *My favourite fantasy is about a large man pinning me against a wall and nibbling against me while playing with my clit and urging me to orgasm with quite foul language – usually in Jamaican patois (I'm Jamaican). With my present partner I try to recreate my favourite fantasy since he's Jamaican too, by urging him to talk dirty and be quite dominant.*

Or we take on roles. We pretend that we are different people from whom we really are: *'We pretend we're both still eighteen and have just met ... we act out being on an aeroplane with my partner the passenger and me an airhostess.'* We may dress up, with clothes from our wardrobe or with ones specially bought for the occasion from a sex shop: *'Stockings ... heels ... a basque ... rubber ... leather ... army uniforms ... schoolgirl.'* A favourite is to combine our fantasies with some mild bondage: *'I imagine being captured by savages and tied up. My partner always rescues me and we have sex while I'm tied up.'* And one of the most tantalising accounts was this comment.

*My favourite fantasy is being naked on the floor and getting my husband who is an artist to paint my body with all types of paints and brushes, preferably edible paint. And yes we do act out that fantasy.*

The majority feeling, then, about having and sharing fantasies is that it is a delightful and extremely unthreatening thing to do with a loving partner. It tells us that we are relaxed and at ease with each other in bed. It reassures us that we are safe — we couldn't possibly act out fantasies with a partner we felt wary of. It shows us that we can be creative and playful, and that we are committed to fulfilling each other's needs, if only in imagination. We have nothing but good to say about a partner who accepts sexual fantasies and about a relationship that includes them.

*As I trust a partner, sex becomes more imaginative: sexual aids, vibrators, dressing up, school girl, rubber. My present boyfriend and myself are getting more and more imaginative, like I have never been before or possibly will ever again.*

VITAL STATISTICS

53.3 per cent of women have used sex aids

45.7 per cent of women have posed for sexual photographs

37.4 per cent of women have tried S and M games

11 per cent have had group sex

64 per cent feel bad about the thought of anal sex

# 19. On the wild side

*The most exciting thing I have ever done sexually has been on various occasions giving myself completely to my partner to do with what he wanted and despite inhibitions going for unusual and challenging experiences.*

WHEN IT COMES to 'variations on a theme' in sex, we are wary. We are happy to make love one-to-one, to cuddle, to stimulate, to give and receive oral sex, to have intercourse. But once we add in extras – sex aids, photographs, ropes, whips, non-vaginal positions or another person, then over half of the women in the survey draw back and are unsure. Certainly the number of interested women is higher than it would have been thirty years ago; but equally that number shows that we don't completely accept all sexual alternatives. There can be a number of reasons for this: we may feel that sex is about two people, with nothing added. We may need sex to be exclusively genital. We may be wary of things of which we have no experience. Whatever the reasons, while fantasizing about many of these things is acceptable, in real life we are still more likely to steer clear as we are to be enthusiastic.

## SEX AIDS

Sex aids make us feel we are lacking in love. Whether a vibrator, vaginal love eggs, a dildo – or anything else that might stimulate us to orgasm – we tend to feel that using such aids, with or without our partner, is somehow selfish and disloyal. Those 50 per cent of women who don't use them at all mainly *'don't think they're necessary'*, though some have been too embarrassed to try. Or they may have tried them and just not liked them: *'The noise was too offputting so it went in the dustbin.'* The overall feeling is that with a good relationship, we won't need or want sex aids.

Even where we do use aids, there is still the same feeling of slight unease. As with masturbation, we tend to indulge less when we are in a steady relationship and more when we are on our own, as if sex aids and partnership love-making are mutually exclusive. As with masturbation too, we may worry that we'll get dependent, or that *'I might get to like sex aids too much and not enjoy real sex.'* We do have a deep fear that if we can pleasure ourselves, we won't need our partner to do it for us. In fact the direct opposite seems to be true; the more we are able to please ourselves, the more we learn about our own response, and so the more we'll be able to enjoy ourselves with our partner. But often if our love-making with him isn't really pleasing us, any alternative that arouses us more also makes us feel guilty.

> *I usually use an electrical massager on my nipples or to stimulate my clitoris. I use a candle to insert into my vagina as well. I usually sit on the floor and often read a favourite erotic book such as* Emmanuelle *while masturbating. I usually reach orgasm when using a massager, though it makes me feel slightly guilty. I'd like to be able to orgasm more just using my fingers.*

Even if we're secure about using sex aids, our partner may not be. He may feel usurped or threatened. The woman who writes, *'I am considering buying a vibrator to use in secret to satisfy myself,'* may sound paranoid, but her action seems more understandable when we read of the woman who *'used a vibrator sometimes alone. When I told my partner, he threw it away.'* Our partners may indeed feel that we don't value their contribution and are coming to rely on our own inventiveness for sexual satisfaction. Maybe if they read those parts of this book that explain just how much more we value partnership sex than any other option, they'll be reassured.

What do we get from using sex aids? Pure pleasure is the main thing; a different sensation from fingers or tongue. We may be able to reach orgasm with sex aids where we can't alone: *'Sometimes I use just my fingers, but I find it more difficult to reach an orgasm this way.'* We also get a sense of naughtiness, of being a bit exotic in our tastes.

If our partner likes the idea, sex aids can also be good for both of us: *'I have two vibrators. My partner knows I have them and jokes about my wearing the batteries out.'* He may use a vibrator himself, on us, as foreplay, or something we can use while he watches. He can use sex aids for extra stimulation during intercourse. And particularly if he thinks that our masturbating is a good thing, a partner may even encourage us to use sex aids when alone: *'I have a vibrator which belongs to my partner. He is keen on my using it even when he isn't there.'*

The final judgement then seems to be that where we use sex aids, they give us a great deal of physical pleasure. But the emotional and partnership side-effects are such that we're only slowly becoming able to enjoy that pleasure fully. Maybe we'll feel better about it in time.

*My ex-fiancé and I used sex aids. We got some underwear and a vibrator from an Ann Summer's party. I also had those love egg things, which was nice. I'd wear them all day to work then he'd jump on me when I got home. I don't use them now, because my ex took them all with him when he went. My current partner doesn't know about that, and he has never mentioned using them.*

## EXOTIC PHOTOGRAPHS

When it comes to sexual photographs, once again we are equally divided in our tastes. Half of us have, and half haven't, half are for, and half are against. Whether or not we would consider posing for a sexual photograph ourselves largely depends on how we feel about our bodies. And, of course, many of us don't feel good: *'I never would pose unless I lost three or four stone in weight.'* For here again we compare ourselves to an ideal – and find ourselves wanting.

Those of us who would like to be photographed are not necessarily happier with our bodies than those who wouldn't. Instead we're just happy with the thought of our partner capturing us on film. We feel that because he accepts the way we look, then we can too. But we still insist on privacy. Time and again women say that they'd love to be photographed, would find it exciting and arousing – as long as it was only for their partner's eyes only.

For we don't mind doing intensely intimate things so long as no one but our lover watches us doing them. We worry that such photos might get into the wrong hands, be seen by people we know personally or professionally. And we are very aware that while a present lover may revel in our nudity, others could use it against us. So we take precautions: we film only our bodies not our faces; we erase the tape afterwards; we burn the negatives: *'My ex-fiancé wanted a photo of my breasts, but I destroyed it when I could no longer trust him.'*

If these precautions are taken, though, we can love being photographed. We want to see how we look, to try out erotic positions. It turns us on to see ourselves naked and posing.

> *I've had photos taken of me semi-naked, dressed like a soft-porn mag woman. I was trying on some new clothes, and I thought I'd like some photos, so I dropped the camera in my partner's lap and asked him to take some. I thought they would all be cringe-worthy, but despite the bad light and setting, and the fact that my partner is crap at taking photos, I was surprised at the way some turned out. We would like to get a camcorder and make our own sex film, just for a laugh really. It would be a turn-on to do it.*

## PARTNER AS PHOTOGRAPHER

There's a sense in which a partner's wanting to photograph or film is a real compliment, a real sign of love. That in itself makes it worth while, quite apart from the fact that taking the photo probably also turns him on. And our partners do want to film us. They love *'catching us unawares . . . in the shower . . . in bed . . . in the bath . . . in my underwear'.* They constantly ask us to pose, loving to capture our beauty, and sometimes so proud of it that they take things a little too far.

> *I had photos taken by a partner. He loved me posing for him indoors and outdoors, naked or semi-naked, in tight, sexy, revealing clothes. But he was so thrilled with them that he used to show them to his friends. I was horrified at that and destroyed a lot of them. I still have some of the nicer shots though.*

When it comes to videoing, not surprisingly we have to cooperate more with our partners; they can't simply 'jump' us coming out of the shower. We have to plan what we are going to film and then carry it out. So, in general, women who say they have been videoed are likely to be in slightly longer-term relationships and tend to be more trusting of their partners.

Videos go one step further than photographs. They can film movement – so, for the first time, many of us can see ourselves making love. We say it feels strange, and once again we may compare ourselves to what we have seen on the media and find ourselves wanting. But it also gives

us a real sense of ourselves as sexual people and can make us feel proud
of our skill and eroticism.

*My husband and I hired a camera to video the children. Then we
videoed ourselves; we put the camera on the dressing table and left it to
run while we had sex. I felt odd watching it afterwards as the feelings
did not show on the video. It turned me on watching it though. I would
do it again.*

It seems as if amateur sexual photography and videoing are certainly
going to increase. Despite our wariness, we enjoy both the actual
experience of filming and the end-results. More than that, some of us
would also be prepared to break the privacy barrier and do the same on
a professional film. Many specified that they wouldn't do it completely
nude, or wouldn't do the full sex act, and most said that the film would
have to be *'tasteful . . . legitimate . . . not porn'.* But they would allow themselves to be photographed sexually and would enjoy the experience — and
that in itself means that our attitudes have changed over the years.

## ANAL SEX

One of the most negative reactions in the whole questionnaire came with
women's responses to anal sex. The words flew off the page, shrieking that
64 per cent of women hate the thought of it and that both among those
who have never tried it and those who have, the verdict is negative:
*'Perverted . . . unnatural . . . unnecessary . . . risky . . . My anus has an exit-
only sign across it.'* We seem to object to anal sex not only because it can
cause disease if wrongly handled but also because it's not real sex. As well
as being illegal, it seems unnatural, as if our vaginas aren't good enough:
*'If I was asked to participate in buggery, I would suggest they find a male
partner or get themselves a plastic doll. Anything other than me.'*

Reaction against anal sex was strongest among those women who
have tried it and hated it. Objections are very specific, describing what
was felt during the experience and what the physical and emotional after-
effects were: *'A tense experience . . . like a painful Chinese burn . . . I cried
for half an hour . . . I had urinary infection after it . . . My husband forced
me to have anal sex. I never forgave him. I never, never want to have anal
sex again.'*

Where we have tried it and liked it though, we feel equally strongly.
This group, 11.8 per cent of women, doesn't seem to agree with the
negative images of unnatural sex or disease. They have instead positive
images of the total intimacy that anal sex offers: *'I have done it to be totally
his,'* and the pleasure that we are able to feel *'fun . . . very different . . . slow*

*and sensual ... incredible ... I was very surprised to discover that I could actually orgasm via the anus.'*

Some women also like the fact that anal sex is one of the very few intimate acts that a man and woman can do to each other equally when using fingers or sex toys. Several women say they brought their partners to orgasm with fingers inserted in the anus. One who enjoys anal sex, even though she admits to discomfort, said: *'I'll never forget one of the first times I did it to him properly. I really went for it in a big way (ha! ha!), and he couldn't believe how he felt the next day, hardly able to walk and having trouble going to the toilet! It felt good that he finally knew how it can make you feel.'*

Our final judgement on anal sex, then, is that for those who don't like it, it is one of the worst possible sexual acts. For those who do get pleasure from it, it's an acquired taste that in the end proves extremely pleasurable.

> *It was something I shied away from thinking it was dirty until I experienced my own pleasure in receiving oral sex or being fucked vaginally while wearing a butt plug. As a way of including more of the body and finding other sensitive and responsive areas, I've enjoyed my experience.*

## TO DO OR BE DONE TO

The issue of 'active or passive' in bed is a broad one. It can include simply preferring to act or to be acted upon, or it can refer to sado-masochism.

In general in bed we divide between those who like to be passive and those who like to share the action with a partner. Only five women from the whole survey say that they much prefer solely taking the lead in bed, and even they like that only if it really turns the man on.

For most of us feel that sharing the action in bed is the most loving way to organize our relationship. We want to both give and receive, want divided control, want *'a meeting of equals'*. We think like this often because we believe in that as a sexual philosophy and often because we find that being able to be both assertive and passive gives us most pleasure. We like to set a varied agenda, with lots of options both of doing and being done to, then to choose which option according to our mood, our sexual desires and our physical state: *'I have no rules ... I think it's good not to have set ideas and to do what you feel like at the time.'*

But while this is the ideal, some of us admit that it takes more energy and confidence to 'do' than 'to be done to'. So if we feel tired and vulnerable, we tend to be more passive. And if we feel inhibited, we may have to struggle against that in order to take the initiative. Some women admit that they have in the past been passive, but as they become more confident, *'I'm gradually doing more in bed.'*

This passivity may well underpin the feelings of the third of women who say that they always prefer to 'be done to'. Perhaps this indicates a lack of confidence, in the same way as it did when we were first starting to have sex; we may prefer to 'be done to' because then at least we know that we cannot help but get things right: *'I don't feel confident about doing.'* Of course there are also totally undistressed reasons why we like to be passive in bed. Quite simply we may like to receive pleasure, in the totally concentrated way we can only when we don't need to worry about reciprocating. And many women report that their passivity complements their partner's wish to take the lead.

## S AND M

When the survey questions move from asking about women's being active to being dominant, from their being passive to being submissive, the answers get a little more wary. When the questions ask about sado-masochism itself, then the answers become positively anxious. And all of a sudden there's a very wide variety of definitions being discussed. We may shriek that we're not into S and M and then go on to say that we don't mind being handcuffed. We may say we've tried heavy S and M – and then describe being handcuffed. In answer to an identical question, we may call sado-masochism *'disgusting ... crap ... perverted ... sick ... people who enjoy this sort of thing have a problem ... and should have their heads examined,'* and *'we tried it and we ended up in a fit of giggles.'* It is likely that these respondents are actually commenting on two totally different aspects of a range of dominance-submission options. And so it's really quite difficult to be clear from the questionnaire answers just what women feel, simply because they may be reporting their emotions about totally different activities.

To be specific though, 40 respondents are into milder forms of S and M such as bondage. And three-quarters of those who've tried them repeat them. They like being tied up, with ropes, ribbons, scarves or handcuffs, and they like feeling helpless. They mention it a great deal when asked what is the most exciting sexual thing they've done.

*The most exciting thing I've ever done was making love to a para. He was in charge of the prison for the night, and I went to see him. He locked us both in a cell and tied me up and made love to me. It was short and sweet but very exciting because of the risk of being caught by his boss.*

Respondents like reciprocal bondage: *'I've tied my partner up and vice versa; we also blindfold whoever is tied up.'* What follows is usually sexual teasing, being masturbated by hand or mouth until the person tied up is writhing but not allowed to come. This is very exciting in the same way as any masturbation from a loving partner is exciting, but with the added bonus of our not being able to control it, not knowing what is going to happen next.

Liking to be tied up doesn't seem to be about not wanting responsibility, as many experts claim; many women who enjoy bondage are also quite happy to turn the tables and take the lead sexually. Rather, being tied is far more about wanting to be surprised, about taking the element of predictability out of the sexual equation for just a little while, about liking to feel slightly at risk: *'When he ties me up to the bed, and I feel totally helpless, this really does make me feel very horny.'*

Equally, liking to do the tying up doesn't seem to mean that we feel any kind of antagonism or cruelty towards our partner: we simply like being in control for a while. In both cases, in fact, there often seems to be an exchange of control. We often seem to prefer what is happening if we take it in turns and experience first being submissive, then being dominant.

*I enjoyed one session in which we had each other tied to the bed in turns. I wore his shirt and tie and his aftershave, mounted him, dismounted and masturbated in front of him with a cucumber. He then tied me to the bed and teased me so much I felt that if he did not enter me I would explode.*

## LIKING PAIN

Just a few women who responded to the survey are aroused by pain itself. The furthest any respondent went along the path of masochism was to say that: *'I like being whipped and hit.'* The furthest any woman said she has been along the path of sadism was *'My boyfriend sometimes likes to be hurt by my gripping hard on his penis and jerking it roughly.'* Neither woman gives any more details than these, and so although both activities sound like real violence, there's no way of knowing whether 'whipping' actually means stroking with a soft leather thong, and whether 'jerking roughly' means no more than a gentle tug.

Other women's accounts suggest that none of the rest of respondents seriously harms their partners at all, and that they allow themselves only to be smacked, slapped or lightly bitten rather than seriously hurt. A partner may act out a schoolgirl/teacher fantasy by putting us over his knee and spanking us. We may tie him up and nibble him, from top to toe, occasionally leaving teeth marks as we go. And we enjoy it: we do get aroused, we do come – and we do enjoy some pain as we climax: *'I enjoy being tied up and for my bottom to be slapped hard during orgasm.'*

It's significant that whereas with bondage both partners often do the tying and the being tied, taking turn and turn-about, with pain-giving there wasn't that kind of equality. Couples take on fixed roles of doer and done-to and aren't really comfortable changing places. In every case, though, both partners have to be equally aroused by what is going on, or sooner rather than later there is a great deal of resentment, and often the relationship ends. Where there is equal arousal, however, both bondage and mild pain seem to create a strong connection between us and our partner.

A final word. Those women who describe enjoying mild S and M activities seem to universally be in control of what was happening – even if they are being tied up or dominated. Many of them stress that both the bondage and the smacking are surrounded by a number of safeguards. It's worth while repeating these: you only do these things with someone you trust; you both agree with what's happening, always; you don't do anything humiliating or truly painful; and if the person being 'done to' says stop, you stop immediately.

## SHARING PARTNERS

As already mentioned in chapter 18, we do quite often like to fantasize about shared sex. We like the thought of having sex with more than one man because we like the idea of being the centre of attention. The idea of group sex is appealing in theory, because we think we might learn sexually and because the thought of all that pleasure turns us on. And when we think of threesomes we feel that we would be 'wife number one', and the other woman or man would be an enjoyable addition, not a threat to our position.

In real life, even thirty years after the sexual revolution, it's actually very different. Only a small number of women say that they have had triangular sex, and the verdict is generally negative. Hardly any of these women speak of the physical pleasure involved, and most of them report feeling strong negative emotions. The first kind of threesome, which a handful of women have experienced, is where a woman's male partner has friends whom he wants to impress or please in some way. He may feel he's showing his wife off, or even that he's showing her how proud he is of her. The woman doesn't like what is happening, but often says little at the time because she doesn't want to upset her partner. Afterwards, often after the relationship has ended, she then feels resentful, angry and degraded.

*My husband's friend started to play with my breast. I did nothing because I knew it was what my husband wanted.*

*He called his friend into the room while we were doing it. His friend was talking to him saying he was getting a hard-on. I felt like a whore.*

*I regularly used to participate in threesomes with my ex-husband and friends of his, at his initiation. It was only after I left my husband and told my sister-in-law that I realized that I was being used. At the time I hadn't seen it like that, and my husband would have been horrified if he'd thought that's how I felt.*

The only completely positive account of a male-male-female three-some that appeared in women's responses is this one. The key to it seems to be that both men had designed the event for the woman's pleasure and weren't doing it to boost their own egos. Also, throughout the proceedings, they made sure she really wanted what was happening. The result is a story so obviously pleasurable to the woman concerned that it could almost be one of her own fantasies.

*They were cousins; one was my lover, and they planned it together for my nineteenth birthday. We all went to L's apartment, and B and I snuggled on the couch; then he suggested that L give me a shoulder rub. It seemed a bit funny, but we were all friendly, and it seemed harmless enough. Then B stood up and hugged me to him, started running his hands up and down my body. L came and stood behind me, hugging me from the back. Suddenly I dared to realize what they were doing. B turned me to L, and we kissed. We swapped the kisses back and forth, L started to touch my breasts – I was pretty hesitant, but let him. Then B started going down on me. I was embarrassed with L watching, but he started whispering in my ear how beautiful and horny I looked. I closed my eyes and just listened and felt.*

*After I came, L asked whether I wanted to sleep with him. I looked at B, and he seemed to be fine about it. So they started foreplay again, and L slipped inside me. It was strange, but exciting to have someone I knew so little screw me – he was smaller than B, but thick, his body weight different. I didn't understand why B started to caress my bottom, putting KY on my anus. I started protesting, then, suddenly I thought, Fuck it, this is unbelievable, and I let him get inside my ass. It was an indescribable feeling – hundreds of sensations. Basically, we kept falling asleep, waking up and doing more.*

## TWO WOMEN, ONE MAN

What happens when the balance of a threesome is reversed, and the third party is female? In our fantasies the experience is full of physical pleasure; in real life, emotions such as jealousy, resentment or disgust are usually uppermost. The physical experience may be enjoyable, in fact on a few occasions we find that we like sex with women more than sex with men. And, just occasionally, we kiss and hug and are able to share almost equally the affection between the three of us.

But far more often such threesomes prove an emotional disaster. It's worst when there is no real agreement on what's happening: we may fall asleep sharing a bed with our partner and a female friend and then wake up *'to find my partner sleeping with a friend. It made me feel ill.'* And even if there is total agreement, and we make love only after much discussion, somehow the balance of emotion always seems to tilt, leaving one person alone: *'She wasn't prepared to share, so I kicked her out ... I watched for a short while, tried to join in some way, but it didn't work. I felt left out by the two people I cared most about sexually at the time ... my girlfriend and I decided to fuck his brains out, then when he wanted more, we refused.'* In the long term it almost always leads to upset and unhappiness: one partner may be satisfied, but the other often feels betrayed.

## PROFESSIONAL SHARING

What if instead of ending up in bed with a friend, we go to an arranged sex party? Here, everyone knows that they are there for sex and not for a relationship. We don't need to worry about what will happen after we've been to bed with someone, because we will probably never see each other again.

If anything, this does make things easier. If we are single, we may be free and want to have sex without bothering with any ritual of courting. The few single women who say they've been to professional sex parties generally found them fun as long as they didn't get stuck with a partner they didn't like. But without the long-term goal of a relationship in sight, the general judgement seems to be that going to a large number of such parties is ultimately boring.

*There was one couple, four men and myself. The man I originally contacted wasn't very nice; he made the others think I was his possession, so the couple, myself and two men moved to the bedroom. Eventually we all got undressed and a group session followed. As the evening wore on, so some people left. At the time when sleep was suggested, there were the couple, myself and two men. The couple moved to one corner, leaving*

*me with the two men. The idea was to sleep, but I didn't; well, would*
*you with two rampant men at your side?*

For a couple, swinging or partner-swapping doesn't seem to lead to
the same feelings of personal betrayal as a simple threesome does, either
because the whole issue has to be so thoroughly discussed beforehand; if
either partner is really against the idea, then usually the couple doesn't
even attend in the first place. The original impetus will often come from
the male partner, with the woman going along willingly but maybe a little
warily. It can be fun; of the few women who'd gone partner-swapping,
some said that they'd found it exciting to think of beforehand, others that
they liked being shown off by their partner, yet others that they'd enjoyed
using their expertise. But the sex itself was not usually all that good, and
it often felt dangerous. One woman says that it has made her realize what
was wrong with her relationship, and she feels it contributed to the breakdown of her partnership. None of the respondents said that they now
regularly attended group sex parties, either singly or with their partner.

The current judgement, then, on sharing is more or less the same as
on most of the 'wilder' options the questionnaire covered. We will dabble
out of curiosity, and we will often enjoy ourselves. But, equally often, we
will get our fingers burned. Sexual freedom may be here to stay, but there
are still many many things that most of us simply don't want to do.

*I've had sex with my partner in front of someone else, on two occasions*
*(but different voyeurs). I did it to please my then partner who loved*
*experimenting with sex. But I did not like it; I felt cheap and humiliated*
*both times. The same partner used to sleep with other women but not in*
*front of me, although he did it very noisily in the room next to me.*
*I found it very humiliating, and I felt used and worthless. He was a right*
*bastard really, God knows why I stayed as long as I did.*

VITAL STATISTICS

70.4 per cent of women have regretted making love at some point or another

57 per cent say yes even when they don't want to

18.5 per cent feel under pressure from partners

19.8 per cent do things in bed that make them uneasy

33.1 per cent say they have been forced to so domething sexual

80.7 per cent of women feel negative when refused sex by their partner

Over three-quarters of women who say no to sex feel guilty about it

# 20. Saying no

*My first husband would cajole me into doing things which I have never repeated. This was usually when he had been reading pornographic magazines. They included my having to dress as a maid; stand naked while ironing; allowing him to push a bottle into my vagina; having to tell him 'dirty' stories while he masturbated. I naïvely believed it was a wife's duty to obey. When I did resist, he plied me with Barcardi.*

THERE WAS A point, during the preparation of this book, when it was necessary to stop and recheck the statistics. It was hard to believe what they showed. The figures said that three-quarters of the women have had sex when they didn't really want to. And over a third of women have been raped or abused.

The picture is of a vast undercurrent of unwilling sex – not a reluctance to have sex or a basic female frigidity, but a sense of sex that takes place with mixed feelings, with regrets, with emotional pressure from a partner to fulfil his desires, with internal pressure from the woman herself to live up to her emotional ideals. The picture is of regular occasions where the woman does not join in the decision to have sex, of so-called love-making that takes place in a relationship that is far from loving. In addition, not merely at the tip of the iceberg but for a massive third of women, there is sex that is forced – abuse or rape, as opposed to unhappy or unwilling sex.

Yet is there a difference? If sex without consent is defined as a woman's opening her mouth and shouting (or whispering) no, then only a third of the women have been so abused. If sex without consent is defined as a woman opening her legs when not all of her, body and soul, wants sex, then 75 per cent have so suffered. The figure is appalling.

Of course these women may not suffer so all the time. In terms of forced sex, we are talking about one incident in a lifetime. But in terms of unhappy or uncertain sex, we are looking at a range, from a woman reporting a single time where she was *'grabbed, jumped or pushed'*, through to regular, often nightly bouts of unwilling coupling within a stable relationship. And, of course, every one of these incidents, however rarely or however often they happen, has repercussions throughout a lifetime. They don't ruin sex – but they spoil the true enjoyment of it. They only rarely create total frigidity – but they frequently take away, often for ever, the potential for a lifetime of uninhibited, confident sexuality. It is as if, along with the freedom women gained in the middle of this century, we also gained an increased potential to be oppressed. Along with the ability to say yes that was given to us through the pill, we have somehow failed to achieve the possibility of saying no.

## NO TO CASUAL SEX

Most of our sexual regrets – and 70.4 per cent of women have had sex with people and regretted it – seem to be around having sex with strangers. We don't want to say yes at the time, but we end up agreeing. It seems to have happened more in the past than it does now. If we are an older woman, we look back to that time just after the introduction of the pill, when sex was not only allowed but also demanded: *'I only ever screwed people who wanted to screw me ... I never used to consider my own feelings.'* If we're younger, we look back to just a few years ago, when casual sex was totally acceptable and therefore expected: *'I've often had sex with a partner even though I didn't really want it.'*

Why do we have sex with people when we are unwilling? Quite a few of us, with some embarrassment, mention alcohol. It overrides our natural objections at the time but leaves us feeling later that we should have said no. We know that, had we been sober, we would have said no.

Or we want to please: *'I was brought up to put men first and always try to please them ... I got my pleasure from seeing their pleasure.'* There's also a sense of obligation. If we hardly know our partner, and we feel we've given him 'come-on' signals or allowed him to kiss us goodnight, then we feel that perhaps we have an obligation to go the whole way. We go through with it knowing at the time that it feels wrong; and as soon as it's over, we regret it.

Or, we are wary that if we don't give out, we'll be forced to. Some 9.6 per cent of women say that, at some time or other, they have said yes to sex on a date because they feared that if they didn't they would be raped. None of them says that the fear was based on evidence of violence by a partner, more on a sense that, having gone so far, to stop would cause trouble.

It can be that, at the time, we don't actually want sex. We want pleasure, comfort or company. We want a kiss and a cuddle or reassurance. We want the evening to be over and the man to give up and go away. What we actually get is sex. Afterwards we realize that it is a mistake, and, to remind us, we now experience an almost physical sensation of nausea or rage when we remember what happened: *'I regret having a one-night stand. I was drunk, and he was very aggressive. It has affected every other relationship since.'*

## NO TO PARTNERSHIP SEX

Even where we know our partner and feel comfortable with him, the issue of saying no can still arise. If our partner wants sex more than we do, or if he wants sex when we don't, then 57 per cent of women do say yes sometimes, even when they want to say no.

Why should we want to say no? It's mostly down to physical reasons – although more than one woman hints that her physical unwillingness hides an emotional withdrawal. We are tired, not well, on our period. We are emotionally upset, or angry. We *'have something to think about and don't want to be interrupted'*. Or we are unhappy with our partner and with the relationship.

Our reasons for nevertheless saying yes pick up on the most selfless motives that we have for agreeing to casual sex. If we love our partner, then we want to make him happy. We also don't want to feel that ours is a relationship where we are pulling back. We feel we have a duty to our partner – and he may agree: *'He believes that a man's sexual needs need regular attention ... My husband says that that [sex] is what a man must have.'* And, all too often, our reason is that if we don't say yes, there will be emotional trouble: *'I get no rest unless I give in ... to keep the peace ... it's an easy way out ... he'd sulk and we'd row ... I never say no. I say yes because he'll go home if I don't.'* Unfortunately, while in the short term we may make our partner contented and reassure ourselves that we are loving women, the long-term after-effects may be unfortunate.

*I regretted having sex with a previous boyfriend because I didn't want it and only he did. Whenever I had sex with him, it was as a result of his nagging me. I only did it because I'd convinced myself (or rather he'd convinced me) I was being nasty and selfish if I didn't. It made me dislike sex, feel self-conscious, nervous, shy and stupid, as if I couldn't do anything right. This mental attitude has continued since I got rid of this bloke, and it's taken a long time for me to feel happy about sex. I still feel I've got further to go before I can feel utterly like letting go during intercourse and foreplay.*

The reasons given by the 76.7 per cent of women who sometimes say no to their partner when they don't want sex are not by contrast selfish and emotionally hard. On the contrary they feel that it is as loving to be honest as it is to be compliant. Many speak of equality. They say that both they and their partner have the right to say no, because theirs is a respectful relationship. Many say that they are sexual decision-makers within the relationship and that this is what makes their relationship special.

Even so, over three-quarters of women who say no feel guilty about it. They try to be assertive, but they don't want to let their partner down. So women vary: sometimes we say no and stick to it. At other times, we give and take: *'Sometimes you do when you don't really want to, sometimes he does.'* We may agree to cuddle, and if that gets us in the mood we can go ahead: *'We do a test where he has two minutes to turn me on – and he usually does.'* Or we trust that in the end, whatever we are feeling at the moment, we will get turned on. So we go ahead regardless of our feelings.

## WHAT TURNS WOMEN OFF

What happens if a partner suggests something that feels wrong to us, that makes us feel uneasy? We are more than likely to say no – 80.2 per cent of women will do. The sexual novelties we are most wary of are fairly consistent: oral sex with ejaculation, masturbation in front of each other; the woman-on-top position, and, above all, anal sex. We hesitate about these, sometimes because of inhibitions but mainly because they feel bad physically – painful in the case of receiving anal sex, nauseating in the case of giving oral sex.

Most of us, in fact, will not say no the first time a partner requests something: *'I would always try something my partner suggested, but if*

*I didn't like it, I wouldn't do it again.'* But if after that we still can't feel good about what he's suggesting, we do say no; where we may feel guilty saying no to intercourse with our partner, we seem to have much less of a problem about saying no to specific sexual requests. We may find ourselves able to 'lie back and think of England' if he wants to have intercourse, but that's just not possible with activities such as oral sex that demand our active cooperation: we say simply that we cannot do anything we don't like, and that is an end of it.

> *If something comes up between us that I am not sure of, he would know I was not prepared to try. I would expect the same from him. And I would not be involved with a person who would want to push me to do something I'm not happy about.*

Once again we may meet negative reactions from our partner: *'He goes silent and cold if he doesn't get his own way.'* And, equally, if once again we do give in it is for the same reasons as we said yes to sex: a desire to please, a need to love, a wish to avoid emotional pressure. In fact, if we are trying new sex techniques simply because our partner is guilt-tripping us, we never really enjoy them. We may carry out the movements, but our heart – and, more importantly, our passion – is never in what we are doing.

Sometimes, though, we gradually learn to like what before we disliked. If our initial reluctance was based on lack of skill and confidence, we may well in time change our minds and become willing. We develop a skill in oral sex. We adapt to new sexual positions. We learn to masturbate in front of our partner. This never happens if we're pressured. But if our partner is supportive, teaches us, gets aroused by what we do and allows us to gain confidence, what was a no can sometimes develop into a yes: *'We've learnt a lot together. I was really inhibited before I met this partner. He doesn't pressure me, but he does give me support and encouragement.'*

## FORCED SEX

Over a third of women in the survey have had sex acts of many kinds forced on them. This is not just a question of being 'gently persuaded'. These acts happen despite the fact that they make it clear on every level that they don't want sex; their abusers go ahead anyway. This figure is higher than it would have been fifty years ago; one of the results of the sexual revolution is that we are being subjected to a greater degree of sexual abuse. And we are having to learn, painfully, how to oppose that.

Such forced sex includes acts of every kind: *'A man grabbed my breast as I was cycling along ... he promised to use a condom and didn't ... a friend took my generosity for granted and pinned me down for a fuck ... he started touching me and the next minute I woke up, and I could feel something inside me ... I was stripped and shagged by a previous boyfriend ... I was face down on the bed expecting normal intercourse, and he entered my anus ... He started to hit me and forced me to have sex.'* Many of us report violence or the threat of violence being used.

Our abusers tend to be people we know. Many women report being physically forced to have sex by their partner, when they have said no to sex, when their partner is drunk or when he wants to act out his aggression. Just a few report date rape, with boyfriends pressuring for intercourse and then turning to rape when, *'I refused to let him stay or do anything to him.'* We are sometimes abused by male friends, who feel safe and untheatening so are allowed to get close and intimate emotionally, and then want to take things further. Five women have been abused by work colleagues, usually by managers or bosses; these men used the trust they have gained and the authority they have been given to force sex on the women who work for them: *'I was too afraid of losing my job to resist ... My boss abused me, and I was too young to tell anyone ... I was raped by my manager whom I trusted to give me an innocent lift home from work.'*

In particular, six women say that their first experience of intercourse was rape. One was a little girl of 8 years old when she was subjected to full intercourse by her babysitter; another was 10 and was raped by her brother: *'I told my mum I had a period because I didn't know what he'd done.'* These women's accounts are deeply moving, and one can only wonder at the courage they show in even being able to retell the horror of their first initiation.

*I remember my first intercourse experience far too well. I was raped. I was 16. I knew my attacker, who was a lot older than me, and it happened in his flat where he had driven me against my will. It was violent and painful and terrifying. I escaped in the early hours and was physically sick for 24 hours. I told no one for many years, convinced that I had somehow deserved it. This act shaped my sexual outlook.*

*I was sexually abused and raped when I was 11 years old by a stranger in a church. I was held for approximately two hours and made to do everything it is possible for a couple to do in bed. It was reported to the police. The second time I was raped, I did not report it.*

## REACTIONS TO RAPE

In response to being abused, those who have suffered feel every negative emotion ranging from *'annoyed'* to *'dirty ... ashamed ... vile ... cheated ... totally used ... If I had got my hands on the poker, I would have caved his skull in.'* It's very noticeable that feelings fall into one of two categories: either anger or guilt. Fear and disgust seem to run through all the accounts.

Those who feel angry are more likely to be those who have suffered violence or who are clear in their own minds that what was done to them cannot be called anything but wrong.

Those who feel guilty often still wonder whether they could have done anything to stop what happened. Frighteningly they often try to excuse their abusers: *'He probably thought I was playing hard to get ... I was really angry, but I have myself to blame as well ... I guess I didn't say no, but I didn't say yes either ... I guess it was rape because I wasn't able to do anything.'* In fact, what has happened to women who speak like this is often just as terrible and abusive as what has happened to those women who feel angry: the last-mentioned comment, for example, is by a girl who was gang-banged by eight men. But, if we feel guilty, we tend to turn our anger on ourselves and feel bad about our own actions more than about those of our abusers.

## TO TELL OR NOT TO TELL?

Those who don't tell anyone about their abuse are much more likely to be those who feel guilty rather than angry: *'I never told anyone because I thought then that I'd asked for it. Now I don't believe I did.'* They're more likely to be related to or in a relationship with their abuser: *'I did not tell anyone because he was also my lover.'* Or, they are likely to see their abuser on a day-to-day basis; very few of the work-related incidents were reported. Conversely, women are more likely to tell where violence is involved, and where they have received physical rescue or support immediately after the event; it seems as if once over a certain threshold of violence, they usually want to go public.

Where we do tell, however, we are in for a nasty shock. It was horrific to read women's accounts of how people they confided in often disbelieved them, tried to diminish the importance of the attack or simply refused to act. These negative reactions are most typical for women who tell friends, family and partner: *'I told several people including my boyfriend; nobody believed me ... I told someone who laughed and said, "You loved it, you tart" ... My partner wouldn't touch me for a week ... I told my boyfriend, and he beat me up.'* Friends and family don't want to get involved because they think we are looking for attention; they don't want to cause trouble; they think we asked for it. If we feel guilty, they may be affected by that and end up blaming us too. Interestingly, those women who report what has happened to the police or other professionals seem to have been taken more seriously; emotionally, they received a much better deal.

## AFTER-EFFECTS

This lack of support from those close to us could well explain why the after-effects of forced sex last so long. Whether the attack was 'rape with threats' or being touched up, it always marks our life. The effect is worse when we are younger; when the attack includes violence; when our attacker is known to us. We may feel *'vulnerable ... worthless ... shy, quiet and withdrawn for a while afterwards'*. We can find it difficult to relate to partners, particularly if the attack happened when we were very young, before we had a chance to form a serious long-term relationship. We become unable to trust our partners, in bed and out of it; we become wary of really letting go in sex. We often find it hard to trust ourselves.

*These episodes have had a tremendous impact on me emotionally, sexually and physically. Every time I go to the family planning clinic, I am reminded of the latter experience. I blamed myself for a long time when any thing happened to me. I also can get myself into dangerous situations to feed that. I am pleased to say that being aware of these things and accepting them is helping me to come to terms with a lot of things, although I still have a long way to go before I will be able to stop my patterns of self-abuse.*

With all kinds of sexual attack, we do need help. And many women who have been actually raped or sexually abused as children have found the courage to accept personal support or to go for professional help. They see counsellors, they ring professional help lines. They work with their partners to reclaim the pleasure in sex, often by spending a long time doing in bed only what feels absolutely right to them. Happily, things almost always get better. Telling other people and therefore ultimately being relieved of their guilt helps them regain confidence. Having control over what happens in bed lets us regain our sense of personal power.

*The affect the first rape had was that I could not do anything with any partner in bed apart from straight intercourse. When I talked to a counsellor from the Rape Crisis Centre when I was 31 years of age, I was able to enjoy all aspects of sex.*

*When my husband manually stimulated me, I would silently cry and feel so dirty and tell him to stop. The problem has been overcome now but lasted much longer than it needed to because I didn't tell and felt it was somehow my fault, that I'd asked for it.*

Sadly, though, some women don't feel able to turn to anyone for help. They often feel that they haven't suffered all that much: it wasn't 'real rape' because they were involved with their attacker; it wasn't real abuse because it didn't involve intercourse or violence. They still suffer, and what happened still affects their sex lives, but because they don't class themselves as rape victims, they feel they don't deserve or need help. It goes without saying that in fact they do; it is to be hoped that reading this book and sharing other women's experiences will encourage any woman who has had any kind of unwilling sex to get support for herself.

## SAYING NO, SAYING YES

We do need to face the very tricky issue of whether we ourselves are adding to the problems. Are we giving out the wrong signals? Should we be looking at the question of whether no means yes and vice versa. Women give very clear answers when asked about this issue. Firstly, and very definitely, no always means no. If men ignore this, it is a violation: *'When I say no, no is what I mean. If I don't fancy him, I tell him ... What comes out of my mouth must be taken as rigid. My word is law.'*

Secondly, there are those very few of us who admit that we have said no when we really mean yes. But we stress that this is never in an ambiguous situation. It is never with a stranger, a new or short-term partner or with any partner who can't pick up the smile and the wriggle and the clear contradictory signs of arousal. It is never said seriously, always with a shriek of amusement as we are grabbed coming out of the shower or a giggly snuggle as we move closer. And we repeat that a no means a no — except in these very particular, safely intimate situations.

*I've played with it and said no when I really mean yes, within the context of a relationship. But then I'd be really aroused, get a rash around my neck, while my body will be giving inviting, come inside me signals.*

The third kind of answer comes from those women who reckon that they have on occasions added to the overall problem — saying yes when what they really mean is no. A vast majority of women say that they have done this at some time or another. For all the reasons outlined above, they agreed to sex when they didn't really want it — and they realize that in so doing, they were allowing themselves to be oppressed: *'I've realized that this was a stupid game to play, and I no longer indulge in it ... Recently when I've caught myself doing this, I've gone back and been honest about it.'* It seems that, now that the social restrictions have been taken away, and women are allowed to agree to sex, we need many years of practice before we can happily, guiltlessly and effectively learn to refuse it.

However, the responsibility for having sex when a woman says yes and means no does not simply lie with the woman; it is a dual responsibility. Women in the survey resent the fact that *'partners have never queried the difference between a congruent yes and an uncertain one. They don't want to know.'*

If partners are interested in knowing when a woman is saying yes unwillingly or not totally congruently, then the signs are there. We can say the word yes and mean something very different. One woman explained it like this:

> *If I say yes and mean no, then I'm lying to myself and lying to my partner as well. My body language doesn't lie. When I'm saying yes and meaning no, I'll be unresponsive, stiff, hesitant, discouraging and unaroused.*

The bottom line, then, is this. Women don't say no when they mean yes, and a no should always be taken as a no, whatever the other signs. But all too often we can say yes when we really mean no, when we're not sure, when we'd quite like to wait until the relationship is more established, or until we are feeling better in ourselves. We are slowly learning to overcome the internal and external pressures that persuade us to say yes when we want to say no, but in the meantime it would be good to get some support from our partners. If we say yes, check that. Ask again; make sure we mean yes verbally and non-verbally. If you're not completely convinced by our passionate response to you, then why not pull back – even suggest that we wait a while for sex. Such a hesitation will do no harm at all, will re-establish our trust in you. And if our yes is genuine, then we'll let you know immediately.

## WHEN PARTNERS SAY NO

There is a final issue, and it is one that will possibly create a great deal of controversy. This is the question of women's reactions when their partners say no to them. It happens to just over two-thirds of women, and of that two-thirds, 19.2 per cent feel fine about it: *'I respect that ... I feel all right because sometimes I say no ... I knew it wasn't personal ... everyone has their off-days.'*

But, rather embarrassingly, 80.7 per cent of women have a negative reaction to their partners' refusing them sex. We find this incredibly upsetting, for a number of reasons: maybe because it happens so very rarely; maybe because women's role is seen traditionally as the one who agrees not suggests; maybe because we are used to 'being the one who allowed sex'. We suddenly feel that our partner isn't attracted to us, that he doesn't love us, or that there are very serious problems between us: 'Rejected ... hurt ... angry ... humiliated ... frustrated ... neglected ... inadequate ... it nearly ruined our marriage.'

> I have tried to instigate love-making with my present boyfriend about five times, but he ignores it or something. He doesn't respond or he pushes me away. This used to kill me, so I don't do it any more. It just made me feel like a complete fool.

We do try to be understanding. We talk the situation through with our partner. We reassure ourselves and try not to nag. Given time, we sometimes realize that if sex is not on the menu it is because our partner is anxious, tired, or upset: 'I assumed I wasn't turning him on any more, but it turned out to be because of worries about his son and about money problems.'

But – and this is hard to admit – quite often women respond with behaviour that, if it came from men, would be called 'emotional pressure': 'I was furious and had a tantrum ... I walked out ... When days turned to weeks, I got rid of him.' Now, there is absolutely no suggestion that we should say yes to our partners if we don't want to have sex. If anything, the worry is more about the women who say that compromise in bed is the loving solution; yet how can we say yes wholeheartedly to our partners if we don't say no when we want to?

But along with learning not to say yes when we mean no, perhaps we ought also to allow our partners the liberty to say "no" when they want to. They, too, have a right to refuse without its being the end of the world. If there are external pressures, maybe they need support with those. If there are problems in the relationship, let us tackle them directly. And if partners simply want to say no because they're not feeling passionate, then maybe we should allow them that option.

> My partner has only rarely said no to me when I have wanted sex. I have not been disappointed or let down by this, but have tried instead to understand why. It's usually down to tiredness, and I've not pushed the point.

VITAL STATISTICS

40.3 per cent of women are actively unhappy with their sex lives

32.2 per cent of women don't touch other people as much as they want to

7.7 per cent consider their failure to reach orgasm a problem

10 per cent consider lack of desire a problem

68.5 per cent of women want sex more than they are currently getting it

28.3 per cent of women say that their partner has had a sexual problem

# 21. Unhappy sex

*If we're heatedly kissing and touching and undressing each other, and I reach down expecting to find a very full erection, and he's limp, it really bruises my ego, even though his body language and breathing tell me he's turned on.*

WE LOVE SEX and we love our sexual partners. And throughout the survey, women celebrate their own and their partner's sexuality. But, just occasionally in some responses and consistently in others, there is no sense of celebration. Instead there are sexual embarrassments, mistakes, unfulfilled wishes and hopes, or real pain and anger at the fact that love-making is not as good as it could be, or should be. We suffer sexual disappointments where things just don't work out the way we want; we suffer sexual problems where we feel blocked or frustrated.

First, at some time during our lives, in bed or out of it, most of us have made sexual mistakes. We've done something embarrassing, something we regret or are ashamed of; it isn't the end of the world, but when we look back on it, we writhe. Embarrassments seem to fall into two categories: being seen when we didn't want to be and doing something that seems rude or dirty. Both are things that are socially unacceptable: the cringe-factor happens because of other people's disapproval. Being seen is a double-edged sword: many of us both fantasize about risky sex in full view and push the barriers to do it. So many women report having made love in loos, on trains, in cars, and how that was doubly exciting because they might have been seen. But in fact, if we are seen, and those people who see us disapprove, the whole event can switch round and excitement can be replaced by embarrassment.

Rudely embarrassing events are usually to do with bodily fluids. For while it's fine to let our vaginal fluid flow, other elements aren't quite so arousing. One woman couldn't stop herself passing urine on her partner's face. Another farted while receiving oral sex. A third was sick while giving oral sex. A fourth accidentally bit a partner's penis and made it bleed. And another 'had anal sex with a partner, and when he withdrew, his penis had faeces on it'. These incidents do make us cringe even to read about, largely because we feel sorry for the women they happened to – unless, of course we are one of the very few women who find things like this arousing. But there's a certain comfort in hearing about them, because we feel relieved that other people make mistakes too.

## UNHAPPY PARTNERSHIPS

Perhaps our deepest and most unhappy feelings are centred not around sexuality itself but around the relationships that give them their context. In order to have good long-term sex that allows us to develop and expand our potential, we need a partner who supports that. Those of us who don't have a partner at all, where 'there is no one on the horizon' feel deprived and blocked. Those of us who have just split up with a partner are not only mourning their loss (see chapter 23) but also want someone to take their place. And those of us with partners who for some reason or other aren't totally available to us feel constantly frustrated that we can't see more of them:

*The man I want lives 500 miles away . . . with my partner being married we don't have enough time to do things slowly, and he always has to get dressed to go home.*

*I miss the closeness and intimacy of sex, but having left a difficult relationship recently, I feel wary of getting involved seriously with someone else (at present). I would like to have a friendly, casual, occasional sexual partner that I could call on when I feel lonely.*

Where we have a partner, we are certainly not all dissatisfied – though 21.3 per cent of respondents claim that they would like some change in their sexual situation. Most of the women in the survey say they are generally happy and only a small proportion actively want to split up. But where we are unhappy, we are usually deeply so, seeing the problem in our relationship to be critical and often unsolvable. We're not simply complaining about his squeezing the toothpaste in the middle of the tube. Instead, we say that he is the wrong person for us completely, *'I would like to have a female lover,'* or that we don't love him but stick with the relationship because we're married to him.

If we are deeply committed, we often feel we miss *'sex without the complications of a relationship . . . lustful sex with a man I'm not tied to'*, while those of us who are having mainly casual relationships are almost always searching for *'consistency . . . stability . . . commitment'*. And where there are problems, they always spill over into our sex lives. We stop sleeping with our partner, we stop wanting or desiring him: *'I don't love him or feel sexually attracted to him any more.'*

## TOUCHING MISMATCHES

Within a perfectly sound relationship, we may have problems simply because we have differing sexual expectations or inclinations. On the most basic level, where we love cuddling and our partner doesn't, or our partner wants to touch and we don't, then there can be friction. Many women who say that they aren't happy with their sexual situation also report a mismatch between their touching patterns and those of their partner.

If from the start of our relationship we have never been keen on touching, this seems to be down to our upbringing rather than any negative feelings towards our partner. But, once involved, if we find ourselves withdrawing from a partner's touch, it is almost always due to some kind of relationship crisis. We may be disillusioned with our partner or angry with him, either because of frustrations that have built up over the years or because of a sudden problem such as his having an affair. If he then keeps on wanting more touch than we can give him, we can start to feel negative, irritated and stifled.

*My husband does get quite frustrated with me because I do not show affection and love very often. He tends to make me feel claustrophobic sometimes with the amount of affection he shows and always seems to be reaching out for intimacy from me.*

Far more usual is that we want to touch or be touched, and our partner doesn't. 33 per cent of women feel that they aren't getting enough touch from their partner, either because *'it doesn't come naturally to him'* or because of some external stress: *'He is preoccupied with work so he doesn't cuddle as much as I would like . . . when he is depressed he tends to withdraw which I hate.'* To add insult to the neglect we're already feeling, some women also say that their partner gets irritated at their need: *'He says I'm too demanding.'*

## DECLINE IN DESIRE

A large proportion of women – almost all those who are in long-term relationships – say that they aren't making love as often as they could be. They put this down to a number of factors. The main one is that they are tired and stressed: 55.2 per cent say that pressure of work is affecting their sex life, so that they either don't make love for long periods of time, or when they do it takes longer to relax, switch off and enjoy themselves.

> *My job now is very tiring, and I have to be at the office for ten hours each day. I think that if I had a relationship at this moment I would struggle to find time for it, not to mention the energy for it.*

The second main 'dampener' is having children. Nearly three-quarters of women who have children say that this makes a difference to their love-making. Childbirth itself seems to lower our sex drive for months or even years: *'I went off sex completely, and our sex life was non-existent after the birth of our child . . . I have lost all my sexual appetite and think that even if I did fancy it I'd be too tired.'* As children grow, it's difficult to have spontaneous sex during the day, and it's tricky to get privacy at night. When we do, either the adolescent child *'is at an age where he sees sex as a perversion'* or *'it's embarrassing to look up from an orgasm and see your small daughter looking at you absolutely fascinated.'*

A whole host of traumas can also put sex off the agenda for many months. Illness, abortion, death in the family, redundancy, depression: all these means that we, our partner, or both are not able to prioritize our love life simply because our physical and mental energies are taken up by the crisis: *'My husband isn't happy at work, and it affects our mood . . . because of the time my partner devotes to work, family and friends, there is little time for me.'*

None of these reasons seems to us to be a major course of worry. It is only when a partner consistently refuses to make love – rather than both of us being, in general, too tired – that we regard it as a issue. And so while 68.5 per cent of women want to make love more often (rather putting paid to the myth that women all have headaches and don't want it), they feel that as long as they and their partner are still sleeping together regularly and enjoyably, then a refusal may be a sexual disappointment, but it's not an actual problem.

*We are making love less often than when we were first together, but that is probably because we used to make love an awful lot. This is a quite natural progression in any relationship I think, and we are both reasonably happy with how often we make love. We would probably both like to feel less tired and see each other more regularly so that we could make love more.*

## SEXUAL BOREDOM

But where our lack of love-making is down to boredom or distaste rather than external circumstances, we worry. Many women complain that *'I'm not interested ... I'm bored with the whole act ... I wish we'd do it less because I'm sick of it.'* For some this may be a simple case of lack of love resulting in lack of passion. Almost every woman living with her husband and sleeping with her lover, for example, says that she hates having sex with the former and adores having it with the latter *'because I love him'.* And in this situation, as with those women who have simply stopped loving their partners, the answer that many of them are contemplating is the obvious one: to leave. We feel – and often we are right – that ending the relationship and beginning again with someone new will solve the problems we are having.

But for many couples it's not love but technique that is at fault. Some of us feel that we aren't experienced enough in bed or, more often, that our partner lacks skill. The result is a static or diminishing sex life. Where we feel we are lacking, we either feel that we don't know enough, or we put it down to not being selfless and loving enough, *'inexperienced ... I have much to learn ... I'm selfish ... lazy ... not always interested enough to participate fully'.* In fact the latter diagnosis is probably the one that is nearest the mark – for if we look at women's accounts of their 'boring sex life', the problem always seems underpinned by a lack of arousal. Whether because an essential sexual spark has died, or because sex is not reaching the parts it should, these women are no longer excited by lovemaking with their partner, and often their partner is no longer aroused by them.

We do blame our partners a good deal. Women's expectations of sex are now higher than they ever were in the past. We want longer, more skilful, more emotional foreplay: *'I am not satisfied with the amount of sex, the lack of foreplay and the mechanical nature of it.'* We want more experimentation, but all too many partners won't *'go further than straight sex ... he says it's filthy and wrong.'*

We come back here to a theme that has run throughout this book – that with the advent of the sexual revolution, women are slowly learning to know what pleases them. But men still often fail to respect that knowledge. We now know that in order to really blossom during sex – and not get bored – we may need lots of foreplay, particular positions, movements or stimulation during intercourse. Perhaps in the early months or years of sex, this kind of love-making is natural because we spend time and energy simply cuddling and getting aroused. But over the years, the process becomes streamlined, and the parts that are important to us are jettisoned in favour of 'getting down to it'. It's little wonder, if we aren't able to stop this happening, that we find sex ultimately boring.

## LACK OF ORGASM

We may also find sex unsatisfying if we have difficulty reaching orgasm. The number of respondents who are able to orgasm is slightly higher than in many sex surveys, but even so there are still 7 who never do so, and another 28 who do so only occasionally. Those who never orgasm seem sad about that but – almost more disturbingly – also quite resigned to it. Many mention trying different techniques or discussing the problem with a partner. But they seem tense and uncomfortable about the fact that they've made no headway; the sexual revolution has put a higher expectation on women to climax, and our guilt at not orgasming often seems to be as much of a problem as the non-climax itself.

Many of us can orgasm when we masturbate, but can't during intercourse. And while we still enjoy intercourse enormously, because of what it means in terms of our relationship, we want to orgasm as well. But again, there is a sense of resignation that suggests that, whether due to lack of knowledge or due to lack of partner communication, many women are simply enduring their non-orgasmic state: *'I used to worry about my inability to climax in intercourse, but I accept it now.'*

Such comments are disturbing for, while mental blocks to orgasm are real and may be intractable, current research suggests that overcoming the physical problems can allow us to make dramatic progress. If that is our situation, then 'accepting' an inability to orgasm is a sad misuse of our energy; it's action by ourselves and our partner that will get results. If we can, perhaps even with professional help, recontact sensual love-making, experiment with different kinds of position and clitoral stimulation, learn our own ways of climaxing and enrol our partners to learn them too, then orgasmic problems can often be resolved.

*I have yet to experience orgasm, although my partner and I have been together a long time, and this is often the cause of upset on both sides.*

*Most of the time it is nearly good enough that it doesn't matter, but at other times it is somewhat depressing. Obviously I would like to be having lots of orgasms. I am sure it will come in time.*

## PARTNER PROBLEMS

If it's our partner who has a sexual difficulty, that will of course affect us. Perhaps he isn't as interested in sex as we are – as mentioned before, many women want to make love more than men do. We do get worried if our partner goes off sex, even if that's temporary. And if his lack of interest lasts longer than a few days, we may suffer a great deal. We feel rejected, undesired sexually. We start acting as undesirable. We get depressed and then angry about that; when we push down our anger, we get depressed again. We also feel powerless – there seems little we can do that won't make matters worse.

We may try talking, and this may help: *'The only thing vaguely like a sexual problem was M's apparent lack of concern if we didn't make love for weeks at a time. When we spoke about it, he hadn't even realized that it had been that long! We suffered no long-term effects because as soon as I talked to him about it, the problem disappeared.'* But if our husband is threatened by our complaints, he may well lose desire even more, so often we keep quiet and consider other options.

*My husband has a lower sex drive than me, which is often frustrating. I have considered an affair but really don't want to be unfaithful to him as he doesn't deserve it, and I would hate him to be unfaithful to me. I can live with this and am happy with my decision to remain faithful.*

When a partner can't get an erection, our feelings can run high. It's happened on occasion to just under half the women in the survey, though only a handful have partners to whom it is a regular problem. If it happens just once, with a casual partner we tend to be very put out, while with an established partner we hardly notice it and stay unworried. If we can track the problem down to a specific external cause, that makes it much less threatening to us. Many of us comment that our partner has failed to gain an erection through *'tiredness ... stress ... medication ... too much alcohol ... too many amphetamines'*, and we tend to take this lack of erection in our stride.

But when we can't see a reason for our partner's problem and conclude that the reason must be our behaviour, things are very different. Some of us try to be supportive, sympathetic and encouraging: *'I was very aware that if I showed any disappointment it was likely to make the problem worse.'* But others say they feel *'unwanted, unattractive and inadequate'* and so acted badly: *'I sulked ... I got angry ... I acted like a spoilt brat.'* Interestingly, we tend to be more annoyed by the lack of erection if we come easily during penetration, as if, when we depend on full intercourse to climax, we see other methods as poor replacements. Those of us who are used to coming more reliably through hand or mouth stimulation are far less distressed and far more easily *'saw it as an opportunity to try something else ... went to sleep ... was happy to cuddle ... let him sub-stitute with oral'*. Most of us, in fact, are quite tolerant, but then most of us don't have the challenge that this woman has.

> *This has been a big problem in my current relationship. I've always thought that men showed their desire with a stiff erection and so I get very put off when my partner doesn't have one in circumstances I believe he should. He explains that he's never been like that and just doesn't get erections whenever he's turned on. I'm trying to understand that he's different and not make matters worse by always questioning it, but a hard-on turns me on and a limp one doesn't.*

Whatever the state of our partner's erection, there can be times when he comes too quickly or doesn't come quickly enough. A few women mention the former problem, premature ejaculation, but go into no detail, simply saying that it irritates them and that they have sometimes tried the 'on top' position to help a partner control his orgasm.

With the latter issue, delayed ejaculation, we are happy to help. Often this is because we feel that we aren't going to come and so want to speed our partner on, though one women did comment that she lent a helping hand *'if children's morning TV is about to finish'!* We seem to be very proactive in finding ways to assist, concentrating on arousing our partner as fully as we can: *'I talk dirty ... become more vocal ... go on top, let him take me from behind ... press harder ... thrust ... hold his testicles ... pull the cheeks of his bottom ... stick a finger up his bum ... add some KY jelly and throw myself heart and soul into enjoying the sensa-tions'*. We love to help in this way; it makes us feel powerful, in control and happy.

## SOLVING PROBLEMS

Do the sexual difficulties we suffer have a happy ending? In fact, they usually do. We are resilient; we are often able to put our mistakes and disappointments behind us. And many of the problems that we've mentioned in this chapter, we deal with ourselves. Over the past decades, along with a new attitude to sex, perhaps women have taken on the responsibility for sorting out the difficulties. We try something new in bed, start making love in a different way, practise relaxing more. Significantly, it is less likely that we can find a solution to a problem if it starts with our partner – 54.5 per cent of partner problems have a negative effect on our relationship.

We also, almost always, talk through what's happening with our partner. And this is a vital part of the way we cope. We feel strongly that if we can't communicate, then there is something lacking in our relationship. Those of us whose partners won't talk about problems complain bitterly that *'he is unapproachable . . . we tend to start arguing . . . he knows about the abuse but reckons counselling would be a rip-off. I don't feel he's very sympathetic about it . . . my ex never used to listen when I had a problem; maybe that's why he's my ex.'*

We solve our problems ourselves because we are able to do so. But we are also wary of going for outside help. A high 77.9 per cent of women don't turn to someone outside their partnership when they have a problem, even though they could have done. They say they're embarrassed or would feel silly. They feel that *'being touched up and abused as a child is something I don't see much point in talking about'*. We feel that only big problems deserve outside help. Or we say we wouldn't know where to go for support or who to ask.

There may well be an added reason why we don't go for help. There's still somehow a taboo on admitting that we have a less than perfect love life. If we go for help for a sexual problem, we are telling the world that we are not the ideal, highly sexed, all-orgasmic woman that the media tells us we ought to be.

This unwillingness to go for help is a worry – and not just because counselling is proved to work. It's also troubling because those women in the survey who did go for help – to a doctor, to a counsellor, to a therapist – say that they did benefit from that. They received medical help for medical problems. Where the issue was emotional, they received support and encouragement.

Respondents are impressively open about the sexual difficulties they have suffered. And maybe there's a lesson to be learnt from that. It would be good if, because of the problems that women have so freely admitted in their answers, because of their openness and honesty, we could realize that we all do have problems at some time or another – and that going for help for them doesn't mean we have failed.

*We worked so hard for about two years that sex became a luxury. It wasn't that it was a real problem, just that we weren't prioritizing it. Through the therapy we got back in touch with what we liked about making love with each other. And for that I have to thank the counsellor.*

VITAL STATISTICS

82.8 per cent of women say they would feel negatively if a partner were unfaithful

69 per cent of women have been unfaithful themselves

59.5 per cent of women have had affairs with married men

55.2 per cent of women have had partners who have been unfaithful to them

38.9 per cent have slept with more than one man in the same day

13.6 per cent of women report that affairs have a good effect on their central relationship

# 22. Being faithful

*I had an affair with a married man which started about three years ago. The attraction was overwhelming; it was a real mind fuck. I've never felt for anyone the way I felt for him, and I believe he felt the same. I knocked it on the head because it was getting too painful, and I didn't want him to leave his wife and kids for me. Funnily enough I bumped into him very recently and the electricity was still there. We talked for ages and had a heavy petting session in the bathroom at a party. But it's still a futile situation and not one I will follow up at all.*

THE CHANGES IN women's sexual freedom may have fundamentally altered our attitude to sex. But we still regard being faithful as the cornerstone of our relationships, just as it was for generations of women before us. As many as 93.1 per cent of women feel that fidelity is important, extremely important or essential, while 82.6 per cent say that having any kind of sexual contact outside their relationship would be totally taboo. And no respondent says that she would feel unreservedly delighted at her partner's being unfaithful.

It all seems completely clear. Fidelity is what holds our relationships together, and it is what makes them worth while. So let's look more closely at what we mean by fidelity, why it's so important to us – and whether we follow through on what we believe.

## WHAT IS FIDELITY?

For most of us fidelity means monogamy. We don't have intercourse outside our primary relationship, we don't have sexual contact up to intercourse. Only one woman in the whole survey says that having full sex with someone other than your partner when you are in a committed relationship is acceptable:

> *Being unfaithful is falling in love with a person other than your partner. I don't consider that having sex with someone other than your partner can always be considered unfaithful; love and sex are not the same thing, and it's the love that counts.*

More than this, if we are faithful, we don't do anything that shows an intention to be sexual with someone else. So we don't hug or kiss, deliberately flirt, spend time with someone privately – or even think about doing these things. For some of us, being unfaithful includes *'having a deep friendship ... emotional betrayal ... confiding things which should remain private'* without any thought of sex. And, for most of us, infidelity means dishonesty. We expect sexual betrayal to include a lie, because most women don't imagine anyone being unfaithful and then telling their partner about it. So when we define infidelity, we call it *'sexual lying'* or *'cheating'*. And, once again, it is the intention that counts: if we are dishonest about contact with someone of the opposite sex, then that is infidelity – even if, in actual fact, nothing sexual or emotional ever happens: *'Even going for a friendly drink with a work mate, can be unfaithful if your partner isn't told about it.'*

We're clear that such behaviour is wrong only within the context of certain kinds of relationship. We can't be unfaithful if we have no committed partnership: *'I see nothing wrong with casual affairs until a stable relationship is involved.'* We aren't unfaithful if we have an arrangement with our partner – though the very fact that we have such an arrangement rather suggests that the relationship is already flawed. We aren't, really, being unfaithful if our relationship is a bad one and we are seeking consolation or a way out: *'If the relationship is good don't rock the boat.*

*If it isn't, what the hell.'* But if we are in an agreed, monogamous, steady relationship and we allow our lust to wander, then we've strayed: *'As for being in a stable relationship, if you've have committed yourself to one person, you should stick to the rules. If you can't handle it, you should not get involved.'*

Only a few women in the survey don't agree with these definitions. They are usually very young women who are still seeing a number of men, or women in their late thirties and forties who have negotiated open relationships with their partners. The former say they want fidelity when they are in a committed relationship, but that at present *'we have no commitments.'* The latter seem to define relationships very differently to other respondents: *'To me, the word unfaithful has little meaning ... it's not a word I use.'* They take pride in having a close partnership that nevertheless allows both of them to see, have sexual contact with, and in some cases have sex with other people. The impression is, however, that this attempt to have open relationships is less common than it was when the sexual revolution first began, and that it is handled a lot more warily.

> *I don't think we feel free to sleep with someone else. But we have talked about infidelity and what we would do if it happened. We've agreed that if it was a one-off affair, it shouldn't mean anything, and we would tell each other. I would rather it didn't happen, but as long as we were honest, we could talk it through.*

## VITAL FIDELITY

The reason we value faithfulness is because we want to be the centre of our partner's world, literally and symbolically. If our partner were to take another lover, that would mean that he's rejected us. He would have chosen to move outside his relationship with us, and so risk its ending. It would also, probably, mean that he had been dishonest and lied to us, and we see trust as an essential ingredient to a loving relationship. Finally, we are worried about disease: the AIDS age means that the implications of infidelity are more threatening to us than to any other generation before us.

> *I think I would feel lost and sad if I were suddenly rejected. I'd want to know why he hadn't spoken to me if he was unhappy. But, most of all, I would feel wary of the possibility that my partner might have caught something. I would try and help him all I could, but no way would I put my life at risk by making love with him.*

What all this means for our current relationship is that, theoretically, infidelity is totally unacceptable. More than one woman, asked how she felt about the possibility of either she or her partner sleeping with someone else, put the words 'NO WAY!!!' in capital letters, followed by several exclamation marks. So the majority of women say that if their partner did actually stray, they would feel *'devastated ... full of self doubt ... ugly ... it would be the worst thing that could happen.'* And in response they would *'leave him ... kick him out ... end the relationship'*; they often talk of being violent:

> *If my current boyfriend was unfaithful to me I would find the girl and beat her. I would probably damage my partner's genitalia also so that he'd never be able to have sex again. Then I would feel like killing myself. I'd probably never want another man again!*

Just a few women say that they would hate it if our partner had an affair, but they would put up with it. They would be more understanding if their partner had been drunk; if the event had been a one-night stand; if he could honestly say that he had done it only for sex not for genuine attraction or love. And most who feel they could tolerate infidelity also have certain ground rules that neatly dovetail with the fears listed above. They would want their partner to have worn a condom, not to have caught any disease, to stay with them and the children. Would they want honesty? Yes, they would want to be told, for it would be far more worrying if he lied to them. But definitions of being told vary: some are sure they would want him to *'tell me anything'*, others are certain that he mustn't *'go into details'*.

## THE REALITY OF UNFAITHFULNESS

This is the theory. What happens in practice when our partner is unfaithful? Just over half, 55.2 per cent, of women who answer this question have had that happen to them. And their response is just as negative as they said it would be – all but a handful of them are devastated.

Our partners have affairs with acquaintances, affairs with colleagues. Many partners have relationships with mutual friends or even our best friend. They have one-night stands, or they run affairs in parallel with their relationship with us. One woman says her *'last partner of 10 years had 20 partners, 3 of whom he lived with without my knowledge'*. Another reports that:

> *My last partner was repeatedly unfaithful. He was in a band and went on tour, and whenever he was in the States he slept around, although he always used a condom. I used to find out, and he wouldn't deny it, and that upset me. Since I have finished with him, many people have*

*told me of more affairs that they knew about but didn't want to hurt me by telling me.*

Many women say that they have no idea what is happening for long periods of time. They stay either totally unaware or, worse, they suspect but their partner lies to them about what is going on: *'I sensed it was happening from different perfume smells, hair on his collar, finding phone numbers ... It is taking me a while to listen to my inner voice, because of denying it for so long.'* When the truth finally comes out, it is often suddenly and violently. A partner returns home *'after being out all night with love bites on his neck'.* A woman catches her partner on the phone to another woman and challenges him.

*He'd been at a party and was meant to be back the night before. He came in at eight o'clock in the morning, had a shower and climbed into bed. I pretended I was asleep, then pretended to stir to wakefulness. I said, 'What time did you get back?' He replied, 'About two hours ago.' LIE!!! His clothes were lying on the bathroom floor, his undies were on top and bloodstained around the crotch area. He asked me what was wrong and I finally confronted him. 'Did you sleep with someone else last night? – Your undies have bloodstains on them and you lied to me about what time you came back in.' He replied, 'Those stains were probably from your period a few weeks ago. Bloodstains don't come out easily.' I said, 'But your undies were clean!!!!' I knew he was lying to me but at the same time didn't want to believe he was. I wanted to believe he couldn't be unfaithful to me. But the circumstances were so sordid. The next day he begged me to come back to him, and for a while we were a lot closer – until the next time he was unfaithful.*

The first main reaction to the news of a partner's affair may well be to disbelieve it completely – which is why a partner is so often able to convince us, at least for a while, that nothing is wrong. But the truth comes out. We are angry at him, we are sad for the relationship. But, often, our main reaction is to feel bad about ourselves. We see our partner's rejection as our failure. We accuse ourselves of being unattractive, fat or bad in bed. We try to examine our personality and see what trait in us could have made him want to stray. We feel that we have let our partner down in some, often undefined, way. And, even if we blame our partner, we still reckon that there is something wrong with us.

*Five out of seven of my sexual partners I found out had gone off and slept with people I knew and friends. Of course they said that I made them, or I didn't take any notice of them. This made me feel I had a problem, and I was very upset.*

Surprisingly, though our negative feelings about our partner are strong, we often act far less negatively than we thought we would. Whereas a large number of women say that they would act with actual physical violence to their partner if infidelity were to happen, hardly anyone says that she actually has, though one woman says that *'the other girl told me, and I blacked her eye.'* This is linked to the fact that we all too readily believe that his action is our fault for not loving him enough. We turn our anger inwards instead of outwards and are able to both stop ourselves from attacking him and, to some extent, excuse him. But what we almost always do, however, is to become unable to trust our partner in the future. We look forward and see a time in the relationship where this might happen again, where we would spend our time checking up on him, where we would worry if he was out of our sight for even a few hours. We realize that we may never feel the same about him again.

## LONG-TERM EFFECTS

Of the women whose partners had had affairs, 81 per cent split up. Usually this relationship breakdown seems to happen spontaneously and almost mutually. The partnership has been going badly, this affair is *'the last straw for our marriage'*, and there is just no way to go on. Or the other woman intervenes: wanting her needs met, she calls or contacts us and brings things to a head.

*My past partner was unfaithful. He had been seeing her for six months before we broke up, but we were living together at the time and had just bought a house. I found out the usual way, lipstick on his shirt, horrible perfume. She also phoned. I asked him about it, and he just laughed at me. Our relationship ended.*

Often the relationship breakdown comes not simply because of the affair, but because that affair carries on after our partner has told us it is finished. What drives us away is the dishonesty as much as the infidelity.

*I found some photographs of my ex-partner having sex with someone while he was going out with me, and after he'd promised to be faithful. I left the photographs in an envelope with a note telling him not to get in touch, refused to speak to him and threw his belongings out of the window.*

Significantly, our unfaithful partner very rarely leaves. He may want to have his cake and eat it, but if he has to choose, he'll choose his daily bread. If the pull of the other woman is very strong, then it may win out over his central relationship but not often.

## RELATIONSHIPS THAT SURVIVE

Just 19 per cent of women who say that their partner has been unfaithful also say that the relationship has survived that. Some of us enter our relationships initially knowing that our partner will have sex with others, and that if we aren't prepared to put up with that, he will leave. However bitter we feel, we submit to that – and when the affair happens, we ignore it and carry on. Equally, many affairs happen within the context of a relationship of many years; we weigh up the fact of the infidelity against the past history of the relationship and the future potential of it – and decide to stay.

*He had an affair which lasted about three and a half years. I guessed. He begged forgiveness and three times more he was unfaithful again. This has affected our relationship so greatly that I cannot forgive or forget or trust him ever again. I want to stay married to him, God knows why! We have been together thirty-six years.*

Or, when the trauma happens, we are able to talk things through with our partner, assess the problem and get a real feeling that things are going to change. In many cases, though not all, the man agrees to end his affair when it comes to light. And he keeps his promise. This makes it possible for the relationship to survive.

*He kissed a close friend on several occasions while they were on a field trip together. He told me. I cried, asked questions and felt heartbroken. It made us both reassess what we wanted, how much we wanted it and make us talk completely openly about our relationship, and where it was going. I gave him an ultimatum. It gave us both a kick up the backside.*

In general, however, we are desolated by a partner's infidelity. Even once our unhappy relationship has ended, we lose trust in other people and in ourselves. The fact of someone we love and whom we thought loved us being unfaithful and lying about it can affect our lives, sometimes permanently. It often has a greater impact than actually losing a loved one.

*When my fiancé slept with my best friend it destroyed me. I tried to take my own life, and I think it has caused a great many emotional scars and*

*totally shattered my life. The anger is still inside me. I can't say any
more because it hurts too much.*

## INFIDELITY IN REVERSE

We would completely expect, then, that when it comes to being unfaithful
to our partner, we would never consider the possibility. If 93.1 per cent
of women feel that fidelity is essential to a relationship, then we would
expect that, allowing for inconsistency, probably 10 per cent will have
been unfaithful in prior relationships. Wouldn't we?

The figure is 69 per cent. As many as 69 per cent of women have,
at some time or another, been unfaithful to a partner. Just under a third,
only, have stayed faithful to their partners throughout their lives. And 5.5
per cent of women who answered the questionnaire are currently having
an affair.

They haven't necessarily slept with another man – but then when
we originally defined infidelity, it didn't necessarily include sex. They
have accepted invitations by other men to go for the night out – without
telling their partner. They have picked up strangers in night-clubs. They
have *'invited a man around when my husband was out, petted and kissed'.*
They have seduced friends, slept with work colleagues, had short-term
liaisons, had 16-year affairs.

We're not talking here about those women whose main relationships
are casual, with no commitment to fidelity on either side. Nor are we
looking at those who have an arrangement with their partners: *'I am
sleeping with someone else, but I don't consider it to be infidelity because
there's no commitment between us ... I was not exclusive and was not
hiding anything. I was very clear that if I wanted sex with others I would
do it.'* The figure of 69 per cent covers only those women who say that
what they are doing is certainly infidelity, in their own definition as well
as their partner's.

Why? Why would we break our own moral code and risk our entire
relationship? A first reason, and one which no woman is proud of, is that
alcohol overcomes good intentions. A second, and often linked reason, is
that lust does the same. These scenarios seem to happen only when there's
no danger of being found out: at a conference, on a course, when our
partner is away. Alcohol takes hold, or we go for the pleasure of the
moment, and it is only after the event that we begin to regret it. We regard
it as a one-off, and, for many of us, the suspicion that our partner may
well have done the same and not told us makes it acceptable to keep silent.

*It was a holiday screw last year. He was totally crap at sex compared
to my boyfriend in fact, compared to anyone! I felt really dirty and guilty.*

*My partner was never told and never will be. I've lied about it for too long to tell him now.*

Up to 22.4 per cent of the women who answered this question have had this sort of casual infidelity, and most don't feel madly good about it. But it isn't a major source of concern or guilt for them simply because they know it is no danger to their primary relationship. They have done what they did for purely physical reasons; like men traditionally are presumed to do, they have had sex. Particularly if the sex wasn't all that good, there is no risk, no weighting up of their old relationship against their new one. They haven't made love, there's no threat to their partnership, and so they haven't really been unfaithful.

## HAVING AN AFFAIR

If simply having sex isn't infidelity, what about affairs? Surely they betray our relationship? In fact, the consistent theme running through every account of infidelity is that affairs happen only when we believe that there is no longer a relationship to betray. Where we have made love with someone outside our primary relationship, it is consistently because we believe that our primary relationship is failing. If our original definition of infidelity is, as quoted before, *'If the relationship is good don't rock the boat. If it isn't, what the hell,'* then we have no compunction at doing a little boat-rocking when things are going badly.

We may be unhappy in our partnership. We are in our late teens or early twenties, and we haven't yet quite learnt to choose the partner who is right for us; we have a one-night stand, and that clarifies for us that we are in the wrong relationship and need to leave. Or, we are older and the relationship we have committed ourselves to has turned out to be a mistake: *'My fiancé was so cruel and vicious that I became promiscuous ... my husband was neglecting me ... I felt I should grab happiness when and where I could.'*

If we expect or are convinced that our partner is being unfaithful to us, then we feel quite happy about being unfaithful in return: *'I suspect he is seeing someone else as well as visiting prostitutes ... I had sex with other partners because I thought it would cushion the blow when he said that he had.'* If our partner is sleeping with someone else simply because he's married, then this may also be a reason for us to do the same. Or we know about our partner's infidelity and want revenge – a sixth of women sleep with others for this reason: *'Before we were married, he rang and said he had seen his ex-girlfriend. I went straight round to his best friend's house and slept with him.'* Or we know that our relationship is over, so it doesn't matter.

*I was unfaithful to a partner with someone I knew, who later turned out
to be my second husband. It didn't bother me as my first husband had
been unfaithful to me. I was then unfaithful in the second marriage. Our
sex life had ceased, so I had a one-night stand and then an affair with
the man who is now my third husband.*

Often we need a love affair in order to continue in our primary
relationship. We *'want parts of both'* as one woman put it, and *'my affair
made my partnership possible,'* said another. Many respondents, particularly those who are married and who are in their thirties or forties, want
to stay with husband and family but at the same time know that there is
something missing in their lives. Much as many generations of married
men have done before them, their answer is to take a lover, to stay with
their spouse, to keep silent and to maintain the status quo. Two generations ago, with little freedom of movement and hardly any contraceptive
protection, this would not have been a real option. Now, it is: *'I don't love
my husband, but he's loving and caring and a good provider. I want parts
of both ... I have not had sexual relations with my husband for the last
twelve years. I am currently involved with another man.'*

## CHOOSING A LOVER

We choose for our affairs someone we know – because if we're in a
relationship, we don't have the opportunity to go out hunting. So we pick
*'an old school friend ... an ex-boyfriend ... a work colleague ... someone
I met at a conference ... a good friend'.*

We are in a situation where no one knows us or no one will worry,
a work conference or an activity holiday. We find ourselves alone with a
friend, late at night, and after a few bottles of wine. We have a quick grope
in the kitchen with our husband's workmate during a New Year party
and then wonder whether to take it further. Or we work in close proximity
with someone and simply get emotionally closer and closer to them; one
day it simply feels inevitable that we will make physical contact.

Sex takes exactly the same course as it does when we are pairing off
as a single woman, but this time with a little more danger attached. We
slip off to a hotel for an hour or pop into the stock room. We end up
making love on the lounge floor. We go off on a business trip, knowing
that once the meetings are over, the fun can begin. We have to be careful,
but often the sex is more fun because it's forbidden.

First reactions can vary. We may feel bad about what has happened:
*'guilty ... dirty ... terrible ... scared ... devious ... I thought it showed
a great weakness in my character.'* If we react like this, we tend to never
see the person again – though whether we don't repeat the event because

we feel bad or feel bad because it was one-off sex can vary. We close ranks with our partner, steer well clear of the 'other man' and do our best to maintain the status quo. We either never tell our partner: *'It was just a drunken immature grope and I didn't think it was worth tearing my life apart for,'* or we face up to things honestly, and often they work out: *'It put a great strain on our relationship, gave us both a shock and in the end made us very strong.'* We often rediscover our commitment to our primary partner. In the future we keep our lust under control – often permanently – with thoughts of how badly our one-off fling could have affected our lives: *'The situation could have got out of hand, and I could have ended up hurting someone I love very much.'*

Or we feel good about what has happened. We like the excitement, we like taking risks and keeping secrets. We feel attractive again, *'which I hadn't for a long time'*. If we feel we are in love, we feel good, convinced that this is the start of something wonderful. We lay plans with our new lover, to keep meeting and continue the affair – almost three-quarters of women who have affairs follow this pattern. We feel aroused and uninhibited, because we are making the decision, we are in control.

*I had an affair with someone I met at a conference. After the first time, I felt confident, happy, thought everything would work out. We hadn't had penetrative but just oral sex, so I didn't really feel I'd been unfaithful. I told my partner exactly what had happened, very honestly.*

## LONG TERM EFFECTS

If we carry on seeing our lover, then sooner or later a preference pattern emerges. This is based on both how we feel emotionally about partner and lover and how we rate the sex with each of them. One-third of women find that sex is actually worse with their new lover than with their old partner. It may feel mechanical, be *'more exciting but less satisfying'*, or *'The sex compared to that with my partner was awful. I stopped it before penetration and left.'* If it's better, it's usually because the lover himself makes us feel good, or because we are the sort of person for whom risk raises excitement.

And, significantly, there is a clear pattern that links how good the sex is with the final outcome of the affair. Where the sex is worse in the affair than in our primary relationship, then the primary relationship tends to survive. It's not quite as simple as saying that we stick with the better sex. It's more that we have often chosen our lover as a temporary measure, never intended to be a real threat to our relationship, and therefore the sex never has a chance to develop and improve. Or we start to realize that our primary partner has more going for him than we realized; we see the sex as a reflection of the emotional link we have, and start to believe again in our primary relationship as being worth while. We may stay, tell our partner and get *'eventual forgiveness'*; if we do, we often say we are closer as a result. It is more likely, however, that we will keep silent about what has happened and hope our partner never finds out: 58.8 per cent of women do this. And, quite often, *'my sex life was reawakened by the affair.'*

> *I was about 18 when I had an affair, and it didn't really develop at all. I had known the bloke since school and we both sort of fell into it. I didn't tell my partner as there was nothing to tell really; it was just a drunken immature grope.*

Where the sex with our partner is worse than that with our lover, the result is what one might expect. The pair-bond we have begins to shift. The fact that we have good sex with our lover convinces us that our primary relationship is lacking, and, particularly if our lover begins to press for a long-term commitment, we do what our bodies and our emotions tell us to. We switch allegiance. We may very well stay with our primary partner for a short while – or until the children grow up. But we begin to avoid sex with him or have sex to keep him happy and unsuspicious: *'When my husband was forcing me to tell him dirty stories to prepare for sex, I could think of my lover.'*

Alternatively, we leave: *'My other relationship was dead sexually and mentally, and I didn't want to be involved with him any more.'* In this situation it's almost as if we have had two monogamous relationships, end-on, but with a short, though regrettable, overlap. If we do tell our first partner in this situation, it is to bring things to a head and force a separation; but if the relationship is on the rocks anyway, we often choose not to tell, but simply to leave. To reveal the infidelity would complicate things, and in any case there is no need – the relationship breaks up, and no one ever knows a thing.

Only ten women in the whole survey say that they are repeatedly unfaithful to their partners, and that is usually because they have an arrangement.

> *I have never been faithful to him. I have never told him I was being unfaithful, and our relationship doesn't seem to alter, despite my repeated affairs. I think that sex with someone new, when perhaps it shouldn't be happening, is always much more exciting.*

But, for most of us, affairs aren't about sheer fun and excitement, with our primary relationship as a backdrop. Affairs are almost always about changing our feelings about our current relationship or about ending it. We need an affair to reconvince ourselves that our partnership is good, to provide the missing pieces so that it can carry on. Or we need an affair as a transition, to convince us to leave, to support us to end our primary relationship. If after that we form a long-term partnership with our lover, that's good. If we don't, the affair has served its purpose, and we have moved on.

## WITH MARRIED MEN

What about those of us who, rather than being unfaithful to our partner, choose to have a relationship with someone who is being unfaithful to theirs? Up to 59.5 per cent of women have at some point had an affair with a married man. Only a few meet married lovers by chance, and only one said she met him through an advert: they're more likely to be work contacts or long-standing friendships. We describe the attraction in exactly the same terms as we do when our lovers aren't married: we find them sexually compelling, we think them wonderful people. And our reasons for sleeping with them are the same as those for entering any relationship; we love them, want them, want to be with them.

Where relationships with married men differ from those with single men is that we have to decide where we stand in relation to his partner. Some 40.5 per cent of women won't do it at all – *'I wouldn't be the bit on the side, it's not right'* – and many more finish with a married partner as soon as they learn he is married or very shortly after.

*I had one-night stands with people who were married, but I only found out afterwards. As a rule I would never do that if somebody was in any kind of relationship, as I would feel it would be betraying the other woman. A man should make a decision, either have one or have all the others, but not both.*

What if we do carry on? It may be because we ourselves are married; we want an affair and having a relationship with someone who is already committed lowers the danger to our relationship. Or we truly believe that we have a deep bond with this man, and that one day we will have him to ourselves. Maybe we believe that *'they were splitting up anyway; our relationship just hurried that along a bit,'* or that *'If he doesn't respect his marriage, why should I?'*

If he is in love with us, then, sooner or later, he must leave his wife for us. If he doesn't, then his love affair becomes shown up for what it is: infidelity. We lose faith in him, and we need to protect ourselves. This is why many affairs have a breakpoint of a year, where it becomes apparent that a partner isn't going to leave. Then we start to pull back: 'I became bored with the lack of feelings and of not being able to do things together ... I couldn't stand the deceit ... It was clear it was going nowhere ... they had a baby.' We move away, finish the relationship, find someone else.

Occasionally his partner finds out. This either ends it all or, much more likely, simply drives it underground: 'His wife found out twice, but we were just more careful afterwards ... it's still current even though both our partners think it's over.' It's rare that a wife's discovery makes the man end an affair; it's equally unlikely that it makes him choose his lover, for had he been going to leave, he would have done so before. This story is unusual.

*We'd always been attracted to each other. When I had a bad car smash and messed my face up, he felt he had to look after me. It was so exciting, lots of sneaking round, treats, motels. It would have been perfect if he'd been single; we were so well matched. I knew he wouldn't leave her, even though he said he would; I was honestly encouraging him to sort things out with her, mainly for the kid's sake. They had a very stormy relationship and eventually split. We got together. After six months we decided to have a 6 month break, and he'd give it another go with her. That was when I met my current partner.*

Just a few women take an affair into its second or third year. They are willing, if not happy, to live with the situation: 'I accepted being the mistress.' And where this is genuinely true, then the relationship can be stable and last for a very long time. As many as 22 women in the survey have formed long-term partnerships with married men: one respondent has had a 25-year affair with one. They are not necessarily happy with the situation – though some of them like the freedom to be themselves in a relationship that is not exclusive. But they have chosen it, and they stick by it. In the end, whether married or not, the man is worth it.

## DOUBLE STANDARDS
We do have to face the fact that there are some deep inconsistencies between our current attitudes to infidelity and the behaviour patterns we have developed along with our increased sexual freedom. As pointed out before, 93.1 per cent of women think that infidelity is important, and 82.8 per cent would feel bad if a partner were unfaithful. Yet 69 per cent of women have been unfaithful themselves, with 59.5 per cent having had affairs with married men.

Some of this inconsistency is down to the fact that as we have grown older, our beliefs have changed. As women in our thirties or forties we may

have grown to value fidelity. But when we were younger, we didn't – and
so over the course of our lives, we have both been unfaithful and grown
to believe fidelity to be vital.

*Yes, my attitude towards faithfulness has changed. Unfaithfulness causes
so many problems, breaks up marriages, affects emotions for many years.
Unfaithfulness can wreck your life or the lives of others around you.
When I was young I didn't care about after-effects.*

*I used to be unfaithful until it happened to me, and I realized how
much pain was involved. Also, my relationship now is far too important
to mess up, and I don't need the thrill either as my relationship fulfils
me enough.*

Despite this explanation, there is a double standard. And we are
aware of it: '*I want fidelity more but do it and get it less . . . I'm never
faithful, but I expect men to be . . . I expect total faithfulness, but am unable
to give it.*' We hate infidelity, but, somehow, faced with the reality of a
new and potentially wonderful possibility, we go ahead. Why?

The key surely lies in the way we see our relationships. For while
we may feel that infidelity is wrong, that only holds true if it happens
within the context of a good relationship. And – here comes the way out
of the double bind – how can a relationship be good if we ourselves are
even tempted to have an affair? Or how can our married lover's relationship be worth while if he has had an affair?

If we sleep with someone, look back and regret it, then we can say
that we haven't betrayed our partner (by recommitting ourselves to him
because of our regret). We can also say that we simply had sex, we didn't
make love. If we sleep with someone and that leads to our falling in love
with them, then by definition our current partnership cannot have been
all that wonderful. Our infidelity was justified.

It seems logical, and it is certainly realistic. As mentioned previously,
the majority of our affairs are within the context of a relationship that
needs changing – or within the context of our needing to change our
feelings about our relationship. And in many ways infidelity achieves these
goals: in the new climate of sexual freedom, it has become a method used
by us frequently to get what we want. By sleeping with someone else, we
either realize how good our partnership is, or we leave it. By sleeping
with us, our married lovers either recontact their partnership strength or
realize that we are best. Or we both of us decide that by having an affair,
we can hang on to the original partnership and stick with it a little longer:
'*Our marriages, especially mine, were kept going longer than they would*

*if I hadn't had a lover.'* This makes sense, and where we are happy with our infidelity patterns, then we see no problem in having an affair.

The only thing is, of course, that it is a problem when it's not we who are having the affair. We don't hear about our partner's infidelity and calmly wonder what he needs to change about his feelings. We feel *'betrayed . . . devastated . . . full of self-doubt.'* We don't listen to him telling us about his affair and coolly analyse the benefits he gets from being unfaithful. Instead, we want to kill him.

There's no easy answer to this. In the past there was one law for men (affairs were possible) and one for women (affairs were taboo): that was a real inequality, and no one should defend it. Now, however, the social 'laws' are the same: infidelity is unilaterally possible if not actually acceptable. We've been given our sexual freedom, and we're using it to the full. But, unfortunately, if we do use it to the full, we can't then expect our partners not to follow suit, can't in all fairness now throw too much of a temper tantrum if they stray too.

What we can do, in the long run, is to create the balance we want between freedom and fidelity. And maybe then, our partners will do the same.

*Yes, I've had affairs in my time, but I've learnt from my mistakes. I now know. End relationship first, then find a new bonk!*

VITAL STATISTICS

78.1 per cent of women have lost an important relationship during their lives

44.3 per cent of these didn't miss their partners sexually

49 per cent who split up with someone had another relationship to replace the partner

30.1 per cent had casual sex to console themselves

Of the 73 women who didn't have sex to replace, only 1 now wishes she had

# 23. Losing love

*Eventually after over two years of a really destructive relationship, I left one partner. I didn't want to leave him even then, I just wanted to stop the way he was behaving. I had tried to leave him many times, but he had such a powerful attraction for me, I didn't stay away long. But I'd heard all the promises before, and my self-preservation instincts must have overruled my emotions that once. I still loved him when I left him, and the thought of him still has a powerful affect on me now. I think I still miss him sexually. Not that he was any good – my present partner is much more sensitive and generally good at sex – but I have never experienced that sort of passion before or since.*

HAD THIS SURVEY been carried out fifty years ago, a very small proportion of women would have reported losing a sexual relationship in the course of their lives. If they had, it would more often have been due to death than to partnership breakdown. But now, things are very different: we have to cope with a new life crisis, relationship breakdown. And so we find that 78.1 per cent of women have lost a sexual relationship that was deeply important to them.

Let's look first at what makes a relationship important enough to mourn when we lose it. The four essential elements seem to be: whether a partnership is a 'first love'; how much emotion we feel about it; how long the relationship has already lasted; and what level of formal commitment and involvement we've made to it.

Our first truly rewarding sexual relationship, our 'first love', may well be important not only because we will usually choose as our first love a person and a relationship that we really want but also because the younger we are, the more likely we are to be devastated by the loss. We not only miss our partner but we also see something symbolic in their having left, as if now a part of our life is over.

Equally, if we have felt strongly emotional about someone, then we will feel that relationship to be important. And this seems to be true whether or not that emotion has been positive. If we have felt immense love, anger or jealousy about a partner, then that's likely to mean that the relationship has become central in our minds. Often the fact of having been hurt by someone makes the relationship vital, as if pain is as much of a signal of importance to us as happiness is.

The loss of a relationship that has lasted for a long time is also likely to affect us deeply. Even if it is fairly casual – although most long-term relationships aren't – we have built up a knowledge of each other, out of bed as well as in it, that is difficult to replace. We are used to being with each other and relating in a way that is unique to us. Whether we have been happy or not, it is painful to break the habits of years.

Finally, the deeper the commitment, the more difficult may be the break. We commit to a relationshp because it is important; but the very act of commitment – moving in together, getting engaged, married, starting a family – all adds weight to the partnership. The more we have invested, the more we feel betrayed if that investment is then taken away – though, at the same time, we may well feel so deeply betrayed that we become disillusioned and glad to let go.

Significantly, if none of these elements has ever been present in a relationship for us, then we may actually feel that we have never suffered relationship loss. Some 21.8 per cent of respondents say that they have yet to undergo the experience. Usually these women are too young to have ever been deeply involved. Or they have gone from relationship to relationship with little strong emotion or hardly any commitment: their relationships have always been casual or transitory. Or, as is the case with just a few respondents, they have committed themselves to their first love and are still with them – in which case they count their blessings.

## MUTUAL BREAK-UPS

The loss of an important relationship is sometimes a mutual thing, though it's very rarely openly negotiated. It happens without our realizing, even though it happens mutually. We may drift apart, particularly if we are young and changing very fast. We grow out of each other, often when we are separated for a while; we may simply let our meetings happen less and less frequently: *'We went to different colleges. The relationship limped along for a year or so, but he hated my new friends and the fact that I was independent of him.'*

Or we have a relationship that has no future, such as an affair with a married man. It's good to enjoy ourselves in the here and now, but sooner or later we realize that there is no point in carrying on, and without really realizing what we are doing we somehow fail to arrange to meet again. Neither of us challenges what's happening, because underneath we both know it's for the best. And in that way the ending is mutual.

There are only three women respondents who say that they openly negotatiated separation with their partner. Two say that they felt they needed time apart from each other; the very agreement they reached made it possible to be separate, though they have suffered. It's probably not a coincidence that these two women speak of their partnerships as being now current, as if a mutually agreed separation eventually brought them closer together again: *'I had a six-month separation from my current partner; he needed to grow up. I missed every single inch of him. But now we're back together our relationship is on a different plane.'* The third woman who mutually negotiated a separation tells this story.

*I split up with my cousin because our families would have cast us aside; at the time it was illegal for cousins to have sex, as it was believed that this led to deformed children. We felt there would be too much peer pressure and scandal if we declared our relationship, so we decided amicably to stay cousins and nothing else. We also stopped seeing each other sexually, though with difficulty. I was about 14 at the time, and he was 19. Then when I was about 16 we nearly undid all of this and got back together; but we managed to hold back and have done ever since. He congratulated me, with sadness, on my marriage, though he gets on quite well with my husband and has had many girlfriends himself.*

## NON-MUTUAL BREAK-UPS

Usually, though, the break-up of an important relationship is down to one or the other of us. Surprisingly, it is not always our partner who leaves. There's a fifty-fifty chance, however important the relationship is to us, that we will go. We usually hang on for a while, perhaps for far longer than we should. We may fight to keep the relationship going, trying to be more patient, more loving, more understanding. We may put up with more than we should because we still love our partner. And if we leave, we may still miss our partner years later. But, in the end, go we do.

*I came to the conclusion I was being used .. After five years of a stormy relationship, I decided enough was enough ... After putting up with violence, I was brave enough to end it ... He was jealous, possessive, verbally and physically abusive; it took me six months to finish the relationship.*

When our partner leaves us, on the other hand, we don't spend years working on the relationship – because we aren't given the chance. More than half the time, we don't even see the end coming: then, all of a sudden, he is leaving. We are often shattered, often wondering even years later just why it happened.

There is a real sense in many of the survey accounts that women don't see the writing on the wall. They may know that there are problems but be convinced that *'we are working through them.'* They may take the rough with the smooth and think that their partner is doing the same. They may expect him, as they do, to try again or to wait and see if things are going to improve. But, in fact, while a male partner is less likely than we are to leave for someone else, he is more likely to leave because he wants to – and hence less likely to stay around when things are going wrong.

## HOW DOES IT HAPPEN?

Whichever one of us is doing the leaving, break-ups seem to follow one of several consistent patterns. Firstly, the relationship may be drifting; both of us know that something is very wrong, but we are long past the point of being able to do anything about it or even wanting to. Our common past makes the partnership important, but the boredom or misery of the present means that we want to get out. Either we or our partner could finish it – and it usually ends with a sudden bang: *'We just weren't getting on any more. My birthday fling didn't help ... We couldn't live together; whenever we rowed, I told him to get out. One day he did.'*

Alternatively, though things are unhappy, we are perhaps convinced that the relationship will still work. It will take a change of attitude, almost a change of heart for one of us to see that it is over.

> *I went on a course from work, got back after the first day and wanted to talk to him about it. I got the usual response; I wasn't allowed to be me, I had to tell him things a certain way. I blew up. I went back to the course the next day and got a lot of support which really helped. We went to Relate to try to sort it out, started communicating for the first time in years, but there was too much between us. I didn't want to be in a relationship with an adolescent-acting man, and two weeks after this, after I had been away for four days to think things over, I decided to leave him.*

It can be that one of us realizes through another relationship that this one is over. The affair or even just the prospect of it completes the break-up: *'I found him in bed with a neighbour ... I had already seen someone I had liked when my relationship was coming to an end ... My fiancé broke it off. I didn't find out until months later that he had met a girl a week before we split up. He had never slept with her but he couldn't cope with the guilt, and I had lost all faith in him.'*

Or interestingly, a relationship can end just when we feel we are doing particularly well. We make a commitment, move the relationship on by buying a house or getting engaged. That in itself sets one of us thinking – realizing that this isn't really what we want to do.

Lastly, there may be a pattern of 'stop and start'. We want to end a relationship, but it doesn't quite work like that first time round. We finish but start up again. We get back together either through fear – of being without him or of simply being alone: *'I waited for him on the way home to beg him to resume the affair. He did ... I clung to the belief that deep down we were meant to be with each other.'* This very rarely works, or if it does the relationship may well die the death slowly a while later: *'I began it again because I still loved her, but we have split up again and are now very bitter. I don't believe people should get back together for the sake of sentimentality.'*

## DO WE MISS OUR PARTNERS?

Only a few of us aren't affected when an important relationship ends. In the rare event that we don't miss our partner, it is usually because we have been totally disillusioned by the time he leaves, or that we have 'seen it coming'. We use the argument that 'he was not right for me' to console ourselves and to look to the future. And we often say that if we have felt hurt, it is only wounded pride and not that we really miss the partner himself.

*Loads of men have broken off relationships with me. Some of them I missed sexually. I felt hurt and rejected, and my pride has been hurt more times than I can remember, but I try not to let it bother me. If I had grown attached to a partner I was upset that he didn't want me anymore, but most of the time I could see it coming and wasn't really bothered.*

Or we realize that we simply miss having 'someone' rather than the flesh and blood person himself. We want 'the thrill of having a regular partner', someone to take out, someone for regular sex, someone to support us when we feel lonely or needy. But we admit that our partner himself wasn't special to us at all; as soon as we find a replacement, the pain goes away.

If we do miss our partner, then it is as likely to be sexually as much as emotionally: 'My body ached for him.' The survey analysis might have indicated that emotions would be placed far higher on the list of important criteria than sex. But, in fact, it showed that by the time a relationship ends, often the emotions are so painful that the only pleasant memories left are sexual ones. Even if we ourselves finish the relationship because we have grown out of, or grown tired of, our partner, we can still miss the sex a great deal.

*I was heartbroken. I lost a stone in two weeks, cried all the time and used to become hysterical. I missed him terribly sexually, mainly because our sex life was better than I'd ever had and I felt I would never have sex as good again. This is the time in my life when I started masturbating alone.*

If we don't miss our partner sexually, it's often because the whole break-up has been so traumatic that we have no sexual feelings left. Maybe we have never particularly valued the sex, or maybe as the relationship has died, so has our sexual contact; in the end 'it hadn't been that good or frequent ... I could masturbate better myself.'

Those of us who do miss our partner emotionally have often based our relationship on being close friends. Sex may not be as important an element in our relationship as discussion, sharing activities, confiding emotions. Typically in these situations it is our partner who ends the relationship; we find it very hard to replace what he has meant to us.

*I missed my first partner very much; he had been my best friend since we were 5 years old, and when we split up he said he didn't want to be my friend any longer.*

## REACTIONS TO LOSS

Because ending many sexual relationships in a lifetime is a new pheno-menon, knowing how to recover from that is something of a new skill. It's almost as if in many ways women are only just finding out how to cope with relationship loss. We may need to go through classic 'bereavement' stages: denial, anger, depression and acceptance. Our physical reactions to our emotional desperation are often very marked. We cry a great deal, get hysterical, stop eating and lose weight, overeat and gain weight: *'When I heard they were living together, I flipped out and got drunk for a whole year.'*

What do we do to recover? Those women who seem to have success-fully worked through the pain have often adopted a number of consistent strategies. First, we take time on our own. While we may need physical support in the first few days or weeks, and we may need people with whom to cry and get angry, in the end most of us withdraw, spend weeks or months being solitary and get to know ourselves again. Many women mention this as being, after the initial shock, the thing that helped most. We may combine our solitude with some destructive patterns, such as those mentioned before – overeating or overdrinking. But these self-hate behaviours will die away if we give ourselves enough time and loving attention.

*Yes, I am still getting over the loss of my relationship. I went from not wanting it to end, to not understanding what was happening, to being bewildered. We were together for 12 years, and I thought we were working through it. I am now trying to go more with what I feel and want.*

The next step is to *'get out into the world'*. Many of us at this stage find comfort in contacting other women, to get a sense of ourselves as female and to get support from our own gender.

*When I finished with David, I wasn't happy. I carried on by making more female friends, which got me in touch with my own life. I'd been with him since I was 17 through to the time I was 30. We'd grown up together and been through a lot together. I had to find a circle of friends to replace the other half of me. I had to become more self-sufficient.*

With the support of others, we can start to rebuild our lives. Many women change things on a radical level – job, house, appearance, *'have moved house, changed jobs. I have put together a life for myself without my partner.'* Many commit themselves to other responsibilities, getting involved in politics or self-development. Over and over again comes the phrase, *'I keep busy.'*

## RECOVERY AND SEX

Sooner or later, given time, we start to consider other relationships. In fact, for many women, this stage overlaps with the others: we don't all wait until our mourning is over before beginning again, and we often use sex as part of our bereavement process.

Many women react to the loss of a relationship by withdrawing from sex completely. They become celibate, for up to two years in some cases, in order to get their strength back. This is particularly likely if they are only interested in sex within a partnership – *'I need to deal with the end of a previous relationship before I am ready to give anything to anyone else'* – or if the contrast between their past partner and those potential partners on the horizon is too great for them to consider having another relationship: *'Having tried the best, you do not want the rest.'*

If we do become celibate for a while, we may instead concentrate on sex with ourselves. Many women say that when they are without a partner is the time they most masturbate; many also say that they develop their sexuality between partners by developing their masturbation skills: *'The only thing I did after leaving my partner was to start to masturbate and have my first orgasm.'*

If we don't choose celibacy, one option is to have a series of casual sexual relationships, what one woman calls *'rebound fucks'*. We want affection, we want attention. We want to learn about sex if we have only had a few partners before. We want to erase the memory of our last partner. We want to get back at men.

*I didn't have casual sex to replace a partner. I did it because I enjoyed the freedom and danger of it all. I loved the attention, being able to have total control and not have to ask permission for anything. I loved just being able to get on with my life without having to answer to anyone.*

After a while, weeks or maybe months, we usually stop having casual sex. We either opt for celibacy or for a more permanent relationship.

And the majority of us, looking back, think the casual affairs were a mistake: *'They made me feel worse . . . I hated myself for it . . . Really stupid, hey?'*

## A NEW PARTNERSHIP

Just about half of women, rather than opt for casual sex, move into a 'rebound attachment' – only one woman comments that she had a 'rebound marriage'! This works as long as our new partner knows what is happening, and as long as we don't convince ourselves that this is true love. Most of these relationships fade quickly, and only one woman said:

> *When I left my former partner I moved in with my present partner as a friend. We became very close and on the rebound we became sexually involved. I think we have worked through all the replacement stuff, and I love him for himself now. That wasn't the case for the first couple of years, though.*

The final possibility is that, in fact, we have been sleeping with someone else before we finish a relationship. If so, then this may act as a kind of buffer to any sexual distress we have. We have probably stopped sleeping with our partner at the end, but we have been sleeping with our new partner for a while – so we don't go out looking for replacement sex because we already have it. Our new lover, however long he lasts, cushions us sexually and emotionally from suffering the loss too much – though, in fact, even if we are gladly leaving one relationship in order to enter another happily, we will still have some mourning to do. And, in the end, one of two things may then happen. Either the new relationship is a true replacement of the old one and lasts a long time; or it is a 'transition' relationship, useful only to prise us out of the old, painful situation. As soon as we are fully recovered, we don't need the transition partnership, and it too dies, leaving us free for a new and more committed one.

Because another commitment is the usual happy ending. Almost all the women who report losing an important relationship also report getting over it, taking time to recover, and then starting again with a new and fulfilling relationship. We meet someone who is good for us, who gives us the love that we need and who wants us to love them. We feel ready to take the risk, and we begin again.

> *For the first couple of months I wasn't functioning. Then I started to get over it. I ate a lot; spent money on myself; went to a writing course; went to political meetings; slept with my ex-husband's best friend; tried dating agencies; started taking A-levels. It was at that point I met my current partner. I'm still with him, and I start university next Tuesday.*

65.8 per cent of women say that relationships get more important as they get older

55.1 per cent reckon that sex is more important to them as they get older

90.4 per cent say that sex has got better with age

# 24. Lifelong sex

*Sex has got better, as I have learnt more and experimented more. Age has nothing to do with it. The best sex is with my partner, but I've had good sex elsewhere. It's more a question of being open minded, adventurous, considerate, uninhibited, conscious of timing and rhythm and capable of giving as well as taking pleasure.*

WHAT HAPPENS TO our sex lives as we get older? We know that as children, we have an inbuilt knowledge of sexuality. But do we build on that? Does natural ageing diminish or undermine it? Do we get disillusioned or lose interest? Even fifty years ago, the expectation largely was that, with middle age, women would become non-sexual. Is this still true?

The news is optimistic. All the evidence from the survey shows that we increasingly develop our capacity for pleasure with age – probably as a direct result of now having the possibility of more sexual experience and more permission to develop our sexuality. Women's accounts speak of passing through every key life transition: of puberty, first relationship, first love, commitment, child-bearing, child-rearing, menopause – each with a little more awareness of their sexual potential.

We feel better about ourselves with age and so get more from our sexual partnerships: *'My relationships changed when I changed my attitude towards myself and gained self-respect.'* We increasingly like being female, value being sexual, or are *'glad to be gay in the nineties'*.

And many of us say that our sexual partners change us. For as we get older and have more relationships, we learn certain lessons. Some of them are pessimistic: *'Love isn't enough ... you need trust and security ... they don't always last.'* But many of the lessons we learn are optimistic; we say that it is only now we are older that we realize just what sex and love are all about.

## CHANGING RELATIONSHIPS

First, how do our ideas about relationships shift as we age? The impression is that it's almost as if women in general have matured in their attitude to relationships. Quite apart from the fact that individual women have altered their viewpoint about partnerships with time, women as a race are becoming more capable of depth and feeling in their partnerships. The vast majority of us say that relationships are either more important, or that they always were important and that we've kept that view. The 13.9 per cent of women who think relationships are less important say that this is because they have learnt to live without a partner and are not desperate for one: they are more self-sufficient.

> *I am a very independent person, and although I love my partner very much and miss him when he is away I don't need him. I take care of myself, the children and whatever needs taking care of without relying on help from a man. I wouldn't want to rely on anyone except myself again.*

> *My present relationship with my husband is important to me, but as I have got older it's not the overwhelming factor in my life. I have come to feel it is important for me to also have time to myself and opportunities to do things by myself and just for myself without always having to justify my actions.*

It seems that as we grow, we change our definitions of relationships. The initial desire to have a boyfriend for status gives way to wanting to share and cooperate. The desperation of needing to possess our first love gives way to a more respectful view of our partner as a separate person. We often leave behind the reliance on casual sex we had in our teens and twenties and look for *'a loving eroticism'*. After that, we may leave behind our reliance on conventional ties and realize that *'marriage isn't important and loving is'*. Those of us who have had lots of relationships and then settled down now say that we value commitment. Those of us who have been through the trauma of divorce say that it is possible to remake a life with a new lover. Almost, the lesson we learn with age is that there is always something new to be learnt about sexual partnerships; just when we think we have mastered the art, we find a new and delightful challenge waiting for us.

That isn't to say that there are no heartaches. Many of us feel that we have been betrayed, by an unfaithful partner, or one who doesn't return our love. And some of us are bitter and unhappy, not able to trust again, unwilling to enter into new relationships. But they are a minority; and even they often believe that in the end things will work out for them.

Many women say that as they have matured, they have become less selfish and more accepting, more able to love. They are willing to do that even if it means not being right all the time.

*When I was younger I was very selfish. It was a game. I used to even cause arguments for fun and wouldn't back down. I don't think I really ever thought about other people's feelings until I was hurt myself. Then I realized it could really hurt, to a degree where you wanted to die. So now I care more about people's feelings. I'll make the peace even if I feel I am right.*

We also realize with age that relationships need working at. When young, we believed that love conquered all. Now we see that even the best partnerships need constant attention: *'I believe that relationships need work as much as a job needs effort.'* And more and more we are, in fact, prepared to work at our partnerships – because more and more we think they are worth while. As is clear from chapter 6, respondent after respondent consistently says that her current partner is better than all previous ones and that her current relationship is better than the ones that have gone before. So we have an increasing motivation to do all we can to make love work.

## DEVELOPING SEXUALITY

About sex, our view is equally optimistic. When we are young, we believe that age will bring a loss of lust. We look at busy adults who don't show their sexual feelings as openly as we do, and we believe that they don't feel passion any more. But 88 per cent of women say that the opposite is true, that, for them, sex has improved with time. They report that being older has made them *'wiser ... more relaxed ... more confident ... more able to communicate ... more experienced ... more knowledgeable ... I've lost my shyness, know what I like in bed and I also know what men like.'* And the fact that they have better relationships has also dramatically increased the success of their sex lives: *'My sex life has got better with time ... due to an incredibly sensitive and understanding partner.'*

As well as being more enjoyable, we think sex is increasingly important to us. This is not because we are addicted to lust for its own sake. On the contrary, as mentioned earlier, the older we get the more we dislike casual sex; we want passion only in the context of a relationship. But as we start to see sex in the context of loving relationships, we also start to see that it is vital to our physical and emotional well being rather than just being something we do because all our peers do it or because our partner wants it. It stops being simply a badge of honour and starts being something that affects our whole attitude to life.

*Sex doesn't seem the same thing as it did when I was younger. Then I was desperate for affection and proof that I was attractive. Now I am much more confident about my sexuality, and I have a lot of mature relationships with family and friends, where I get the affection I need. So sex has lost some of the excitement of discovery. Yet it's much more fun now: I know what I like, and I know what works on men, I know my limits and things I am really good at. I think overall, sex is more important to me in a more mature way.*

There are, of course, some exceptions to this trend. Some women have suffered the trauma of physical and emotional abuse and still bear the scars. But even they often comment that with supportive friends or partners, or the help of professional counsellors, things are getting better. They learn to have orgasms. They discover masturbation, oral sex or fantasy. They gain the confidence to ask for what they want in bed. The *'emphasis changes, quantity to quality'*, and in the end they learn to make love rather than just simply having sex.

## THE LATER YEARS

But let's be specific. So far in this chapter we have talked about how things improve with age. But do we simply mean that as we move from teenage to twenties, we get more skilled? Or are we actually saying that this improvement can last throughout our lives — through to middle and old age? The common belief is that at this time, women cease to become sexual people. Many younger respondents say that, for example, the menopause will probably have negative effects on their sex life: *'I won't feel desirable any more ... I suppose my libido will drop.'* But is this correct?

Eleven of the women in the survey are over 50, ranging in age through to 69. Many were part of the first contingent of women to benefit from the movement towards increased sexual freedom. Others were already married by the time the sexual revolution happened but benefited after a first marriage ended or because they and their partners learnt to change their own approach to sex. None of these women has remained uninfluenced by the social changes over the past decades.

To explore this point further, it was helpful to look in particular at their stories. Many of them, in fact, begin their accounts by saying that they have answered the questionnaire just in order to make the point that *'for the record older women do not always go off sex. We can be adventurous and sexually active.'*

And the impression that they give is the one that comes through from all the other respondents – that, crises and trauma apart, relationships and sex do get better as life goes on. Sex is less important in life for only two of these older women; most say it has improved increasingly as time passes. They speak of *'more intimacy, more long-term intimate knowledge, more romance and mellowing'*. They talk happily about experimentation, trying different positions, oral sex, masturbation and having multiple orgasms. They give detailed accounts of their

> *afternoons in bed with my partner, gently stroking each other and teasingly taking time before slowly performing oral sex and culminating in a fierce, frenzied penetration with mutual orgasm. This is performed in front of a video camera, then together we watch the playback.*

When we look at the effect of the menopause, in fact those women who have been through it don't report dramatic drops in libido. Of admittedly a small sample, most reported no change. Some said that the removal of any risk of pregnancy made sex more relaxed and less inhibited, one said that her only real problem was vaginal dryness, and another extolled the virtues of HRT. Another replied, in answer to the question, 'Has the menopause affected your sex life?', an outraged, *'We both like to continue our sex life and enjoy it!'*

Most of these women put their continuing interest in sex down to their having a continuing loving relationship. Our oldest respondent, 69 at the time of answering, says that her sex life constantly improves because she and her husband *'are at ease with each other . . . are content with our marriage . . . enjoy the give and take of a good partnership'*. She has been married for 43 years.

## TO OTHER WOMEN

Finally, then, from our growing knowledge of sex, what do we have to say to others? The very last question in the survey asked women to pass on, from their own experience, words of wisdom to other women. The answers were an amazing mix of humour, compassion and eroticism.

Their first key message to other women is to resist pressure. They feel very strongly that, over the years, women have been motivated by pleasing men in general and specific partners in particular. And this not only makes them less able to enjoy sex ourselves but it also blocks them from real love-making. So over and over again they want to tell other women to 'say no if you want to ... don't be pressured'. What they are saying here picks up on a theme that has become clear throughout this book – women now are starting to become sexual decision-makers. Not only is it better for our emotional self-esteem to be in control – or in mutually negotiated agreement – of what we do in bed, control also, in a very real sense, enhances our pleasure. If we do what we do unwillingly, then passion becomes blocked. Doing only what we want to, when we want to, frees our potential.

Secondly, respondents want other women to let go of guilt and start to enjoy themselves. Whether that is letting go of early experiences that are causing problems, or whether it is regretting what they have done, they see guilt is a one-way trip: 'Never be ashamed about anything you have done.' Equally, they feel women should revel in sex without inhibition: 'Be a lady in everyday life and abandon yourself in bed.'

As regards sexual relationships, many respondents have warnings for others. They caution against casual sex: 'Don't do as I do – it hurts emotionally even though it's physically satisfying.' They caution against ending up with the wrong partner: 'Don't stay with a bastard when you could be getting out and about and living.' They caution against possible infidelity: 'Nurture strength of spirit to shield you when your man is unfaithful.' And they caution against enforced celibacy: 'Don't continue in a relationship without sex if you don't want to.'

Above all they say again and again that relationships need striving for, and that as women we may have to be prepared to work at our relationships '24 hours a day for the rest of our lives'. It may be hard, but the message is that it is worth while.

When it comes to what happens in bed, respondents advise abandonment: 'Practise ... experiment ... don't restrict yourselves ... don't be afraid to act like a whore.' If it is lack of confidence that is holding women back, then they should start to believe in themselves sexually and do what feels right. Women should never blame ourselves if orgasm doesn't happen – as one woman says: 'Some of us experience it later than others do. And we should never be ashamed to try something that we find pleasurable and arousing – whatever that is.'

Lastly, survey respondents want to encourage other women to rely on their own sexual knowledge: 'Forget about pleasing men and please yourself.' This is not advice to be selfish, but exhortation to find out what

gives us pleasure and to go for it, to allow ourselves the luxury of whatever
we want in bed that makes us happy.

*Sex has got better as we have grown older together. We have had our
ups and downs in 22 years of marriage, but we have managed to
communicate and sort things out, and I think I am really lucky to have
such a good lover in my husband. Although I enjoyed sex the first six
to eight years of marriage, I did not have an orgasm. Then, when
I explained my needs to my husband, he became able to hold himself
back until I could climax, and then we would have an orgasm together.
Now still, thank God, we still find each other attractive sexually. And
we still keep the romance in our lives.*

## LAST WORDS

These accounts of women's sexual knowledge have, hopefully, offered not
only insight but also awareness, reassurance and some surprises. They
explain what women think and feel about sex, here and now, in the
nineties; they explore how women's potential for sex has changed as a
result of their changing sexual roles and their new sexual freedoms. They
pass on experience and life-views from women to women and possibly also
to men. And it is likely that they will provide some clues as to how female
sexuality will continue to change in the future.

But these women's accounts in this book are only the starting-point.
They are a catalyst for you, the reader, to start to explore your own
knowledge about sex and your own approach to it. They are an
encouragement for you to respond to the changes in attitude and
approach as they increasingly take hold. They are an inspiration for you
to make the rest of your lives full of passionate and loving sexuality.

# Appendix 1
# The methodology of the book

THIS BOOK WAS compiled from the written questionnaire responses of 200 women. You may be interested to know something about the way the questionnaire was put together, and the survey handled.

The original idea, for a book that allowed women to speak directly about their sexual experiences and attitudes, came from David Sloane and Lorna Hastings. They were very aware how fascinating it is to hear other people's thoughts and feelings about sex. So they put together a list of compelling questions about women's sexuality in the nineties and over nine months, refined these questions through discussion and a series of face-to-face interviews. The result was a questionnaire of over 300 sub-questions, covering every aspect of female sexuality (see appendix 2).

## DESIGN AND DISTRIBUTION

When Lorna and David had got together with the publisher Robert Smith and through Robert contacted myself as author, we were faced with the task of validating the questionnaire, getting responses and then transforming those responses into a book. We did wonder whether to opt for a simpler-to-answer format, maybe including multiple-choice questions that would allow women to answer much more quickly and easily, which would make the job of compiling statistics a thousand times more simple. But though this would have provided numerous figures and facts, it would have given us no thoughts, opinions or feelings. We decided to opt for a qualitative rather than a quantitative approach, where women would be encouraged to answer in their own words as fully as they wished.

We wanted to reach as wide a cross-section of women as we could, and one that would be honest in their answers. So having put the questionnaire together, Lorna started a campaign to receive editorial coverage: the survey was highlighted in 4 national women's magazines, 17 regional magazines and newspapers and several local radio stations, giving broad-based coverage in both area and age group. Questionnaires were sent out either to women who wrote in directly, or, via those women, to their friends or colleagues. Once a questionnaire had been sent off to a woman, she knew that her name and address would be deleted from the records. She was therefore guaranteed total anonymity – though there was a section at the end of the questionnaire that allowed her to give her name and address if she wanted us to have them.

## THE WOMEN

The women who responded represent a mixture of those in Britain today (see table). The youngest was 17 when she filled in the questionnaire, the oldest was

69. Most have lived their entire course of their sexually active lives in post-pill times – but even the very few women who haven't said that their sexual lives have been changed by the pill's existence, either because they had taken it or because the sexual revolution had affected their relationships. These women came from all walks of life: some saw their main role in life as *'domestic engineer (housewife and mother)'*, others worked in professions as varied as office worker, barmaid, travel representative, computer programmer, lollipop lady, courier, nanny and 'pornographer'. Their household incomes ranged from £30,000 per year to £33 per week.

These figures show some basic details about the 200 respondents when the survey was conducted in 1993.

| Age | No. of women | % |
|---|---|---|
| Under 18 | 2 | 1 |
| 18-20 | 24 | 12 |
| 21-24 | 44 | 22 |
| 25-29 | 53 | 26·5 |
| 30-34 | 28 | 14 |
| 35-44 | 31 | 15·5 |
| 45-54 | 12 | 6 |
| 55-59 | 2 | 1 |
| 60-69 | 4 | 2 |

| Occupation | No. of women | % |
|---|---|---|
| Unemployed | 23 | 11·7 |
| Student | 26 | 13·3 |
| Housewife | 22 | 11·2 |
| White collar | 97 | 49·5 |
| Blue collar | 28 | 14·3 |

| Household earnings | No. of women | % |
|---|---|---|
| Below £5000 | 42 | 22·1 |
| £5-10,000 | 51 | 26·8 |
| £10-20,000 | 52 | 27·4 |
| £20-30,000 | 35 | 18·4 |
| over £30,000 | 10 | 5·3 |

| Religion | No. of women | % |
|---|---|---|
| No | 130 | 66·7 |
| C of E | 23 | 11·8 |
| RC | 11 | 5·6 |
| Christian | 17 | 8·7 |
| Jewish | 1 | 0·5 |
| Non-Christian | 13 | 6·7 |

| Region | No. of women | % |
|---|---|---|
| London | 57 | 29·4 |
| Anglia | 21 | 10·8 |
| Midlands | 25 | 12·9 |
| North West | 13 | 6·7 |
| North East | 22 | 11·3 |
| South East | 15 | 7·7 |
| South West | 11 | 5·7 |
| Wales (HTV) | 19 | 9·8 |
| Scotland/Ulster | 11 | 5·7 |

The respondents were in a broad range of partnership situations. Most were single or married, the longest for 43 years. One had been engaged for two days and another for ten years when they sent in their responses. Many, usually older women, had been divorced 'and happily too'. Many lived alone, with their children or with a partner, though a small contingent of younger women lived with their parents. Three women are widowed.

The majority of women, 66 per cent, were in one sexual relationship. Some 9.8 per cent had more than one partner. And 24.2 per cent of women had no partner. Two women had never had intercourse; they and the several respondents who have chosen to be celibate added an important minority angle to the survey results.

The questionnaire itself was not originally targeted at lesbian women or designed to cover the lesbian experience; hopefully another book will specialize on this topic. Hence the vast majority of respondents are essentially heterosexual, and, because of this, I have in general referred to partners as 'he' throughout the book. I have, however, included a chapter on woman-to-woman sex; in addition, in those cases where lesbian women's accounts seem to parallel heterosexual women's experience, I have added them to the statistics and quoted them in the main text.

## ANALYSIS

By spring 1993 we had collected 200 responses, totalling over one million words of text. Most women wrote about 3000 words and often took weeks or even months to complete the questionnaire. The longest single reply was 25,000, the length of a short novel, and many women wrote nearly as much as that. The accounts piled up, and we began to type them into our computer system.

We had a data base specially designed for us that allowed us to key in and then code each response, gathering them into themed groups, which allowed me to see what the overall patterns of belief, attitude and feeling were in the answers to each question. What I, as author, had in the end were responses to every question, visible on screen, so that I could not only view the statistics for each question but also read every woman's answer, take notes and cross-reference.

Our final step was to make things slightly more personal. Perhaps there was more that women wanted to say – or perhaps there were gaps in what we had asked. I contacted 20 (10 per cent) of the 200 women. Some were happy to fill in a further, short questionnaire (see appendix 2), others were willing to talk, and so I was able to add to the in-depth written accounts by hearing at first hand what women wanted to say. Only then did I start to write the book, combining the material into 25 chapters, using the statistics, the themes and – most importantly – women's own words to put together an account of sexuality in the nineties.

## EFFECTIVENESS

How effective was the approach we adopted? From my point of view, as the author of the book, I found that the questionnaire and the coding process gave me both statistics and 'flesh on the bones'. The questionnaire gave me a broad spread of replies but with a significant set of themes within them. The coding process took many months, but the end result enabled me not only to draw out broad statistical trends but also to gather subtrends from the responses I saw on screen and to back up these trends with quotations from actual accounts.

How did the respondents judge the questionnaire? We included a question asking for feedback on this, and the answers were very clear. The length of the questionnaire was an issue: many women got bored or longed for the tick-box approach. Despite this, most women gave us full and, as far as we could tell, honest replies. (We cross-checked for obvious inconsistencies in responses and for places where women were obviously exaggerating or fantasizing; we found almost none.) And more women complimented us on the way the questionnaire allowed them to give us full and extended answers than criticized its length: even women who complained about having to write so much often added that they realized that the result would be a much better book. Most respondents said that when it came to the book itself, they would be much more interested in reading personal accounts than simple statistics.

## ACCURACY

Is the approach accurate? The number of 200 women is statistically significant, and we have aimed to get a broad and representative range of age, economic background and sexual approach. However, the survey makes no attempt to parallel the large-scale surveys such as those done by Kinsey (1953), Hite (1976), Sanders (1985) or the Welcome Foundation (1992-3).

There are also three vulnerabilities in the approach, though these are also true of every sex survey that has ever been done. First, it's more or less impossible to get a totally random sample, one that is completely representative of the general population; even with the benefit of anonymity that we had, people self-select. Respondents are, by definition, women who are happy to reveal their sexuality, so can never be totally typical.

Secondly, some women did not answer all questions – occasionally they felt a question wasn't relevant to them or they weren't prepared to answer it: so both the statistics and the anecdotes can only ever show the opinions of those women who answered a particular question. Thirdly, of course, in writing up results, there is always an unavoidable element of interpretation. Readers' attention will be drawn to the statistics I report, as opposed to the minority ones I fail to mention; to the anecdotes I use, as opposed to the ones I filter out; to the way I present and explain women's thoughts and feelings, as opposed to the way any other author would have chosen to explain them.

The bottom line, however, is that this is not a quantitative but a qualitative study. And, qualitatively, we feel that we have been honest in our approach. The anonymity, length and immense depth of each response does, we feel, give new and valuable detail about women and sex in Britain today. It answers questions that readers may have about how women feel and think. In addition, we have made a real effort not to preclude from the book women who don't fall within the broad range of respondents and to explore both majority and minority opinions. Finally, as author, I haven't concentrated only either on the hard figures or on the unanalysable emotions of the women's responses. I have tried to combine the two, letting the statistics draw my attention to points that need to be made but then also exploring the reasons, judgements and feelings that reflect those statistics. I have, in short, tried to be an 'honest broker' of what the respondents want to say, and, because of this, I believe that the qualitative fidelity of the book is extremely high.

In the end, then, the aim of the survey, and the aim of this book is to provide a snapshot of women and their sexuality in the nineties. And, as such, I hope it enables readers to hear clearly the true voices of women on sex.

# Appendix 2
# Survey questionnaire

## 1. PERSONAL DETAILS

**1A.** How old are you?

**1B.** Are you religious? If so, which religion?

**1C.** Which ITV region do you live in?

**1D.** Which newspaper do you read?

**1E.** What is your occupation?

**1F.** Are your current household earnings below £5000 per year, between £5-10,000, between £10,000–20,000, between £20,000-30,000, over £30,000?

**1G.** Are you married or living with a partner; Are you separated, divorced or widowed? Are you single or not living with a partner; If married or living with, how long have you been with this partner?

**1H.** Are you currently celibate, currently in a number of sexual relationships, currently in one sexual relationship? (If you are currently in a number of sexual relationships, please take questions in this questionnaire which use the word 'partner' to mean the partner most important to you, or the one about whom the question is most relevant. Alternatively, please give answers about several or all of your partners, but make it clear in your answers which partner you are referring to.)

**1I.** Are you happy with your current sexual situation? If so, what do you like about it? If not, what would you prefer it to be?

**1J.** Is there anything else about you, such as your education, race or upbringing, that you would like to mention?

## 2. DATING

**2A.** Is the age of your partner important to you? Do you prefer to go out with an older/younger person? What is the difference in age between you and your youngest partner, and your oldest partner? What age were you when you were with each?

**2B.** Do you have any pre-set sexual rules when going out on a date, and do you stick to them? Do you ever have intercourse with a partner on a first date? If so, how often does this happen and what dictates this happening?

**2C.** Do you think that women are pressured into having sex (not necessarily intercourse) on a date? Do you consider it a form of prostitution if a man takes a woman out for dinner and she sleeps with him that evening?

**2D.** Have you ever agreed to intercourse on a date fearing that, if you said 'no', you would be raped?

## 3. PRE SEXUAL-INTERCOURSE EXPERIENCES

**3A.** Do you think your family shaped your sexual outlook. If so, how and why? Do you think your friends shaped your sexual outlook? If so, how and why?

**3B.** When was the first time that you looked at your genitals? When was the first time you realized that a man had a different body from yours?

**3C.** What was your first experience of feeling sexual sensations? Do you have any memories of sexual feelings or experiences when you were a child? At what age do you consider you became sexually aware?

**3D.** Where and from whom did you learn about sexual behaviour?

**3E.** Who initiated any pre-sexual experiences you had before you had intercourse/lost your virginity: Generally, were your partner(s) in these pre-sexual experiences more sexually experienced than you? What did you do, eg masturbation, oral sex, petting of the upper body, full petting? Were you aware of what you were doing? Where did you usually do it? What would you not do or allow to be done to you? What were you happy to do, and what were you not happy to do? What do you remember enjoying and why? What do you remember disliking and why? Did you have an orgasm? If so, were you aware of this at the time or are you only aware of it now? Were you using any form of contraception?

**3F.** Did any form of sexual activities (before you had intercourse) ever take place in front of other people or where you could be seen? Please give details, eg at parties, sharing a room. Did your boyfriends ever ask you to show any part of your body unclothed to one or more of his friends?

**3G.** How many boyfriends did you have prior to sexual intercourse? Did you feel that you sexually progressed with each successive partner?

## 4. BODY AWARENESS

**4A.** How do you feel about your physical appearance? How do you feel about your genitals? Are you comfortable being naked in front of other people? Who?

**4B.** Are there any parts of your body you would like to be different, and if so, how? Have you ever done anything (eg dieted, had a perm) to change the way you look? If so, what?

**4C.** At what age did you reach puberty? How did you first find out you were menstruating? How did you feel about that? How do you feel now about menstruating? Do you have any problems, eg pain? During what stage of your monthly cycle is your sexual appetitite at its strongest? Do you have intercourse during a period?

**4D.** Would you prefer to be medically examined by a male or by a female doctor? Do you feel the same way about an internal examination?

**4E.** Where is the female G spot? Where is the male G Spot?

## 5. FIRST EXPERIENCE OF INTERCOURSE

**5A.** Do you remember your first intercourse experience?

**5B.** Where did intercourse take place, eg bedroom, parents' lounge?

**5C.** What age were you? What age was your partner? How long had you known this partner? Was he a regular boyfriend, your future husband, or a casual acquaintance? Was your partner a virgin? Had you previously discussed intercourse with this partner?

**5D.** Describe what happened. Who initiated it? Were you embarrassed to show your body in the nude to your partner? Did you take all your clothes off? Who did what, and to whom? Was there any pain or bleeding? Did you enjoy the experience? Did you orgasm? On this first occasion did you have intercourse more than once?

**5E.** How did you feel later that day/night or the next day?

**5F.** Approximately how long was it before you had intercourse on another occasion with the same partner?

**5G.** Did you use contraception, and if so, what?

**5H.** Did you feel that with this partner you sexually developed? Did you develop emotionally with this partner? Did you do things then which, now you are more mature, you would say 'no' to? Are there things that, at the time, you said 'no' to, but which you now wish you had said 'yes' to?

## 6. LOVE & AFFECTION

**6A.** Have you ever been in love? How did you/do you feel? Was this a sexual relationship?

**6B.** Do you have a pattern of emotional relationships developing in a particular way, and if so, what is this pattern? How do you/have you found love changes as the sexual relationship continues; how does sexual satisfaction change as the love relationship continues?

**6C.** Is emotional affection important to you? Why?

**6D.** How important do you find touching other people (without having sex with them)? Do you touch people as much as you want to? Do you kiss, cuddle and show affection or physical contact other than immediately prior to or during sexual intercourse? Have you ever had sex with someone in order to touch and cuddle them? Does your current partner touch and cuddle you less than you would like? More than you would like?

**6E.** Do you find it difficult to get sexually aroused without love and affection from your partner?

## 7. THE IMPORTANCE OF SEX

**7A.** How important is sex to you? How important is sex to your partner?

**7B.** Do you think making love/having sexual intercourse should be kept within special relationships only? Please explain. What emphasis do you place on a relationship before love making?

**7C.** If you had to choose between being able to have orgasms only for the rest of your life but no cuddles or loving affection; or being able to have the cuddles and loving affection, but no orgasms, which would you choose?

## 8. FOREPLAY

**8A.** What does foreplay involve for you? What do you do? How long do you generally like foreplay to last?

**8B.** How important is foreplay to you? Is it more or less important than intercourse? How important do you think foreplay is to your partner?

**8C.** Does your partner use foreplay as a matter of course? Do you think your partner does it only for your benefit? Are you happy with the amount of foreplay your partner gives you?

**8D.** Is there a foolproof way to get you aroused? (This could be mental or physical.) Do partners know and use this foolproof way?

## 9. MASTURBATION

**9A.** Do you masturbate now? If not, have you ever masturbated?

**9B.** How old were you when you first masturbated? Did you orgasm? How did you learn to masturbate: on your own, from reading, from someone else?

**9C.** Do you think masturbating is important? If so, why?

**9D.** How often do you masturbate?

**9E.** What do you do when you masturbate? For example, what do you use, how do you lie, where do you touch yourself, what do you do, in what order? How does masturbating make you feel? Do you usually reach orgasm when you masturbate?

**9F.** Have you ever seen another woman masturbating; how did she look?

**9G.** Have you ever masturbated in front of your partner? If so, was this because your partner asked you to? How did you feel? Did your partner assist you? If so, how? Do you get aroused, do you orgasm? Do you enjoy it?

**9H.** If a partner has masturbated in front of you, how did you feel? Did you assist your partner? If so, how?

## 10. ORGASMS

**10A.** How often do you have an orgasm? Never, rarely, occasionally, frequently, always?

**10B.** When did you first orgasm? How? How old were you when you had your first orgasm with someone else? How?

**10C.** If you do orgasm, is it easy or difficult for you to have an orgasm?

**10D.** How do you reach orgasm: through penetration, manual stimulation, oral stimulation, using sex aids? Please explain this as fully as you can. Is there any difference in the ways you reach orgasm when you are alone and when you are with your partner?

**10E.** If you reach orgasm through penetration, what particular way(s) do you have to move, or what particular positions(s) do you have to take up in order to orgasm? Do you also have to have another sort of stimulation at the same time (eg pressing your clitoris through the movement of intercourse; you or your partner touching your clitoris; long foreplay) in order to come? If so, please describe.

**10F.** Describe what an orgasm feels like to you. What does your body do at the moment of orgasm?

**10G.** Do your orgasms vary in kind or intensity and why do you feel this is? Do you have more than one orgasm during a period of love-making? Do you have multiple orgasms?

**10H.** How important is it for you to reach orgasm while with your partner? If it is important, why? How important it is to your partner for you to reach orgasm, while making love or during foreplay?

**10I.** What happens if you move towards orgasm and then fail to reach it? How do you feel? When does this tend to happen?

**10J.** Do you show any signs of orgasm; do you think your partner knows when you have come?

**10K.** Do you/have you ever faked orgasms? Why? What were the circumstances?

**10L.** On average, does love-making last long enough for you? On average, does intercourse last long enough for you?

**10M.** Have you ever been disappointed that your partner did not have an erection when you wanted intercourse? If so, how did you react?

**10N.** Do you ever wish your partner would climax more quickly? Have you ever or do you do something that you know makes your partner climax more quickly – what was this? If so, how did you feel?

## 11. ORAL SEX – Giving oral sex

**11A.** Do you naturally give oral sex or does your partner have to ask you to? If you do not perform oral sex on your partner, what are your reasons?

**11B.** If you perform oral sex on your partner what exactly do you do? Do you bring him to orgasm or just allow him to experience the sensation? If he orgasms, do you pull away or let him come in your mouth? When you give oral sex, do you only give it to the penis? If not, please explain.

**11C.** Do you enjoy this form of oral sex? If not, why not? If so, why? Do you sometimes say 'no' to giving your regular partner oral sex; if so, why? Do you say 'no' to a casual partner; if so, why?

**11D.** Can you get HIV from oral sex?

### Receiving oral sex

**11E.** If you receive oral sex, what exactly does your partner do to you? Does oral sex for you confine itself to the vagina/breast area only? If not please explain.

**11F.** Do you enjoy having oral sex done to you? Do you think your partner enjoys doing this to you? Does your partner naturally perform oral sex or do you have to ask?

**11G.** Do you orgasm with oral sex? How frequently?

## 12. SEXUAL ACTIVITY

**12A.** Does sexual activity with men usually follow a pattern? (Things you do, when you do them, how long you do them for.)

**12B.** In intercourse, what is your favourite position/movement/rhythm? What positions/movement/rhythm do you not like and why?

**12C.** Do you try out new positions/movements with your partner? If so, who is the instigator? You, your partner or both?

**12D.** Do you ever feel uncomfortable during intercourse? Do you get more or less excited the longer intercourse goes on?

**12E.** If you had to choose between penetration and clitoral stimulation, which would you choose and why?

**12F.** Have you ever had to masturbate to orgasm after intercourse? If so, have you done this in front of your partner, or not? Describe how you feel when this happens.

**12G.** Have you/do you participate in anal sex? What are the deciding factors? What are your views on anal sex?

## 13. FREQUENCY OF MAKING LOVE/SEXUAL ENJOYMENT

**13A.** Are you happy with your sex life? If not, why not? If so, why?

**13B.** How would you rate yourself as a lover?

**13C.** How often do you and your partner make love? Would you or your partner like to make love more often? What gets in the way of your making love more than you do?

**13D.** Do you normally make love on a particular day? Is there a particular time of day that you enjoy making love? How many times per session do you make love?

**13E.** How often do you and your partner spend the night together (if you are not living together)?

**13F.** What is your favourite setting to make love (outside the bedroom)? Please describe such a setting where you have made love. Please describe your fantasy setting. What places have you had sex outside the bedroom, eg office, beach, etc; was this with a regular partner/a one off occasion? Please give full details of circumstances, what you did and whether you enjoyed it? Where is the most exciting place you have ever made love other than in the bedroom?

**13G.** Are there any preliminaries to making love that you enjoy (food, drink, music, a bath, sexy talk)?

**13H.** Do you prefer to have the light on while making love?

**13I.** Do you enjoy intercourse? If so, what do you enjoy about it? Does it lead to orgasm always, usually, sometimes, rarely or never? If not, what sexual activity do you enjoy more?

**13J.** Is the size of your partner's penis important to you? If so, please explain why.

**13K.** What is the most sexually enjoyable thing you have done? What is the most exciting thing you have done sexually?

**13L.** If you are making love less often than you used to, is there a reason that you want to make love less often? Are there outside pressures that you think have made you lose your sex drive?

**13M.** What is the longest time you have gone without making love? What were the reasons for this?

**13N.** Do you ever worry about not enjoying making love?

**13O.** Would you wish to change anything about love-making with your current partner? What would you change and why?

**13P.** Has your mind ever wandered to other things when you are making love?

**13Q.** Is there a sexual activity you have done with one partner that you would not do with another? Please give details of the act and your reasons.

**13R.** What is the most embarrassing thing you have done sexually? What have you done sexually that you are most ashamed of? What have you done sexually that you would never repeat?

**13S.** Have you ever regretted having sexual intercourse? Why did you regret it? Has this affected any other relationship? If so, please explain.

## 14. WHO INITIATES SEX

**14A.** Who makes the first move? Do you/have you ever made the first move? If you make the first move, is your partner happy to let you take the leading role or does he feel threatened?

**14B.** Have you ever seduced a man? If so, how, and why? Is this a regular occurrence?

**14C.** Do you usually have sex with people you want to have sex with, or with people who want to have sex with you, whether you want to or not?

## 15. DISCUSSING SEX

**15A.** Do you think women talk more frankly to female counterparts than males do?

**15B.** Do you and your partner talk openly about your sexual relationship? If not, do you think this is a problem? If so, what do you feel the problem is?

**15C.** How easy or difficult do you find it to ask verbally for what you want in bed? If you do ask, how do you ask? If you don't, do you have other ways to get what you want in bed?

**15D.** Have you or would you discuss previous sexual partners and experiences with your current partner? If not, why not? If so, would you also tell them honestly the number of previous sexual partners you have had?

## 16. PREVIOUS SEXUAL PARTNERS

**16A.** How many sexual partners have you had? How many of these were casual partnerships and how many were relationships? Are you happy with the number of previous lovers you have had? If not, do you wish you had more lovers or less lovers?

**16B.** If relevant, do you wish you had remained a virgin until you formed a permanent relationship/marriage?

**16C.** Have you ever had sexual intercourse with a virgin?

**16D.** How often do you have holiday romances involving sexual activity? Please describe a typical one.

**16E.** Have your partner(s) ever told you about previous sexual experiences? If so, how did you feel when they told you? If not, are you curious as to how many previous partners and sexual experiences they have had?

**16F.** How would you define a woman who 'sleeps around'? Do you think such a woman is cheap if she does so: within a stable relationship; while having casual affairs? How would you define a man who 'sleeps around'? If your partner has slept around previously, how does this affect you emotionally?

## 17. SAYING NO

**17A.** Do you think men assume that you are sexually available if you are single?

**17B.** Do you ever say 'no' if your partner wants you to make love? What generally is the reason for refusing? Do you ever say 'yes' when you really don't want to make love?

**17C.** Does your partner put you under pressure to be more free towards him in your sexual activities?

**17D.** Have you ever done anything sexually that you really hated and do not wish to repeat? Do you ever do anything that makes you feel uneasy but do so because you know your partner really enjoys it? If so, please explain what you do and why.

**17E.** Do you consider you have ever been raped? Who by? What made it rape? Did you tell anyone? If so, what happened?

**17F.** Can you tell your partner exactly what you do enjoy and don't enjoy during love-making?

**17G.** Has your partner ever said 'no' to your request for love-making? How did you feel about being turned down?

## 18. CONTRACEPTION

**18A.** Do you use contraception? If so, what type? Do you feel competent/happy about your knowledge of contraception? Does the type of contraception you use affect lovemaking?

**18B.** Have you ever had sex without using contraception?

**18C.** Have you ever had a miscarriage or an abortion? If so, how did this affect you emotionally? How did this affect you sexually?

## 19. SEX AIDS/FANTASIES/GAMES

**19A.** Do you ever use sex aids? When with your partner? When your partner is not with you? What sex aids do you use? Does your partner know about this?

**19B.** Do you fantasize about sexual activities during lovemaking? Do you fantasize about other things than sex during lovemaking? Describe your favourite fantasy. Do you share fantasies with your partner? Do you and your partner act out your sexual fantasies/roleplay.

**19C.** Do you ever have sexual dreams? Please describe.

**19D.** Do you read porn magazines and watch porn videos? Do these things turn you on?

**19E.** Have you ever been into: a sex club, an orgy, partner swapping? Whose idea was it to go? Did you participate? What did you see and do? Did you or would you ever repeat it? Please explain.

**19F.** In sex, do you prefer to do or to be done to, or neither? What do you think of sado-masochism or dominance/submission games? Have you ever tried them? How do you feel about them?

**19G.** Have you ever had group sex? Who initiated it: you, your partner, or someone else? What was the number and combination of genders involved? Did you enjoy group sex? If so, what did you enjoy about it?

**19H.** If you have not been to any of the above, do you ever fantasize about them? Should the opportunity arise, would you go? Why would you go?

**19I.** If you have been to one of the above, please describe how it affects/affected your sex life? Did you go with your regular partner?

**19J.** Have you ever performed a sexual act on a partner's friend to please your partner? Have you ever made love with someone else in front of your partner? If so, please describe the circumstances, who did what and your emotions afterwards. Have you ever watched your partner make love with someone else, in front of you? If so, please describe the circumstances, who did what and your emotions.

**19K.** Have you ever had your photograph/video taken without your clothes on? Please describe the circumstances. Have you or would you pose for a sexual photo/video?

**19L.** If you had a picture in your mind what would be the most erotic that you could think of?

## 20. SEXUAL PROBLEMS

**20A.** Have you ever been troubled by sexual difficulties? If so, what was the problem?

**20B.** Did you ever seek professional help? If not, why not?

**20C.** Can you discuss openly with your partner what you consider to be a sexual problem?

**20D.** Has your partner ever had a sexual problem? How did you react short-term? How did this affect you long-term?

**20E.** Have you ever been sexually abused/forced to perform a sexual act or raped by anyone, including a member of your family? If so, please give details, eg what they did, their relationship. Did this occur on more than one occasion? Did you report this to anyone? If so, to whom and did they resolve the problem? What effect has this had on any subsequent relationship(s)?

## 21. SEXUAL DISEASE / HIV & AIDS AWARENESS

**21A.** How aware would you say you were with regards to sexually transmitted diseases? If you have recently become more aware, what do you think has made you more aware.

**21B.** At what age did you become aware of sexually transmitted diseases?

**21C.** Have you ever had a sexually transmitted disease? If so, which did you have and how did you feel about it? Do you know who was the cause of it?

**21D.** How aware of HIV/AIDS are you? Do you feel that you may be at risk of contracting the virus and why? Has this changed your sexual behaviour in any way? If so, please give details. Has HIV changed your attitude towards casual sex? If so, please give details.

## 22. OTHER INFLUENCES

**22A.** Would your parents allow you to sleep at home with your boyfriend?

**22B.** Have you ever had sexual feelings for a member of your own family? If so, what happened, and how did you feel about it?

**22C.** Do you think it is important for a woman to have sex before marriage? Do you think that it is important for a man to have sex before marriage?

**22D.** Have you ever lived with a partner? If your current partner is your husband, did you live with him first?

**22E.** Do you have any children? If so, did pregnancy or childbearing affect your sexuality? If you have children, how do they affect your sex life now?

**22F.** What sexual advice would you pass onto your children?

**22G.** What affect does pressure at work have on your sex life?

## 23. UNFAITHFULNESS / AFFAIRS

**23A.** What do you consider is meant by the word 'unfaithful'?

**23B.** How important is it for you or your partner to be faithful to one another? Essential, extremely important, fairly important, not important?

**23C.** Have you ever been unfaithful to a partner?

**23D.** How did you feel after the first time you were unfaithful? Was it with someone you knew, or a casual acquaintance? How old were you? Did this situation develop into an affair or was it a one-off? Did you tell your partner? If so, how honest were you? How did this affect your relationship? How did this sex compare with that of your relationship?

**23E.** If you are in a regular relationship/living with a partner, would you or your partner feel free to have sex (not necessarily intercourse) outside your relationship?

**23F.** Are you presently being unfaithful to your current partner? How is this other relationship affecting you emotionally?

**23G.** Have you had an affair with a partner who is living with someone else or is married? How did this affair begin? Is it a current situation? If so, how long has it been going on? If not, how long did it go on for and why did it end? Has the other partner found out? If so, how did this affect the affair?

**23H.** Are you repeatedly unfaithful to your partner?

**23I.** Have you ever been unfaithful to get back at your partner? Describe what you did to find someone to have an affair with, and what you did sexually with them. How did you feel afterwards.

**23J.** Have you ever made love with more than one person in the same day/night? What were the circumstances? How did you feel?

**23K.** How do you feel about the thought of your partner being unfaithful to you? Has your current or a past partner ever been unfaithful to you? What happened? How did you find out? What happened? How did this affect your relationship?

## 24. LOSING AN IMPORTANT RELATIONSHIP

**24A.** Have you ever broken up with or lost an important partner in your life? What were the circumstances? Please describe. Did you miss him sexually?

**24B.** Did you indulge in sexual experiences to replace your partner? If so, was it casual sex or an attachment?

**24C.** If you have children living with you, have they hampered your developing new relationships?

## 25. WORK RELATIONSHIPS

**25A.** Have you ever had a sexual experience with one of your work colleagues?

**25B.** Please describe the first occasion and what happened. Where did this happen? Was this person a more senior member or more junior member of staff? Did your colleagues find out and what were their comments?

**25C.** If not confined to one occasion, how long did the affair go on for and how did the relationship develop? How did the relationship affect your working environment?

**25D.** If the relationship finished, how did you cope with your work situation afterwards?

**25E.** Have you repeated the situation with another work colleague? What were the circumstances and how did that affect your work and your emotions? Please give details.

## 26. GROWING OLDER

**26A.** As you grow older do you feel that sex becomes less or more important in your life?

**26B.** If you have not passed through the menopause, do you think it will affect your sex life, physically or mentally? If you have passed through the menopause, has it affected your sex life? Has it affected the way your partner feels and acts towards you sexually?

**26C.** If you have had a hysterectomy, has this affected your sex life? How?

**26D.** Has your attitude towards relationships changed, particularly with respect to how important relationships are to you and why? Please explain.

**26E.** If you have retired, has the frequency of sexual activity changed with the additional free time you have available? Do you have intercourse more often, less often, or the same as when you were working? Has the routine of your sexual activity changed, eg time of day? Have you become more active and do you now have intercourse in more adventurous positions?

**26F.** Have your attitudes towards faithfulness changed as you have got older? If so, please explain.

**26G.** Has sex got better with time – ie as you get older, or as you and your partner have developed your relationship? If so, what do you think has made it get better?

## 27. LESBIAN AFFAIRS/RELATIONSHIPS

**27A.** Have you ever had a sexual experience with another woman?

**27B.** If so, how old were you when you had your first lesbian experience? How old was your partner? What did you do sexually? Did you enjoy it? Did you have an orgasm when, with male partners, you don't? Why do you think this is?

**27C.** Is it something that you will repeat should the opportunity become available?

**27D.** Have you repeated this with the same woman or with a different woman? Please describe.

**27E.** Are you currently having a lesbian relationship? Is this your only relationship? Are you also having a heterosexual relationship?

**27F.** If you have not experienced lesbianism do you/have you ever had the desire to? If the opportunity arose would you carry out your desire? If not, what would stop you having a lesbian experience?

## 28. END QUESTIONS

**28A.** Is there anything we haven't asked about that you would like to mention? If so, please do.

**28B.** Are there any sexual messages you could like to give to other women?

**28C.** Are there any things you do in bed that you would like to tell other women about and recommend that they do?

**28D.** Thank you for answering this questionnaire. If you want to, please tell us why you answered it and what your experience was of answering it.

**28E.** We are very interested in finding out more about women's attitudes and experience. Would you be prepared to be interviewed face-to-face about your answers to this questionnaire? If so, please give your name and address and contact number in the space below. (Otherwise, of course, your contribution to this survey is completely anonymous.)

# Appendix 3

# Supplementary questions to a selected cross-section

1. What is your opinion of men?
2. What, in a partner's body or looks, turns you on? What else is important when you're choosing a sexual partner?
3. How can a partner 'impress' on you on a first date?
4. If you have ever chosen to be celibate for a while, why have you taken that option? What, if anything, made you decide to opt for a sexual relationship again after your period of celibacy?
5. How do you communicate sexually with your partner? What ways have you of showing what you want?
6. Have you ever been happily seduced – ie, willingly persuaded into sex? What did your partner do that persuaded you?
7. Does your partner pick up and use your sexual fantasies, if any? If not, how would you like your partner to do so?
8. Have you ever yourself ended a sexual relationship – and then begun it again? If so, what happened to change your mind and persuade you back into the relationship again?
9. Have you ever said yes and meant no? or said no and meant yes? How could a partner tell the difference – from what you say or from your body language?
10. Have you ever experienced a relationship ending unhappily and then got over it? What did you do to help yourself recuperate from the loss?

# Resources
# Further reading and support

If reading this book has made you want to know more about female sexuality, or if you feel you need support on anything specific, these resources may help.

**General**
*The Mirror Within*, Anne Dixon, Quartet, London, 1985.
*Women's Experience of Sex*, Sheila Kitzinger, Penguin, Harmondsworth, 1983.

**1 First knowledge**
Incest Crisis Line, PO Box 32, Northolt, Middlesex UB5 4JC (081-890 4732).

**6 Men in our lives**
*Men and Sex*, Bernard Zilbergeld, Fontana, 1978. Aimed at getting men to enhance their sexuality but interesting for women to read as well.

**7 Women in our lives**
Lesbian Line, BM Box 1514, London WC1N 3XX (071-837 7324). A helpline for lesbian women that can refer you to local lesbian lines.

**8 Body image**
Women's Health, 52-54 Featherstone Street, London EC1Y 8RT. A resource centre on all aspects of women's health that will also answer basic queries over the phone. General telephone line 071-251 6333. Health enquiries: 071-251 6580.
SPOD, 286 Camden Road, London N7 0BJ (071-607 8851). An association to aid the sexual and personal relationships of people with a disability.
*Fat is a Feminist Issue*, Susie Orbach, Hamlyn, 1979.
*The New Our Bodies Ourselves*, Angela Phillips and Jill Rakusen, Penguin, 1989.
*The New Sourcebook for the Disabled*, Glorya Hale, Heinemann, London, 1983.

**9 Pleasure alone**
*Sex for One: The Joy of Self-loving*, Betty Dodson, Crown, 1974. There is also an accompanying video. Both are available from Blue Moon, Chippings, Single Street, Biggin Hill, Kent TN16 3AB (0959 572756). Celebrates masturbation and shows you how.

## 16 Orgasm

*The Body Electric*, Anne Hooper, Virago, 1980.

*Women's Pleasure, or How to Have an Orgasm as Often as You Want*, Rachel Swift, Pan Books, London, 1993.

## 17 Taking precautions

Brooke Advisory Centres, 153a East Street, London SE17 2SD (071-708 1234). With centres in major cities, they offer sexual help and advice to young people.

Family Planning Association, 27-35 Mortimer Street, London W1N 7RJ (071-636 7866). Provides information about contraception and will refer you to your nearest Family Planning Clinic or Well Woman Centre.

Irish Family Planning Association, Half Penny Court, 36-37 Lower Ormond Quay, Dublin (010-353 18725033).

National AIDS Helpline (0800 567123); Wales (0222 2233433); Scotland (031-558 1167); Eire (0232 226117).

## 18 Dreams and fantasies

*My Secret Garden*, Nancy Friday, Quartet, London, 1979.

*Women on Top*, Nancy Friday, Quartet, London, 1991.

## 20 Saying no

Rape Crisis Centre, PO Box 69, London WC1X 9NJ (071-837 1600). Twenty-four hour help line gives support to those who have suffered assault, harassment and rape.

## 21 Unhappy sex

Relate, the National Marriage Guidance Council, Little Church Street, Rugby CV21 3AP (0788 73241). Whether you are married or not, Relate can refer you to their nearest branch for counselling about any aspects of relationships or couple sexuality.

You can also contact:

Catholic Marriage Advisory Council, 1 Blythe Mews, Blythe Road, London W14 0NW (071-371 1341).

Jewish Marriage Guidance Council, 23 Ravenshurst Avenue, London NW4 4EE.

Redwood, 83 Fordwych Road, London NW2 2TL (071-452 9261). Runs women's sexuality and assertiveness groups throughout the country.

Marriage Counselling Scotland, 26 Frederick Street, Edinburgh EH2 2JR (031-225 5006).

Northern Ireland Marriage Guidance Council, 76 Dublin Road, Belfast BT2 7HP (0232 223454).

*Sex Problems: Your Questions Answered*, Martin Cole and Windy Dryden, Optima MacDonald, 1992.